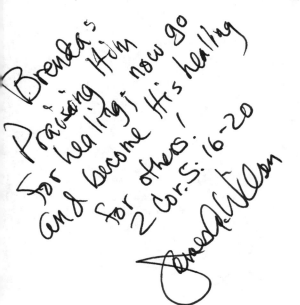
Living as Ambassadors
of Relationships

LIVING AS AMBASSADORS OF RELATIONSHIPS

Reconciling Individuals, Families, Genders, Denominations, Cultures, Liberals and Conservatives, Jews and Gentiles, and the Generations

JAMES WILSON

DESTINY IMAGE® PUBLISHERS, INC.
P.O. Box 310, Shippensburg, PA 17257-0310

*"Speaking to the Purposes of God for this Generation
and for the Generations to Come."*

This book and all other Destiny Image, Revival Press, Mercy Place, Fresh Bread, Destiny Image Fiction, and Treasure House books are available at Christian bookstores and distributors worldwide.

For a U.S. bookstore nearest you, call **1-800-722-6774.**

For more information on foreign distributors, call **717-532-3040.**

Or reach us on the Internet: **www.destinyimage.com.**

ISBN 10: 0-7684-2587-5

ISBN 13: 978-0-7684-2587-1

For Worldwide Distribution, Printed in the U.S.A.

1 2 3 4 5 6 7 8 9 10 11 / 11 10 09 08

ACKNOWLEDGMENTS

I am deeply grateful to more people than I can count or acknowledge for sharing the insights, the inspirations, and the occasions that I have tried to bring to life in these pages. I honor them, give God the glory, and accept responsibility for whatever foul balls I may have hit.

First up would have to be my gratitude to John and Gina McNaughton. John has been a close friend and supporter of our ministry and of my vision for more than twenty years. When he married Gina, she stepped right into the gap along with him. Diana and I don't ever want to find out where we would be without them.

I want especially to thank Ray Shelton and the crew at the JH Ranch and Nick and Kristin Sorani for providing me with places to write and for giving me lots and lots of encouragement. I am more than grateful to the pastors and lay leaders of the gathered churches of Shasta County who nurtured the concepts of a city-wide church and Holy Spirit transformation of a region that was God-planted in my mind and heart. Among them, I must single out Bill and Beni Johnson, Kris Vallotton, and the people of Bethel Church, Redding, for modeling a culture of revival; Tim and Carole Moore and Dawna Groves who have prayed for decades for some of the sacramental outbursts that we have seen only now in the first decade of the twenty-first century; and the many who helped to found transformational ministries such as Faithworks Coalition, Restoration Enterprises, and the Carenet and LifeLight ministries of compassion for people in crisis pregnancies. These ministries are founded and sustained in vision rather than agenda; they breathe reconciliation across the board because they are steeped in Great Commission ambassadorship. Much of what is written in these pages is rooted in the crucible of praying and serving with them and the Christians who gather with them to worship the Lord our God.

It is to Jill Tahauri Rogoff, Tia Tahauri, Kahu Vince Colleado, Suuqinna and Qaumaniq Suuqinna, and (most especially) Lynda Prince that I owe a debt of gratitude for leading me to rethink and repent much of my own cultural, generational, and denominational background—not in order to reject those gifts of God, but in order to permit Him to redeem and resurrect them in me.

I am also deeply grateful to the men and women who have served God and mentored me within a particular part of the Body of Christ. Through them I am given the vocabulary to speak what God has downloaded about a new creation, viewing others through that lens, and the call from God to become

His ambassadors of reconciliation—as He says in Second Corinthians 5:16-20. That branch of the Body—mired as it currently is in sin and apostasy—is also promised redemption and resurrection by the Lord, who never gives up. Indeed, the seeds of that resurrection are already planted in the Word of that same Lord and the revelation He gave to that Body part over a decade ago.

I am greatly indebted to Destiny Image and to Ronda Ranalli for taking a chance on an unknown author, and to Michael Phillips, who introduced me to Destiny Image—one of his publishers—and stuck his neck out to bring me to their attention. Alistair Petrie, John-David Schofield, and Mike Flynn have mentored me over years—what can I say about them to express how thankful I am? Ron Archer and Fawn Parish have served with me and helped to shape my ministry. Cindy Martinusen has served as an example of what you can do when you take your calling to write and your doubts about it to God, and ask Him to do something through you. I am blessed to know these people.

I am blessed to know my two living children. Fathering them has been the greatest adventure of my life. Parenting provides lots of need and opportunity for practicing reconciliation; Diana and I have joked for years that those who claim to be experts on children don't have any. My children are a whole lot smarter and more broad-minded than I will ever be. They are two different kinds of miracle.

I owe more to my wife, Diana, than to any other human being. She has been the love of my life for more than three decades, showing me what love means, what it says, and what it does. She has mothered my children: Christopher, Malorie, and the ones who met God before they met us. She has lived and practiced the principles of reconciliation for all of her life—long before we knew how to talk about them. The only One of greater influence and impact in my life is God Himself—Father, Son, and Holy Spirit. To Him be the glory forever and ever—on earth as it is in Heaven.

ENDORSEMENTS

My friend Jim lives what he speaks. Jim is privileged to live in a culture of revival, and his stories will astonish you. My favorite chapter (of course) is Chapter 6! That chapter would be a great lecture for the International School of Reconciliation Studies. It's been said that God's one item agenda is reconciliation. Jim has lived God's one item agenda for years. You'll be educated, enriched, and entertained as you read this book.

—Fawn Parish
Director, International School of Reconciliation Studies
Author, *Honor, What Love Looks Like* and
It's All About You Jesus, A Fresh Call to an Undistracted Life

One of the things I value most is believers who *do* the Word of God instead of just knowing it. Jim Wilson is such a man. This book is full of stories—and the truths they permit—concerning a most important part of God's plan for mankind. I would gladly recommend this book to those who want to live in obedience to the Lord and His agenda. In addition, the book is written in a conversational style which makes it easy to read. But its truths may sometimes be difficult to put into action, in which case I urge the reader to follow Jim's examples.

—Rev. Mike Flynn
Director, Fresh Wind Ministries
Author, *Holy Vulnerability, The Mustard Seed Book,*
and *How to Be Good Without Really Trying*

Jim Wilson succeeds in taking us effortlessly through unexpected spiritual breakthroughs, in his and his wife's experiences, to the deep principles that form our lives and our perceptions of others. Based not only on personal experience but also on the solid foundation of Scripture, this book invites us into the wonder of healing and restoration that God alone makes available to us as we seek Him in renewed relationships with family, with cultures totally foreign to us, and even with those whose current lifestyles are known to be destructive and without the blessings that we are shown how to release. This is not a book for those who wish to remain members of Christ's Body who are secure from challenges or spectators at arm's length from all that the Holy Spirit will do through those brave enough to surrender their lives to Him.

—The Rt. Rev. John-David Schofield
Bishop of San Joaquin, the Central Third of California
Cofounder, The No-Name Fellowship

Being called the people of God is not a casual phrase but one that assumes identity, purpose, and activity. When God says "If My people…" there is an implication that He is waiting for us to respond to our call and purpose. In this book, Jim Wilson challenges and encourages us to move into our destiny as God's people in a day and age when we need practical answers to challenging questions, answers that equip, inform, and encourage. If you really want to see the transforming power of God at work in your lives, your churches, your cities, and your nations, then this book needs to be read cover to cover and then honestly implemented! Paul the Apostle said "For the kingdom of God is not a matter of talk but of power" (1 Cor. 4:20). The contents of this book are a blueprint to reveal how the Kingdom of God releases its power and authority in our very midst. Be warned: this book is not for the faint of heart but for forceful people who forcefully want to advance the Kingdom of God!

—Rev. Dr. Alistair P. Petrie
Executive Director, Partnership Ministries
Author, *Transformed* and *Releasing Heaven on Earth*
www.partnershipministries.org

Reconciliation is the paradigm of the twenty-first century. Jim Wilson is a cherished colleague and dear friend. I was privileged to be part of a couple of the "prayer journeys" mentioned in this book, and I experienced a deep and profound encounter with the Lord and His Body as we worshipped, listened, and prayed together for the healing of His Bride. *Living as Ambassadors of Relationships* is a serious book and an important contribution to the literature and process of reconciliation. Because of Jim's conversion experience and liturgical background, he brings fresh eyes, language, and perspective to many of the issues that are increasingly divisive in our own society and world. This book is clearly, concisely, and compassionately written, is full of poignant personal stories, punctuated with a relevant biblical foundation, and offers hopeful strategies and solutions to many of our most pressing conflicts. I pray that many will not only read this important book but will also prayerfully put its principles into practice and experience the miracles of the grace, redemption, and reconciliation for which our Lord Jesus died. "God was in Christ reconciling the world to Himself..." (see 2 Cor. 5:19). Should He desire any less from His Church?

—Ron Archer
North American Coordinator
International Reconciliation Coalition

Jim Wilson's passion for reconciliation is contagious. He lives in daily pursuit of this expression of God's love. The insights and examples given in *Living as Ambassadors of Relationships* are sure to inspire the reader to rise to the challenge and embrace the ministry of Jesus—the ministry of reconciliation.

—Bill and Beni Johnson
Pastors, Bethel Church, Redding, California
Best-selling author including, *When Heaven Invades Earth,*

Supernatural Power of a Transformed Mind, and
Face to Face with God

Jim Wilson is all about reconciliation. It is his life work, and it is where his heart lies. His message is like arms reaching across the denominations to bring them into the warmth and beauty of unity. Written in a beautiful form, the message is perfect for our time and world. This book will impact many, just as Wilson continues to do.

—Cindy Martinusen
Award-winning author including
Winter Passing and *The Salt Garden*

More and more, many people are coming to understand the scope and meaning of the truth of sowing and reaping. This present day and our immediate future are securely tied to the generations that sowed before us, even as future generations will surely be affected by our sowing today. This is serious business, spiritual business, for all generations to consider. Some books are ahead of their times. Some are immediate in their timeliness. This book is past due, not to the fault of the authors, but to our own blind spots about the scope and meaning of history. We have needed, desperately needed, this work for some time now. Maybe Yahweh will extend His mercy and grace by allowing us to absorb these truths and enable us to act upon them with swift obedience. A friend once said, "You only really believe that which activates you." Reconciliation is about action and not simply words or sentiments.

Thank you for writing this book that will lead us all toward a hopeful future as we partner together in His glorious Kingdom.

—Rev. Qaumaniq Suuqiina and Dr. Suuqiina
Indigenous Messengers International

CONTENTS

PREFACE

WHEN we went to war with God—back in the Garden of Eden—we broke fellowship with ourselves as surely as we did with God and with our neighbors. We are made in His image; thus, when we rejected His image in us, we also rejected it in the rest of His creation. It is fair to say that the history of humankind is the story of every man against all others—including himself, if we count our many suicidal behaviors ranging from auto-immune disease to self mutilation—peppered with numerous attempts (often with demonic assistance) to cope with the problem without solving it. These attempts are called religion—a poor substitute for relationship with the living God—or at least Jesus the Son calls them that. He calls them that and then substitutes Himself on the cross for all of our religion. He opens the door to relationship with Him and His Father through relationship with the Spirit, and He invites us to walk through it. This renewed relationship is what we call reconciliation.

But before we can understand reconciliation, we need to come to grips with what we have substituted for it. When God first gave me vision for this book, I believed it was to be called *If My People*. The name comes from Second Chronicles 7:14, in which God says, "If My people, who are called by My name, will humble themselves and pray and seek My face and turn from their wicked ways, then will I hear from Heaven and will forgive their sin and will heal their land." If we did a word study of the Hebrew, we would find that what we translate into English as "wicked ways" is more akin to *inadequacy* than to moral evil. Yet, the translation is appropriate the way it appears in our English Bibles.

Reality is that we all too often worship our inadequacies. We decide that we are doing the best we can with a tight schedule when we decline to seek God regularly in the pages of His Word, making our schedules the ultimate reality of our lives and the altar where we worship. We declare that everyone should understand that we cannot let go of this or that grievance because we are only human, and we make our flawed incarnation of humanity the measure of our expectations for ourselves. (Reality is that only Jesus was fully human; we are still working on it.) We determine that the best we can do is the best we will offer to God instead of asking Him to transform our lives and our offerings, which is all He has ever insisted on doing in us. Truth is that whatever we designate as the ultimate reality of our lives is the god we worship. That renders the best we can do into the idol we worship—until and unless we permit our best to be transformed into His.

He is after more than the reconciliation of individual men and women with Himself. He takes restoring our relationships with one another so seriously that He says we cannot be serious in saying that we love Him without being just as serious about loving our brothers and sisters (see 1 John 2:9-11). He says that if we cannot treat each other the way He treats us, we cut ourselves off from that treatment from Him (see Matt. 6:14-15). He will settle for nothing less than His best in each and every one of us. To that end, He populates His Kingdom with those who take no offense at His Son being both the modeler and enabler of authentic humanity. It is the Son who forgives sin and restores relationship wherever He goes.

How central to the gospel is reconciliation? "All this is from God, who reconciled us to Himself through Christ and gave us the ministry of reconciliation....And He has committed to us the message of reconciliation. We are therefore Christ's ambassadors...," says Paul in Second Corinthians 5:18-20. But there is more at stake than the reconciliation of God in Christ to each one of us. Paul goes on, in Ephesians 2:19-21, saying, "Consequently, you are no longer foreigners and aliens, but fellow citizens with God's people and members of God's household...with Christ Jesus Himself as the chief cornerstone. In Him the whole building is joined together and rises to become a holy temple in the Lord." In other words, God holds our reconciliation to one another as inseparable from our reconciliation to Him. In case we miss the point, Jesus Himself hammers it home, saying repeatedly that if we do not forgive our brothers, we cannot receive His forgiveness (see Matt. 18:21-35). Reconciliation—becoming ambassadors of reconciliation across the board—is our calling and the making of our resurrected humanity.

Today the Body of Christ is hopelessly divided—as we count hope in terms of human ingenuity, resources, and good faith effort. Yet the Lord, who commanded His disciples to be perfect, as our heavenly Father is perfect (see Matt. 5:48), has ingenuity, resources, and good faith of which we know nothing. He is calling us today—as we near the end of today and await His glorious return—to step out in faith as the priests stepped into the Jordan River under Joshua's direction (see Josh. 4:18). This book is about identifying several lines of division within the Body and about what the people of God can do to open the door for Christ's reconciling work to flood our lives. There is no more important spadework for living out the Great Commission, which is our reason for being.

The first chapter will make a case that part and parcel of paving a straight highway in the desert for our God is the repentance toward one another visualized by John the Baptist in Luke 3:6-14. Reconciliation does not supplant confession with our lips and belief in our hearts that Jesus is Lord. But a commitment to reconciliation with all from whom we are separated, in fact or in terms of the factions with whom we identify, welcomes Him, and its achievement confirms the reality that He is in our hearts and lives. It cannot be separated or held over and away from receiving the lordship of Jesus.

The subsequent chapters, excepting the last one, will deal with some (though not all) of the separated lives and communities that presently exist inside and outside of the Body of Christ. Each will make the point that we all live in glass houses—that none of us are worthy of casting the first stone—and detail some practical ways in which we can lay down our stones without laying aside our integrity.

The last chapter will offer a Kingdom vision that can transform our communities into His community—even while we await the coming of the Bridegroom. This process is underway around the world, and it is His heart's cry that none should miss it.

Chapter 1

Ambassadors of Reconciliation

Some years ago, a woman from my congregation asked me to pray for the healing of her heart. Stephanie had been consumed with guilt for nearly twenty years, since the afternoon her daughter had been hit by a car in front of their home. The little girl, not more than two years old, had run out of their driveway and into the path of the car, and this mother had always believed that if she had only been more vigilant the accident would not have happened. The fact that the girl had miraculously survived after a full frontal collision with two tons of hurtling metal machine did not comfort Stephanie; she was too busy dwelling on the limp her daughter still carried, and the limpness in one arm. The always-volatile relationship between the two, which stretched over two decades, only made things worse. She had come to ask Jesus to intervene in the very history of her life.

We sat down and prayed that Jesus, and only Jesus, would enter into her mind and imagination, showing her what He had been doing the afternoon of the injury. Jesus came and showed the mother how He had imposed His body between her toddler and the bumper of the car. He showed her how His cushioning of the impact saved the little one's life. Stephanie figured out for herself that the permanent injury—with which the daughter coped quite well—was a permanent reminder that her daughter's life was a miracle. She left my office in peace, but the miracle of inner healing had not yet run the whole of its course.

I asked her how things had changed when I ran into her a couple of weeks later, and she couldn't wait to tell. She had a newfound depth of knowing God's love for her and for her daughter. For the first time in a long time, she was not ashamed to face Jesus, even when she had fresh sins to lay at His feet. But the most astounding thing she said was this: the relationship with her daughter, who knew nothing of the inner-healing session that had so changed Stephanie's life, was itself being resurrected as mother and daughter developed a new appreciation for each other. Reconciliation with her daughter—which the mother had not even dared to ask for—was part of the resurrection of her walk with Jesus the Christ.

Stephanie had lived in a personal relationship with Jesus Christ for years before the afternoon she visited my office. But in that afternoon, she experienced reconciliation with God and with her daughter. The issue of whether or to what degree she might have been responsible for the accident somehow never came up during the prayer encounter with Jesus. The issue of her estrangement from the God who loved her and her daughter more than she ever could took center stage. For the truth that she had never before spoken was that she resented God in the midst of her guilt, just as much as she resented herself and her daughter for failing to bond to one another.

It was necessary for her to repent, in the true meaning of that word, before she could receive the gifts of faith and trust in God, even for His management of her history. It was necessary for her to turn away from her hopeless and fruitless efforts to somehow atone for her past. It was crucial that she turn even her past over to Jesus with no strings attached. When she did that, she saw the truth of what God in Christ had been doing the day of the accident. She had never seen it before—not even on the day itself—because her focus was on what she had done or failed to do. She had been obsessing about the horror of the crash, so she failed to see the wonder of the deliverance. The new reality that she saw as we prayed in my office was the only possible explanation for the fact that her daughter had lived to reach adulthood.

It was not truth alone that set her free. It was her agreement to let God reconcile her to Himself and to her daughter that both revealed the truth to her and set her free. She agreed to that reconciliation the moment she agreed to submit her past to God—just as she desired to submit her present and future to Him, the moment she agreed to take even her thoughts about her guilt and resentment captive to Him in prayer. That freedom also permitted reconciliation to become a lifestyle for her—beginning with her daughter—as she became more and more a person created in the image of Him for whom she is called to be an ambassador of reconciliation.

It was her obedience to God in Christ that both revealed the truth and set her free. Jesus said, "If you hold to My teaching, you are really My disciples. Then you will know the truth, and the truth will set you free" (John 8:31-32).

Paul spoke the Word of the Lord when he said, "All this is from God, who reconciled us to himself through Christ and gave us the ministry of reconciliation....And He has committed to us the message of reconciliation. We are therefore Christ's ambassadors, as though God were making His appeal through us...." (2 Cor. 5:18-20). When he spoke these words he was, of course, characterizing the Great Commission as a call to join in the reconciliation between God and man that Jesus won on the Cross. But he was also hitting a favorite theme of Jesus in the Gospels—that sin versus righteousness is much more than a question of debits weighed against assets in some heavenly ledger.

If we understand religion as a human effort to close the gap that we created when we abandoned God for a piece of fruit in the Garden of Eden, the question becomes one of relationship weighed against that very religion. The Old and New Testaments can then be seen for what they are: the histories of God's effort and our responses to renew the relationship for which He created us in the first place. Thus, religion is that thing the Pharisees interposed between themselves and Jesus when He challenged them to get real and relational. But God will not let us get away with the false claim that we only feud with our neighbor out of devotion to Him. The

Apostle John poses the famous question: How can you claim to love God whom you cannot see, when you fail to love your neighbor whom you can see? (See 1 John 4:20-21.) Jesus consistently measures the degree of our repentance—our effort to renew relation with God—in terms of our willingness to forgive our neighbor for what we see as the neighbor's abandoning relation to us.

Just what is reconciliation, and how central is it to the Gospel? And how is it inseparable from the Great Commission? The meaning of the term is easy enough. To *reconcile* is "to renew relationship." It is "to refresh and reconstitute a relationship that has been broken or decayed." It is what Jesus accomplished on the cross when He accounted for all of the garbage of our sin that has fouled His connection with human beings. It is to engage with us in a new covenant that is a fundamental renewal of the old one, only better because the promised Holy Spirit is supplied as the glue that binds us together, even in the face of history that post-dates the cross. But how is it that we must believe that reconciliation between the people of God, one to another, is inseparable from the Great Commission to baptize and teach one another all things that He has commanded?

FIRST GIFT—FIRST OBLIGATION

For one thing, the authority to reconcile with separated brothers and sisters is the first gift that Jesus gave to the disciples after the resurrection. When He met them in the upper room, He twice called them to peace—and the Greek word actually means wholeness or integration. Then He said, "As the Father has sent me, I am sending you....If you forgive anyone his sins, they are forgiven; if you do not forgive them, they are not forgiven" (John 20:21,23). At first blush, this passage may appear to list forgiveness as an option; but when it is read in the context of the relationship Jesus has already established with His friends, nothing could be further from the truth.

In Matthew 18 (which is just one example), Peter asks Jesus how many times he must forgive his brother who sins against him. Jesus replies that seventy-seven times would be a good number to start with (see Matt. 18:21-22). But the parable of the unmerciful servant, just a couple of verses later, takes things a whole lot farther. Jesus illustrates his injunction to Peter with the story of a man who is forgiven a great debt by his master. As he joyfully leaves the master's house, he runs into another servant who owes him a small amount. Instead of sharing his joy by offering the same kind of mercy to the one who owes him, he grabs the other servant by the throat and demands full payment. The master then canceled his own act of forgiveness and sent the first servant to prison (see Matt. 18:23-34). Jesus told the disciples, "This is how my heavenly Father will treat each of you unless you forgive your brother from your heart."

I suspect that anyone witnessing the violence of the exchange between the servants would have seen the peace and joy drained from the unforgiving servant's face before the master ever said a word. When we focus on our imagined rights—like the right to judge one who belongs to another—it is pretty hard to remember and live in terms of the real blessings we have received. When God gave us free will, He also gave us the renewable choice to live in terms of His revelation of our life or in the residue of the choices we have made and the prerogatives we have claimed. It is this choice for fantasy over reality that cost the servant his abundant life. He robbed himself of that peace, which is about wholeness or integration—with God, with neighbor, and with self, in that order.

Yet, choosing God's reality—for God's revelation—as normative for our lives also opens the door for many others to obtain salvation. Just a few years ago, a number of the unrecognized American Indian tribes of northern California made a decision to sign a covenant with one another to provide mutual assistance in their dealings with the federal and state governments. I was honored with an invitation to speak at an event at which many in attendance would see the Church I represented as a symbol of oppression. They associate Christianity with the church-run boarding schools that their children were forced to attend to learn the white man's ways, enduring many beatings and humiliations. (Many American Indians resent these schools more than they resent the slaughtered buffalo and massacred villages.) When it was my turn to speak, even though I had never participated in the horrors that formed their corporate memory, I apologized for the many times that we had misrepresented the gospel and the Lord Jesus. I quoted Micah 6:8, "He has showed you, O man, what is good. And what does the Lord require of you? To act justly and to love mercy and to walk humbly with your

God." I said that I knew that we had been called to walk out that Scripture and that we had all too often failed to do it. I begged them to blame us, if they must, but not the Lord who loved them more than life itself. I pledged myself to become a truer man of God for having known these people.

I have since had the privilege of baptizing several members of one of the tribes represented, and I have shared the gospel with many more. Repentance for the sins of my people is not a ploy; it is not an agenda. It is a walking out of the obedience that leads to truth and freedom (see John 8:31-32) in light of truth that if my brother has anything against me, dealing with that issue should be the top priority (see Matt. 5:23-24). It is what we are commanded to do, and it bears the fruit of Him who commands it. This is true across the board.

Some years earlier, when I was fresh out of seminary, I taught the junior high class for an interdenominational community Vacation Bible School. Two of the girls in my class had been dropped off for the summer session by parents or caregivers who were too busy to spend time with them and much too busy to have ever exposed them to the love of God before. But God had other plans for these girls.

During the Vacation Bible School, I decided to teach the class a method of visual prayer that would enable them to draw closer to Jesus by inviting Him to literally inhabit their imaginations. As these two pre-believing girls asked Jesus to show Himself to them, He appeared to one in His kingly robes and to the other in blue jeans and a white t-shirt. When they reported what they had seen, each was overjoyed at how Jesus had "become all things to all men" (see

1 Cor. 9:22), or in this case, to a couple of adolescent girls. The one had never heard of a King who would invite her to enter His service. The other had heard of Jesus as a forbidding judge, but the man in the casual clothes had spoken softly to her of how much He loved her. Both of the girls received Him as their Lord, and I had the privilege of baptizing them a couple of weeks later. But Jesus Himself had paved the way for the witness. Jesus Himself, who never sinned against these girls or anyone else, made reconciliation the leading edge of revelation.

In the Sermon on the Mount, Jesus placed a premium on seeking reconciliation through forgiving and obtaining forgiveness. In Matthew 5, He stated that anyone who is angry faces judgment (see Matt. 5:21-22). He advised adversaries to settle their disputes before facing the judge, unless they preferred prison and torment for themselves once the case was heard (see Matt. 5:25-26). He commanded His disciples to love their enemies and pray for their persecutors if they would be men and women cast in the image of their Creator (see Matt. 5:43-48). He reserved His highest commendation for those who do not receive what they are due—the mourners, the meek, and the hungry—and he named those who make peace the authentic sons and daughters of God (see Matt. 5:3-10).

He said of such men and women,

You are the light of the world. A city on a hill cannot be hidden. Neither do people light a lamp and put it under a bowl. Instead they put it on its stand, and it gives light

to everyone in the house. In the same way, let your light
so shine before men, that they may see your good deeds
and praise your Father in Heaven (Matthew 5:14-16).

Clearly, Jesus was speaking of people who seek across-the-board reconciliation with other people—as they have received reconciliation with God—to be His ambassadors and the carriers of the gospel message to all nations and tribes. But His most radical pronouncement came in Matthew 5:23-24. Jesus said, "Therefore, if you are offering your gift at the altar and there remember that your brother has something against you, leave your gift there in front of the altar. First go and be reconciled to your brother; then come and offer your gift."

I am personally as self-righteously certain as the next man that if my brother has a problem with my behavior it is usually his problem. Jesus simply blows my mind when He calmly informs me that my gifts, even my worship, are not acceptable to Him so long as I have made no effort to reconcile with someone who claims I have offended him. Yet that is exactly what Jesus is saying. There is no hearing, no trial, and no judgment; on the contrary, Jesus tells me that I do not want to risk going to judgment over my brother's claim. He insists that if there is a problem, my job—as a disciple created in the image of my Lord—is to seek forgiveness and reconciliation from the other one. I can only be a light to the world, a bearer of the Great Commission, an ambassador of the reconciliation of Almighty God, if I am willing to be transparently vulnerable to the opinions and prejudices of people who are just as self-righteous as I am.

And they wonder if God has a sense of humor. They also wonder if what God commands His people as individuals should be applied equally to the Church as a whole. Is the obligation to pave the road for carrying out the Great Commission a corporate one? Is God calling His people to engage in what is called *identificational repentance* and *reconciliation*—seeking atonement with people and groups who may have sustained injury in another time or place from people who are long dead or otherwise unavailable? How far and wide does God plan to spread the net of grace depicted in Matthew 5:23-24?

CALLING OUT THE CALLED OUT

Is the Sermon on the Mount preached to individuals or to the Church? Did Jesus engage in identificational repentance when He mounted the cross for us and for our sins? Certainly we know the answer to both of these questions. Surely we know that bearing one another's burdens is our responsibility—corporately and individually—if we would live as ones made in the image of God. Scripture says as much—undeniably—in Galatians 6:2. Our world is a seething mass of old and new resentments, many that are fully justified on the basis of fact, and many more that may or may not pass a reality check. We are divided from each other on the basis of denominational practice and cherished belief. We resent the generation that is older than we are and the one coming up behind us. We have ancient and modern grievances against the people of ethnic and cultural tribes other than our own; and in the present day, the limits of the tribe we claim may not be any broader than a particular circle of friends or family or those who share a common job, hobby, or political passion. We litigate and look down upon the people of geographical regions other than our own, genders other than our own, and economic groupings other than our own. We fiercely resent those who follow a code of ethics and morals to which we do not subscribe. We remain split between Jew and Gentile.

God has something to say about this—and it is not to be sure we are right before we continue the conflict. On the contrary, He says,

> *Why don't you judge for yourselves what is right? As you are going with your adversary to the magistrate, try hard to be reconciled to him on the way, or he may drag you off to the judge, and the judge turn you over to the officer, and the officer throw you into prison. I tell you, you will not get out until you have paid the last penny* (Luke 12:57-59).

Nowhere in the Bible does God ever ask us to compromise our pursuit of truth. But He says again and again—in the strongest language—that seeking His face and judging our brothers simply are not compatible activities. And a house divided against itself—even the house that He calls a temple of the Holy Spirit and that I call my own body—cannot stand in the condition of division against itself.

The good news is that God, who loves all of those He has created and desires neither death nor suffering for any of us, came into the world not to condemn but to save (see John 3:17). His patience with us as we struggle to bend Him to our will (just as we seek to control everybody else) seems to be inexhaustible. But the really challenging news is that He does not budge from His conviction. His conviction is that He, through the Son, died and rose in order to bring about reconciliation between Himself and all of mankind. He will not rest until that baptism is accomplished, and He will not consider it accomplished until each of us has left our gift at the altar and gone to be reconciled to our brother and our sister. That is what is meant by teaching one another all that He has commanded us (see Matt. 28:20).

In John 9, Jesus and the disciples encountered a man who had been born blind. The disciples, just as steeped as any Pharisee in the cultural construct that if we suffer it is because we have transgressed, want to know who sinned, the blind man or his parents, to bring about the tragedy before them. Jesus, who never shied away from calling sin what it is, yanked the rug out from under his self-righteous followers. "'Neither this man nor his parents sinned,' said Jesus, 'but this happened so that the work of God might be displayed in his life'" (John 9:3).

It is not the case that neither this man nor his parents sinned. All have sinned, and all have fallen short of the glory of God (see Rom. 3:23). We know that—and certainly Jesus knew that. But He also knew that we tend to obsess over the sins of others and pay less attention to our own. The speck in my brother's eye is so much easier to see than the log in my own eye (see Matt. 7:3-5). Jesus was saying that it was not the sin of the man or the parents that accounted for the condition of blindness. God had brought all of them together within the circumstance of the man's disability so that (and solely so that) His glory might be displayed. It was the man's choice to worship the One who healed him, just as it was the parents' choice to curry favor with the authorities by pretending they didn't know what had transpired. The implication—and the application—is that we can now choose to seek reconciliation with those from whom we are estranged, regardless of who we think the injured party is. Or we can say that it was all too long ago—and we are too confused or too ignorant—and besides, they were just as wrong as we were. Either approach will bear fruit after its own kind for the salvation of many— some in multiplication and some in division.

Not many years ago, there was a wave of hate crimes in northern California. It began with the murder of a gay couple in Redding, and it came to include the burning of three Jewish synagogues in Sacramento and the bombing of an abortion clinic. Spokespersons for the gay and atheistic communities denounced the crimes as being the work of Christian fundamentalists. They organized rallies and gave interviews full of bile and invectiveness.

The Jewish synagogue in Redding received warnings from the FBI that they might be the next target, and they asked the Christian community for help. It was quickly decided that a peace garden—instead of the security fencing recommended by the FBI—would be built around the synagogue grounds. Many churches volunteered to work alongside the Jewish congregation as the garden was planted, making a very public statement about how they viewed both hatred and the people originally chosen of God for covenant. Eight years later, the gay and atheist communities are still fulminating against the Christians as dealers in death. But there was never an attack on the Redding synagogue, and the congregants thanked the churches that helped in a wonderful way.

A few weeks after the garden was planted, the synagogue leaders invited the pastors and volunteers who had worked on the planting to come for a ceremony of dedication. We pastors were given five minutes each to address the crowd in any way we felt led by the Lord. It was my privilege to remind everyone that we all worshipped the God of Abraham, Isaac, and Jacob. I then confessed that the blood of Moses flows in my own veins and that I wished that everyone present would discover the Messiah of Moses as I had. I spent my five minutes thanking God and those Jewish people for what we already shared and for the fulfillment of our faith in the Messiah I hoped we would one day share. After the speaking was finished and the partying was well underway, a number of synagogue members came up to personally thank me for my words. They said that they had never heard a Christian speak like that before, had never heard the gospel spoken like that before. The gospel was indeed preached from my mouth on that day, but it could only be heard in the atmosphere of reconciliation that preceded and enveloped it.

So who sinned, the blind man or his parents? Or was it all about Jesus and the glory He shares only with the Father and the Spirit from start to finish?

PAVING A HIGHWAY IN THE DESERT

I know this much, John the Baptist told us what we were to do in preparation for the coming of the Messiah in Luke 3: "'Prepare the way for the Lord, make straight paths for Him. Every valley shall be filled in, every mountain and hill made low. The crooked roads shall become straight, the rough ways smooth. And all mankind will see God's salvation'" (Luke 3:4-6). He morphed the poetic depiction of God's vocational vision for all of His people into (paradoxically) the simplest and the most comprehensive terms: "Produce fruit in keeping with repentance..." (Luke 3:8).

If we seriously believe that we are closer to the end than to the beginning of human history, if we seriously believe that the return of the King cannot be far off in time, then are we not called to listen again to the Baptist's message? He echoes down the centuries, "...And do not begin to say to yourselves, 'We have Abraham as our father.' For I tell you that out of these stones God can raise up children for Abraham. The ax is already at the root of the trees, and every tree that does not produce good fruit will be cut down..." (Luke 3:8-9).

When the crowd asked John for specifics, he told them, "'The man with two tunics should share with him who has none, and the one who has food should do the same'" (Luke 3:11). He added that tax gatherers, soldiers, and others wielding civil power should not abuse their power by over collecting or extorting (see Luke 3:12-14). But the thrust of his preaching was that we should empty ourselves of prerogative and entitlement for the sake of our calling as ambassadors of reconciliation—for the sake of the reconciling gospel of Christ crucified. This is the high calling against which the apostle Paul rated all other things as rubbish (see Phil. 3:8).

Jesus Himself, in the Sermon on the Mount, told the disciples, "If someone forces you to go one mile, go with him two miles" (Matt. 5:41). This is not so that we can accept or enable injustice but so that we might by all means win some to Christ. To go the extra mile is a choice for radical engagement. It is a choice for relationship as much as a choice for reconciliation because the two are made of the same stuff. It is not a legalistic requirement (How could it be such in a just world?), but it is a choice that Jesus typically makes and typically awaits in us, if we would be called by His name. He is so invested in radical engagement that He asked a man who was obviously blind what he wanted before giving him the sight he so obviously desired (see Mark 10:51). (Jesus wants engaging conversation more than the blind man wants his eyes.) He is so committed to encouraging engagement under any circumstances that he promised paradise to a crucified thief in response to a verbal acquittal from the thief (see Luke 23:43). He forgave the sins of the prostitute who wept over His feet and dried them with her hair, not because she had been atoned for or had even yet repented, but only because she loved (see Luke 7:38-44). He has decided that from within the relationships He has established will come all of the repentance for which the Father could ask.

A legalist will say that the naked gospel has all of the internal power for salvation it needs. He will say that the mere proclamation of God's saving grace and atoning sacrifice is all that anybody needs to hear in order to choose life instead of death. He will add that all past history is covered by the blood that was shed on Calvary and that any necessary reconciliation is effected the moment the sinner confesses his sins and throws himself at the foot of the cross. Of course, this is all perfectly true. And of course, the legalist gets it all perfectly wrong again, knowing neither the Scriptures nor the power of God. This is because the sinner will not likely hear the gospel until one or some who have already heard it become willing to break into that sinner's life the way Jesus broke into the life of the Samaritan woman at the well, engaging with her on her own territory instead of waiting for her to visit Him in Galilee (see John 4:1-42).

When legalists quote Scripture, they are usually correct as far as they go. But they invariably commit one or more of three errors—and they cling to their errors with the tenacity of the average wolverine. Legalists tend to be selective in their reading of the Word. When the Pharisees criticized Jesus for healing people on the Sabbath, they got it right that He was working and that the law says to leave our work for the other days (see Matt. 12:10-12). But they got it wrong inasmuch as they managed to forget that the very Scriptures they revere make specific exception for acts of mercy—such as hauling an animal out of a well (see Exod. 23:4-5, Hos. 6:6,

Micah 6:6-8). The law has always required that full attention be focused on God during the Sabbath—but it has never established an absolute method for maintaining this focus. God knows where we are paying attention when we care for one of His own. If this was not generally so, the clergy would always be in trouble for working on the Sabbath—Christian or Jew.

Legalists tend to be hypocritical in their application of the Word. When the Pharisees pointed out to Jesus that Moses permitted divorce when he fleshed out the commandments in the various legal codes of the Old Testament, they got it right (see Matt. 19:3-9). But they got it miserably wrong when they forgot that the very passage from Deuteronomy that they cited accepted divorce only in cases of infidelity—which effectively poisons the covenant between a man and a woman by introducing another person into the marriage bed (see Deut. 24:1-4). Jesus pointed out that the legal codes are meant to support God's Word that a man and a woman are to become one flesh; only a people with hard hearts would find in this material a license to cancel a covenant because of a change of affection.

Legalists tend to be innovative—harvesting provisions of the Word that God never planted. When the Pharisees (always the villains except when the Sadducees got into the act) accused Jesus and the disciples of impiety for not washing their hands before eating, they were answered with the naked fact that no such requirement exists in the Word of God (see Mark 7:1-8). The Pharisees were talking about human traditions of many generations that were intended to show piety but that were not laid down as law or gospel.

Jesus went even further in castigating His enemies for making up God's law as they went along when He pointed out that they even evaded their responsibilities to care for aging parents by simply dedicating their wealth to the Temple— whatever was left when they were finished enjoying it (see Mark 7:9-13). When the Pharisees justified what they called the Corban law, they got it right when they said the law required that oaths be kept (see Num. 30:1-2). And they got it utterly wrong when they imagined that one piece of Scripture could negate another. Evading God's will regarding caring for our families by taking a pious oath is still evading God's will—and God doesn't like it.

The bottom line is: never permit a legalist to instruct in the law. Always remember that anyone who speaks authoritatively about what Jesus believes while ignoring what Jesus did is probably a legalist.

Even more fundamental to an understanding of the relationship of reconciliation to establishing the Kingdom of God is the Parable of the Talents. Jesus tells this wonderful story in Matthew 25:14-30, a story in which three servants are given treasure amounting to five talents, two talents, and one talent of silver respectively. Those with the five and the two talents invest their wealth for the benefit of their master, and upon his return from a journey, he commends them and entrusts them with even greater wealth. The servant entrusted with the single talent does nothing with what he has; the master berates him for failing to invest what he had and orders him stripped of his one talent.

The only difference between the servants who are commended and the one who is cast out of the master's presence is that the former risked all to invest all and the latter risked nothing to invest nothing. The master had no concern about how much of a profit was returned—he rewarded the investing itself to an equal degree. But what has a story of the investment of material wealth, measured in the weight of talents of silver, to do with the carrying out of the Great Commission for the establishment of the Kingdom of Heaven?

Saint Lawrence was a third century deacon who functioned as treasurer of the Church in Rome. Hauled before the pagan authorities during a time of persecution, he was threatened with slow death if he failed to turn over the treasure of the Church at once. Lawrence gestured out the window—at the poor and the sick and the hungry—and declared that they were the treasure of the Church. He knew what his captors could not comprehend, as they roasted him to death, that the most precious features of the Kingdom are those people who will be raised from the dead, healed, given their sight and their hearing, and given the best news in the world. He knew what his torturers could not imagine, that one entered the Kingdom simply by taking no offense at the Lord of it. And if those precious ones needed some extra outreaching care before they could hear that good news—if they needed some renewed ground for relationship in order to renew their fellowship with the bearers of the good news before they could receive it—then a worthy investment would be to leave our gift at the altar and go to be reconciled with our brother.

The Parable of the Talents has always been understood to refer to the Kingdom calling, packaged as material wealth for the sake of the story. The chapters that follow will provide a sample of the many dimensions within the life of the Body of Christ that cry out for healing and reconciliation in order to enable the Kingdom to come and God's will to be done. They will offer expression of what I believe needs to be done on both sides of these relational gaps so as to enable our talents to multiply for the glory of God. They will also embody my own conviction that, as we become willing to do whatever God allows for the reconciliation of the people for whom He gave His only Son, we will become more and more like the servants who multiplied the five talents and the two talents. I am just as convicted that to fail to make this effort is to become the servant who buried his single talent in the ground because he was offended at the Lord of the Kingdom.

Jamie was a client of mine some years ago when I was serving a marriage and family counseling internship in southern California. He had been sexually assaulted by a male relative over a period of years. When he finally worked up the courage to tell his story to his pastor, he was ordered to keep silent and avoid rocking the boat. By the time this young man entered my office, he was full of hatred for God and for His Church.

On our first visit, he told me of his hatred for the representatives of the God he hated. He said that he had noticed the title Reverend on my business card, and he wanted me to know he would not come back if I was going to "throw the Bible at him." I replied that I would not do that at all. I added that I would respect him for who he was if he would allow me the courtesy of being who I am. We began a relationship on that basis.

For seven months, we saw each other weekly. I allowed him to ventilate all of the rage that he had for people he identified with me. He allowed me to say with freedom things like, "The only way I know to express what is on my mind right now is with a Bible story. May I share that with you?" Eventually there was enough trust between us that I could offer him the ministry of inner healing for some of his searing memories. I let him know that I could only do that in the name of Jesus—and he consented to that. A few weeks later, he permitted me to lead him into a living relationship with that same Jesus that he had rejected as a boy.

It took seven months of painstaking relationship-building and reconciliation to bring one new citizen into the Kingdom of Heaven while the ninety-nine waited on the hillside (see Matt. 18:12-13). We both engaged in repentance—in the original sense of letting go of the entitlements we imagined in favor of the real grace and gifted life that Jesus offers the willing ambassadors of His reconciliation. He required Jamie to walk an extra mile of grace and me to share an extra tunic of respect. Was Jamie worth it? Am I? Aren't we all, according to the Lord of life?

Chapter 2

GATHERING THE STREAMS

THERE was a man shipwrecked on an island. The island had everything he needed except company, and he lived there alone for twenty-five years. He was a Christian and worshipped God regularly—always giving thanks that Jesus had died and rose for him and for the fact that he had been well provided for while he was marooned. He also thanked God that he had the skill and know-how to build the things that he needed from the materials he found on the island. And he always fed the signal fires that he burned on the highest bluff on the island.

One day his faithfulness was rewarded. A ship saw the fire and landed a rescue party on the beach right in front of where the man lived. When the boat came ashore, the crew immediately noticed the three huts the man had built, but before they could look inside, the man came running and shouting down from the bluff—thanking God that he was about to be returned at last to civilization. The leader of the rescue party embraced the castaway and told him they would return to the ship as soon as the others in his party could be located. "But I am the only one," said the man. "I have been alone on this island for twenty-five years, and I am going home at last. Oh, to see my own kind again! Thanks be to God!"

The officer pointed out that there were three huts on the beach. Were there not others who lived in the huts? "Oh," said the man with a slightly embarrassed laugh. "I built all three of those huts for my own use. Actually, I live in the hut on the right. And I am a Christian. I go to church every Sunday in the hut in the middle." When the officer asked about the hut on the left, the man blushed and looked at the ground. "Well, uh, that is where I used to go to church, but I felt like I wasn't being fed there."

My mother-in-law has a favorite saying: "Wherever I go, there I am." We seem to have an unlimited capacity to blame others for our own shortcomings—as Adam blamed Eve in the garden for bringing him the forbidden fruit, and Ahab blamed Elijah for bearing to him the bad news of his repeated idolatries and their consequences—"Is that you, you troubler of Israel" (see 1 Kings 18:17). Yet as it was in the beginning, is now and ever shall it be until the last trumpet sounds; wherever we go, there we are. We bring our character flaws and fluctuations with us, and we devise creative ways in which to blame our faults on others. With so many denominations and ways of believing and ministering within the bounds of orthodox Christianity, the fields are white for the harvest of possibilities for pinning some group other than our own with responsibility for the fact that the Kingdom has not been established in all the earth over the past two thousand years.

The only difference between the man on the island and the rest of us murmerers and malcontents in the Church is the degree of imagination required to discover that the sin is not in me but in thee.

In the beginning there were no denominations. There was the Church in the city—understood as a branch of the Body of Christ—the *ekklesia*—the called out or gathered people of God. There were often multiple congregations of these city-wide churches; each had a distinctive identity, as gatherings will, but each understood itself as a localized expression of the one Church. (That is where the word *catholic* comes from; it means "universal," and never mind that one or another denomination may attempt to own the word.) There is no way to argue logically that our present divisions were in any way intended by God. Jesus' prayer for the Church was that we might be one (see John 17:23), and He never prayed that we might maintain integrity within our divided state. On the contrary, He maintained that the totality of our life was in our connection to Him, just as a branch is connected to the vine.

He knew and celebrated the fact that we are different. He said through Paul that the Spirit bestows different gifts on the various members of the Body and that the reason for this diversity is for the up-building of the whole as we grow into maturity (see Eph. 4:4-16). As molecules coalesce into collections that form elements, and elements combine into gases and liquids and solids that become a harmonious ecosystem (one that both lives and bears living things within it), so the

Author of creation spoke to the gifting of individuals for personhood and gatherings of people for communities larger and more complex than the sum of their gatherings. What He said to the disciples when they jockeyed for leadership in the band of His first faithful intimates, He has always applied to the congregations of the faithful. He told them repeatedly that the Son came to serve, not to be served (see Mark 10:45). He said and demonstrated time and again that this applies to those we love easily and to those we love with difficulty—to those we recognize as family and to those we are called to choose to recognize as family—because that is how He applies it. He said to go and do as we saw Him do—just as He did only and all that He saw the Father doing (see John 5:19).

Denominations came in the course of history, all believing they had something that all of the others lacked, and this much is true. But each denomination, from within itself, fails to see that the others also have something that (whoever we may be) is lacking in us and in ours. The congregations within a denomination vie with one another for the supreme expression of their peculiar and distinct identity. Because we resist genuine repentance, just as our fathers always did, we still seek to climb to the top on each others' backs while He waits for us to accept His invitation to climb to the top on His back—and to go and do likewise for our brothers and sisters.

God expected and enjoyed the reality of distinctive expressions of the Body in each city inhabited by the Body. The New Testament Church celebrated His joy and sent apostles from one city to another to capitalize on all of their diversity—whether it was to impart the Holy Spirit to Antioch by way of a Jerusalem delegation or to contribute money for sustenance in Jerusalem by way of delegations from many cities. When we divided more radically into denominations, after centuries of threatening such splits, God found a way to bless us even in that division because He is a God of redemption. He is ever One who works all things together for good in those who believe.

God gave gifts to each of our denominations, so that some specialized in signs and wonders and others in delving deep into the Word and still others in expressing His majesty in their worship, so that we could be contributing branches of the tree of life. He specially blessed each of our congregations so that we could be constituent members of the Body of Christ. In our zeal to blame others for our shortcomings, we created denominationalism, which is simply the same old yeast of the Pharisees. Denominations and congregations celebrate the varieties of gifts at their best. But when we add on the *ism* to those perfectly good nouns, we produce the same old legal-ism that declares that it is not who you know but what you have mastered that qualifies you for the abundant life Christ died to bring.

We make the implicit (and sometimes explicit) declaration that, unless your distinctive features and emphases are our distinctive features and emphases, you just are not right with the Lord. That way, some of us can tell others that they are unclean if they baptize infants and others of us can tell the rest that they are unclean if they do not. We can make a Kingdom issue out of whether or not one speaks in tongues or drinks coffee or enjoys a glass of wine while the call to go into all of the world and make disciples waits on the outcome of the argument.

It need not be so.

I will never forget the gift that I received from Phil, a member of a denomination I could scarcely comprehend, much less appreciate at the time. Diana and I were having a very bad time in our lives. We wanted children as much as any couple we had ever known, and we had faced only death in our efforts to begin a family. Beginning in 1977, with our stillborn daughter, Alyssa, we had conceived seven children by 1981. None had been born alive, and most had not survived past the third month of pregnancy. And to pour salt on wounds already as deep as they were raw, some members of family, friends, and the medical profession told us that we were only imagining the pregnancies. They urged us to relax at the same time that they let us know that we could not be a completed couple until we gave birth. We even had "friends" in our church who urged us to literally buy a baby so that we could be fulfilled in our marriage. Then we conceived an eighth time—in the fall of 1981. This time, I believed; I had a word from the Lord that the baby would be born healthy.

This child died in the third month—as had all of the others. By this time, we were under the care of a fertility specialist (who, incidentally, assured us that we had indeed been pregnant all of those other times), and it was necessary to collect the remains of our child and bring them to the lab for analysis. I remember standing in my garage with what was left of my son, cursing God to His face for misleading me about my son's chance at life, shaking my fist at the One who had died to give me life. Tears like a salt water runoff mixed with my rage, and I knew that I would have to confess my sin to someone I could not expect to understand. Understanding, much less excusing, could have no part in this transaction.

Phil was a colleague of mine at the high school in which I taught. He was one of two identified Christians on the faculty (I was the other one), and he was what I called a fundamentalist. I didn't really know what that meant, but I was pretty sure he took the Bible quite literally—something about which we were sometimes a bit cavalier in my denominational background. I was quite sure he would be quite literal about the blasphemy passages. I was absolutely convicted that I had to find the nerve to confess my sin outside of the sacramental system to which I was accustomed, to someone who would not just assign me a couple of prayers and a passage from the Bible or a hymn to recite. I had been angry enough to rail at God; I needed to be brave enough to let Him shout back. And so I went to see Phil.

I poured out the story of my deep disillusionment with God over the death of my son after the deaths of all of my daughters. I told him how my wife grieved (but never cursed God), how I seemed unable to grieve the way she did, and how I had cursed God to His face. He asked me if I was sorry, and I said that I was. He said that he figured God could handle my occasional outburst, that it was better to be honest about things than to pretend a grace I did not have. He said that he was glad I was willing to repent, and he prayed with me that the next child would be born alive and well. He helped me into a restored and renewed relationship with the Lord my God. And he did not know where I was coming from spiritually or doctrinally, but God used him to come looking for me anyway. He could not have made a better choice.

TWO SIMPLE COMMANDMENTS

Jesus gave exactly two general orders to His Church, His Body that is to remain on the earth until He comes again. The first was that the members love one another—*that* would be the sign that authenticates our life as His ambassadors. The second was that we would baptize and teach everyone we could draw into this fellowship of the crucified and resurrected people of God, counting on the enduring presence of Jesus through the outpouring presence of the Holy Spirit, sent by the ever-creating presence of the Father to sustain, inform, and empower us. He also gave a promise that we would do the same wonders we had seen Him perform and even greater things, but only as we acted in His Name. Acting in His Name, of course, means acting in accordance with the orders He left when He commissioned us as an apostolic band of brothers and sisters.

The first general order was as unqualified as it is pervasive throughout the pages of Scripture. The most explicit expression comes in John 13:34-35 when Jesus says, after having washed the disciples' feet and fed them with His own hand, "A new command I give you: Love one another. As I have loved you, so you must love one another. By this all men will know that you are my disciples, if you love one another."

There is no opportunity to parse the command to suit our needs or our limitations. He does not ask us to love as we understand the concept but as He understands and demonstrates it. "As I have loved you, so you must love one another." That means that we are called to wash each other and feed each other: "Now that I, your Lord and Teacher, have washed your feet, you also should wash one another's feet. I have set you an example that you should do as I have done for you" (John 13:14-15). It also means that we are called to unconditional and unlimited forgiveness of one another, as He makes explicit in Matthew 18:21-22 when He answers Peters' question, "How many times shall I forgive my brother when he sins against me? Up to seven times?" with the words, "I tell you not seven times but seventy-seven times."

It means conversely that, when a brother is having difficulty forgiving me, there is nothing more important than an attempt at reconciliation, regardless of whether the grievance is believed to be justified. "Therefore, if you are offering your gift at the altar and there remember that your brother has something against you, leave your gift there in front of the altar. First go and be reconciled to your brother; then come and offer your gift" (Matt. 5:23-24).

Through Paul, He calls on us to esteem all others as better than ourselves (see Phil. 2:3). He repeats the order to love one another with an added dimension in John 15:12-13: "My command is this: Love each another as I have loved you. Greater love has no one than this, that he lay down his life for his friends." In such a radical call to love, where is the permission found to look down on a Christian brother or sister because of a variance in belief or practice that yet falls within the bounds Scripture sets for membership in the Body of Christ?

It has been this way ever since the Father said through Hosea, "I desire mercy, and not sacrifice" (Hos. 6:6) and through Micah, "He has shown you, O man, what is good. And what does the Lord require of you? To act justly and to love mercy and to walk humbly with your God" (Mic. 6:8). Not one of these injunctions to love is qualified by words to the effect that they only apply when the brother is worthy of them.

The second general order is even more explicit than the first. The Great Commission calls us to do three things—in order. First, we are to worship the Lord at the place He directs, bringing our doubts with us. Matthew 28:17 reads, "When they saw Him they worshipped him; but some doubted." Second, we are to baptize and learn from one another. Matthew 28:19-20 exhorts, "Therefore go and make disciples of all nations, baptizing them in the name of the Father and of the Son and of the Holy Spirit, and teaching them to obey everything I have commanded you...." Finally, we are intended to depend on the eternally continuing presence of the Lord Himself in our midst, not on our own abilities to approximate what He would be like if He were actually with us. Matthew 28:20 assures us, "...I am with you always, to the very end of the age."

The doubting part is as interesting as it is explicit. The Scripture is clear that those who came to worship, even as they doubted, were welcomed no less warmly than the others. Jesus offered the same instructions and promises to all who showed themselves on the holy mountain. Yet we know from the Epistle of James that a double-minded man can expect nothing from the Lord (see James 1:6-8). There is a sharp distinction between the doubter such as Thomas—who offered to die with the Lord when he failed to understand the righteousness of Jesus' commitment to show Himself in public (see John 11:16) and who was the first person in the Bible to address Jesus as God (see John 20:28)—and doubters such as Simon Magus who offered money for the power to work miracles just in case that might improve his personal standing (see Acts 8:9-25) or the pathetic King Herod who begged Jesus to work just one little miracle for his entertainment (see Luke 23:8-9).

When I lashed out at God in my garage over the death of our child, I was expressing doubt, salty language and all. When I confessed my sin to my friend, Phil, I was simply bringing my doubts with me to the altar. We agreed that what I had done was sin, but we also agreed that the only way to resolve that breach in my relationship with my Lord was to bring it before Him in a way that I understood as leaving me vulnerable. Waiting until my hands are clean before coming to the Lord implies that I believe I can clean my own hands. It is not so; it is not required.

There is no place in Scripture in which God rejects a person for bringing honest doubt with him to the meeting, although the signs with which God resolves doubt can be as brusque as when Zachariah loses his voice for the nine months of his wife's pregnancy (see Luke 1:20) or Moses finds himself temporarily stricken with leprosy (see Exod 4:6-8). But God only rejects those who exhibit apathy toward Him, and He says as much in the Book of Revelation. It is the Church of the lukewarm, the apathetic, that He threatens to spew forth from His mouth (see Rev. 3:16). For those who are seeking God and are not yet sure they have actually found Him, the only reception they will ultimately find is the one that awaited Thomas on that evening a week after the Resurrection. Jesus said, "Put your finger here; see my hands. Reach out your hand and put it into my side. Stop doubting and believe" (John 20:27). In our shared commitment to denominationalism, we behave as though the gift of God's grace must be earned through the manufacture of certainty as a state of our being. Jesus does not agree.

If the doubting part is interesting, the baptizing and teaching part is fascinating. Although it has been the practice of the Church since the earliest times to give a prolonged period of instruction in the faith before admitting new members through baptism, there is not a hint in Scripture that this was the intention of either the Lord Jesus or the apostolic leadership from the beginning. On the contrary, the typical New Testament story of baptism is found in Acts 8, in which the deacon, Philip, is directed to intercept an Ethiopian who is reading the Book of Isaiah at the same time he is driving his chariot home from a trip to Jerusalem. The Ethiopian questions Philip about the application of what he is reading, and Philip shares his faith with the man. The next thing we know, the Ethiopian has made his own profession of faith. Without further ado, they stop the chariot and Philip baptizes a new citizen into the Kingdom of Heaven (see Acts 8:26-40).

A similar scenario plays out in the city of Philippi and is recorded in Acts 16. Paul and Silas were placed in prison, and that night, while they were serenely engaged in worship, an earthquake blew open the doors and they were free to go. Rather than leaving at the first opportunity, they waited to see what would unfold. Soon the prison warden announces his intention to commit suicide rather than be executed for losing his prisoners. Paul and Silas assured him that he had not lost any prisoners, and his response was to ask what he could do to gain salvation. They shared their faith with him and then, at his request, baptized the man and his family on the spot (see Acts 16:16-33).

Yet again, the pattern of Holy Spirit activity leading to salvation worked its way out in Joppa in the story of the centurion. Peter had a vision in which the Lord told him to lighten up on his inhibitions regarding what foods are clean for him to eat (remember that Jesus declared all foods clean in Mark 7 during the debate over corban and whether what goes in or what comes out can defile a person). God was clearly preparing Peter for his next assignment, which was to answer the call of the centurion for answers about the Kingdom of Heaven. While Peter was visiting the centurion in his home and sharing the Gospel with the man and his household, the Holy Spirit fell spontaneously on all of those gathered. Peter responded to the Lord's initiative by ordering that all present be baptized at once; he had only known the centurion for a few hours, but that had proved long enough to confirm the hunger in the man's heart. And then Peter remained in the house for several days, presumably instructing the new disciples in the basics of the faith after the fact of their entry into the Kingdom (see Acts 10).

The New Testament pattern was that the baptized ones would spend the rest of their earthly existence learning and practicing the implications of what they pledged in Christ when they received Him as their Lord and announced their commitment through the sacrament of baptism. Scripture visualized preparation for the Kingdom as coming *after* receiving citizenship by the free gift of it. But in our commitment to denominationalism, we want to insist that converts be fully prepared for the privilege before it is conferred. Although no two denominations agree on just what knowledge is essential for living eternal life, they all insist that it be earned in some way before it can be bestowed.

The Scriptures do urge all of us to be prepared to give an account of the faith that is in us, but we are not expected to give that account before we receive the faith. On the contrary, faith is given in response to the hunger for it; grace is bestowed as a free gift; and we are instructed to seek knowledge with all of our hearts now that we can receive it.

The words of the Great Commission that we translate as "teaching them to obey," actually come from the Greek word for instruction, which is *edukos*. It implies such a thoroughgoing mutuality in the power of the Holy Spirit that it should be read in English as "teaching one another to obey." We are not called to transfer the knowledge of the Kingdom, but to share it in the First Corinthians 12 sense, in which all parts of the Body have equal value as instructors and equal need for instruction after their fabulously variegated kinds!

If the baptizing and teaching part is fascinating, the part about Jesus staying with us is sublime. He simply will remain with us for as long as it takes Him to draw us to Himself. Nothing brings that reality home to me more forcefully than communion at a pastors' prayer summit some years back.

THE CHURCH IN THE CITY

When we moved to Redding, California, in 1996, it became quickly apparent that God was creating a church in and for the city. (Actually, in this case, it was for an entire county.) I found myself invited to three different pastors' prayer groups, one made up of primarily charismatics, another of evangelicals, and the third a grand mix of all three streams of the river of God (evangelicals, charismatics, and liturgical types). They met at different times and in different locations, yet their very existence crossed denominational lines and testified to God's move to gather. Over the coming months, we would become more and more aware of each others' existence, even though only a couple of us belonged to more than one of the groups. As we began to come together more and more, for this project or that, some remarkable features emerged.

We began to learn from one another. This learning was not just some quaint appreciation of how someone else lived; we found that the Lord really had planted gifts in others that all the rest of us could incorporate for the blessing of the whole. For example, the bunch of us in the mixed prayer group that met in the south part of the county shared a conviction that the Body of Christ was called to a major role in the coming reform of the federal welfare system. The year was 1996, and a new law had just been enacted but had not yet gone into effect. We knew that we were not called to a mere taking up of the slack when a fatally flawed system went out of existence, but rather, we were called to demonstrate the across-the-board power of God to meet the practical needs of families at the same time that He was meeting their spiritual needs. We understood that we needed nothing less than a vision from God to show us what He expected from us and what He meant to do through us.

We scheduled a retreat in which we would simply worship and seek a vision from the Lord. We made covenant with one another that we would not plan or brainstorm (using the brains God gave us to process our own ideas about how to image a Kingdom welfare reform approach) until the Lord had given us a recognizable and supernaturally sourced vision. We would then use the brains God gave us to process the revelation that He had given. We prayed and read Scripture together, and then we closed our eyes and begged God to speak to us. What emerged was a composite vision of grandiose proportions. One piece actually showed trucks coming in from the countryside loaded down with produce on a road that was constructed as they drove over it, which ultimately resulted in an interdenominational ministry called Faithworks Coalition.

The concept that was birthed in the hearts of half a dozen pastors gathered in a school gymnasium is now a coalition of more than seventy churches in California's Shasta County. In the first eighteen months of its existence, the ministry partnered with the county social services department to cut welfare roles in half. It has cloned itself in several locations around the country and has been recognized by the federal government as a point of light and a model for faith-based ministries worthy of competition for government grants. It has just built and dedicated an apartment complex that will house families for up to twenty-four months as they emerge from dependence to independence, with mentoring and support from the larger community. (A spinoff ministry under the Faithworks umbrella was the only agency, public or private, to build housing for the uninsured victims of a wildfire that swept our county in 1999.) Faithworks offers a larger life in Jesus Christ to every client family it serves, and it serves them with a smile whether or not they receive Jesus. Families are placed in churches when and if they desire it.

The governing philosophy behind Faithworks is that we are a full-service welfare ministry in ways that the government welfare system can neither imagine nor comprehend. But the revelation behind the philosophy is that God used an Episcopalian (who learned it from a bunch of tongue-speaking Charismatics) to teach the rest that God meant it literally when He said that without a vision the people could only perish (see Prov. 29:18 KJV). He used the Catholics in the group to teach the rest of us how to operate a social services agency. And He used the evangelicals to teach us to keep the Great Commission as our focus, even when we are feeding, clothing, and providing jobs for people.

We began to sow into each others' ministries more and more. When one congregation found itself without a home, another would welcome the people into their building (usually rent free) with open arms and a flexible schedule that would permit worship and ministry to go forward. Pulpit swaps became commonplace, and weddings and funerals were conducted in each others' buildings when the home facility was not suitable for a coming event. When one had a financial need, another would take up a special offering to help meet that need. In 1998, more than twenty local churches began making monthly pilgrimages to each others' sites in order to pray God's blessings on each other as an interdenominational group. The beauty of these visits is that the power of the Holy Spirit, which is bestowed on the whole Body, is unleashed in submission to the particular pastor who has been anointed by God in a particular congregation from a unique tradition.

We began to identify with one another, as the Church in the city, more than with our denominational polities. That meant simply that more and more of us saw ourselves as our denomination's representative within the larger mix of our region and as a necessary component of the whole. But as the Episcopalian in that gathering, I identified more with my brothers and sisters in Shasta County than with the Episcopal Church in northern California, which was centered two and a half hours away in Sacramento. We tended to socialize, minister, study our Bibles, pray, and worship together more than we sought those opportunities in settings where all we had in common with the others involved was a denominational background. But the communion service was where the rubber met the road, at least for me.

About sixty-five pastors and their spouses had gathered at a regional conference center near Chico for three days of shared prayer and worship. About midway through the second day, the leader approached me to ask if I would lead the group in a service of Holy Communion. I was deeply honored that he would ask me to do this; the only problem was that we had no wine.

For an Episcopalian, communion is always celebrated with bread and wine; juice simply does not work. We cherish our adherence to what we believe was the original practice of the Church (indeed, of Jesus and the disciples) just as much as any Evangelical loves the sinners' prayer and the four spiritual laws and with the same bedrock devotion that Pentecostals reserve for praying in tongues—and for the same reasons. Yet here was an opportunity to be the whole Body in a special way, and my brothers and sisters were asking me to lead the way. I understood that God's reign is exercised in sacrifice. I also knew that His principles are never to be compromised. Was I being asked to sacrifice God's principle or my own? I asked for a moment to pray, and the Lord spoke quickly and clearly. "What is more important—doing it right or doing it for my Kingdom?"

By phrasing His answer the way He did, of course, the Lord left open the question of whether *right* was a subjective or an objective term at that moment. He also left open the opportunity for me to sacrifice my comfort and my personal expertise in this most central act of my priesthood—at least in my own understanding of that priesthood. I told the leader I would be honored to lead the communion service even though I knew (as he did not) that I was releasing into the air the very core of my understanding of the greatest gift, the gift of sacrament, that God had entrusted to my branch of the family for the sake of giving that gift to the rest of the family. I found myself thinking of Peter in Acts 10, when the sheet came down from Heaven three times, as I prayed over the bread and the juice and as the people later told me that they had never before seen such a reverent and majestic supper of the Lord.

In the context of my participation in the leadership of many regional and statewide associations, I am often privileged to celebrate communion in interdenominational gatherings. I make it a point to consecrate both wine and juice so that people are free to choose how they will participate and be honored in conscience as they do. I usually ask ministers of various streams to lead with me (there is no greater privilege), and every time we do this great act together, there are few dry eyes in the house as the Body both comes together and recognizes how much we lose when we do not. But it begins—for me—with the memory of the afternoon I obeyed God when He invited me to sacrifice my identity within my tribe in exchange for a gift of the Holy Spirit in a wholly unexpected shape.

REALITY CHECK AND CHALLENGE

But all of this is not business as usual. Look how far we Christians have traveled down the road of separation from one another without realizing that we separate ourselves from Him as we travel. We have denominations that believe real Christians will only baptize adults who have made a mature decision for Christ. And we have others who believe just as strongly that baptizing infants makes them more able to grow into mature Christians who will make that decision for Christ and that anyone with the slightest theological insight can see they are right. We have church bodies who think it a sin to take communion with real wine; they will tell anyone listening that Jesus used a non-alcoholic beverage at the last supper. And we have others who believe the Lord's presence in the sacrament is fatally compromised unless even the ingredients are identical to those used two thousand years ago. There are legions of Christians who know that a congregation is apostate if it permits women in the pulpit or at the altar. And there is a growing multitude who are just as convinced that the men-in-leadership-only crowd is too obsessed with law at the expense of the gospel to ever amount to anything in the Kingdom.

Everyone recognizes that the Holy Spirit was transmitted through the laying on of hands from the beginning. But multitudes of believers are utterly convinced that this kind of transmission today is only for the setting apart of designated clergy. Other multitudes are just as convinced that leadership can only be legitimate if the one laying on the hands stands in tactile succession to the successors, back down two millennia, of the original apostolic band who first laid on the holy touch. More millions, in their denominations, believe the wonder-working gifts that accompanied that laying on of hands disappeared centuries ago and that it is stark heresy to think otherwise. Other millions know beyond the reach of rational discussion that the gifts, especially tongues, are so very much for today that salvation must surely be questioned in a Christian who does not exercise at least one of the gifts listed in First Corinthians 12-14, Ephesians 4, or Romans 12.

I will never forget the day I shared the story at a pastors' prayer meeting about the dedicated group of intercessors who had prayed every day for the abortion clinic in a city nearby. They had spent the past decade praying nothing but God's blessing on those who came in and those who went out from that clinic, remembering that what God blesses He also transforms into His likeness. They had seen the number of abortions performed each year in their city drop by two thirds, and they were determined to keep praying and blessing until the total zeroed out. One of the pastors blurted out that he knew of a small group who prayed daily at our local abortion clinic, and wouldn't it be great if we all began to stand with them in prayer. But one of the other pastors muttered that the prayer group at the clinic was mostly Catholic nuns and he didn't think he could bring himself to pray to the Virgin Mary. The fact that no one had mentioned (much less encouraged) prayer to Mary was lost in the thunderous silence that followed. Just as lost was the opportunity to break a deadly stronghold over our city by standing together over time and theological disparity.

Not one of the roadblocks we throw against one another will bear up under biblical scrutiny, yet by clinging to them, we protect ourselves from both the opportunity and the obligation to storm the gates of hell. By refusing the fullness of fellowship with those Christians whose practice differs from ours, whether through open scorn and distrust or through the mere indifference of a smarmy co-existence, we encourage the waiting world to distrust the gospel and the bearers of the gospel. This should arouse in us nothing but remorse.

On the other hand, imagine the power of the Holy Spirit regularly unleashed in communities all over the nation as it was in my community on the day that representatives of each of the streams of the Body of Christ (evangelical, charismatic, and liturgical) gathered to bless a public middle school. It was a Saturday, but the principal was so excited that people would give up their Saturday to bless his school that he gladly gave up his day to meet us on campus. He asked us to pray over the violence that was so pervasive (the athletic field had been the site of a rape just a few weeks prior). He asked us to pray for release from drug abuse that was common amongst his students, aged eleven through fourteen. He asked for blessing on a new reading program in this school since they were far below the standards set in the new federal No Child Left Behind Act. Finally, he asked for a miraculous boost to the morale of his faculty—a group of deeply dedicated men and women who had labored for many years in a dead-end school with little evidence that they were making a difference. We prayed on site and in unity for several hours and went home having seen no more evidence of Holy Spirit activity than would visibly accompany the average communion service. It was only on the occasion of our next visit, the following year, that we heard the spectacular testimony of this principal about what God had done on his campus.

Drug use and violence were dramatically reduced. The reading program had taken off like a shot. But the most gratifying feature, to the principal, was that the faculty and staff had returned from summer vacation more pumped-up and energized than he had ever seen a staff in his entire career. But it has taken another three years for the fullness of God's grace to unfold on this campus. In the Fall of 2004, the school launched itself as a magnet school for the performing arts, now a major league beacon of light in a public school district in which it had been the black hole just three years earlier. Today this school is listed as a California Distinguished School.

Two things transpired. The faculty and staff continued to faithfully carry out their duty to care for and educate the young people placed in their charge. And a cross section of the gathered Body of Christ functioned as that Body in the very midst of the fallen world to which we are called. In that gathering, the Kingdom comes.

Chapter 3

ENGAGING THE DENOMINATIONS

RECENTLY I had the privilege of leading an interdenominational team of intercessors (people who pray for others) as we visited several churches who are under heavy fire from their own denomination because of their stand for the truth of the Word of God. The national branch of their denomination has made an institutional decision to tolerate and even endorse the sexual misconduct of some of its members. This national leadership has gone even further, declaring in public responses to international member bodies of their denomination and to most of the Body of Christ that their perspective holds a theological enlightenment superior to the rest of the Body. They claim a better revelation due to what they call their better education and deliberative acumen. The orthodox churches we visited had withdrawn from this national branch, and the national leadership had filed suit to confiscate their property in retaliation.

Once again, we went as representative samples of the charismatic, liturgical, and evangelical streams of the Kingdom. We went to bless the churches rather than to fulminate against those who would attack them. We went entirely dependent on the Holy Spirit to give authority and power to the prayers and prophecies we released into the atmosphere of these church campuses. And God showed up.

When we arrived at the first church, we took out the bottle of anointing oil we had brought and found that it had spilled in its carrying case, leaving just one drop in the bottom of the bottle. Although disappointed, we covenanted to spend what we had in anointing, just as we were determined to spend what we had in prayer and presence—for as long as we had any to spend—leaving the outcome to God.

We spent the next eight hours in unselfconscious praise, worship, and deep petitionary prayer with the staff and pastors of these congregations. We anointed with oil anything and anyone who would hold still for us. We declared in the Spirit that we were so identified and intertwined with our brothers and sisters that we were them and they were us. (We were not content to just support them in prayer—we declared that there was no *them*, only an *us*. This embodies or walks out Second Kings 3:7, in which the King of Judah says to the King of Israel, "I am as you are, my people as your people, my horses as your horses.") We saw God reveal old bondages in these congregations that compromised their ability to minister the gospel with power, and we forgave and re-commissioned them for mission. We prayed God's overwhelming blessing and transformation on the parent body that sought to do them harm, and they joined with us in for-giving. At the end of the day, we looked at that pathetic bottle of oil that had contained only a drop of oil at the beginning, and we saw that it now held a quarter of an inch of the stuff of anointing. The jury was in, and God had voted for resurrec-tion, not just in Heaven but on earth as well. As I write, these churches have prevailed in the lawsuits brought against them. More importantly (much more) is the fact that these churches are now ministering in their communities with a power and authority that they have not previously known. Such is the power of spiritual warfare that is grounded in the blessing of all parties and the forgiveness of sin.

What if we had said, "I don't know if I can pray with these guys without compromising my own doctrinal integrity," as that pastor in the last chapter had said of the intercessors for the abortion clinic? Christians made no such demands on each other for the first thousand years following Pentecost. There were plenty of squabbles and debates, and uniform agreement was required on the foundational creedal state-ments dealing with the persons and placement of the Trinity. But it was only required on such basic issues that, without that agreement, it could be truly said that they were not even speaking the same language. Uniformity of worship practice, baptism, what goes on during and in the communion, and so forth were left to local option so long as the parties agreed that the Bible was the authoritative Word of God and the struggle was over how best to interpret that revelation. Both thought and practice differed widely (and peacefully) throughout the world until the western branch of the Church presumed to re-write one of the foundational summaries of the Faith and the eastern branch drew a line in the sand. Since that time, our treatment of people who differed from us while claiming the same Lord has varied from burning to ostracism. But it has never been pretty. Typically, when one faction separates from another, the urge to separate from those within the separating faction who are not perfect in their understanding (as we are) prevails again and again.

The Kingdom can only diminish from this, even if our particular group gains more members. The world holds us up to ridicule as did the great American Indian leaders Red Jacket of the Iroquois (in 1805) and Spotted Tail of the Brule Sioux (in 1876) when missionaries from many denominations asked their commitment not just to Jesus but to the missionary's denomination. Their objection had not changed in seventy years, and it has not changed today: "When your leaders finally agree on what you believe is true, come back then and we will talk about it. While you fight among yourselves, how can we be expected to choose?"[1]

What are some of the issues that divide us? And can any of us claim such unimpeachable integrity that we can afford to write off the rest?

Take the issue of baptism for openers. Each and every identified person in the Scriptures who received baptism is an adult who had made a mature confession of faith in the Lord Jesus, from the Ethiopian eunuch of Acts 8 to Cornelius the centurion in Acts 10 to the Philippian jailer in Acts 16. Paul said that in order to be saved, we must confess Jesus with our lips and believe what we confess in our hearts, and that implies strongly the need to understand the confession we make. A very good case can be made for adults-only baptism.

On the other hand, the Scripture is clear that the family of the Philippian jailer was baptized along with him; we are compelled to infer that the children were included. It is equally clear that the large gathering of people in the home of Cornelius the centurion were all baptized. Indeed, three thousand people were baptized on Pentecost after hearing Peter speak of the Lord and His resurrection for their sake. The clear implication is that children were present and were included, especially if we recall Jesus' own words about children—that the Kingdom was composed of them and their like (see Matt. 19:14). John the Baptist leaped in the womb in the presence of his unborn Lord, proving once and for all that what we regard as responsible faith is not necessarily the vision of God. An equally good case can be made for baptizing any who are willing or who are presented by their guardians or those who have charge of their welfare.

Responsible faith on our part impels us to choose to simply respect the decision the respective churches make about their own baptismal practice and make no judgments about their orthodoxy from that practice. The only thing that is crystal clear in Scripture is that we are to use water and the Trinitarian formula when we baptize. In the absence of a clear and irrefutable biblical mandate for one direction or the other in deciding eligibility for baptism, we have few choices and many opportunities.

Take the communion issue, as a next step. There is simply no room for reasonable doubt that Jesus used real (read alcohol-laced) wine at the first recorded service of Holy Communion. The use of wine was so pervasive in the cultures of the day and of the region that terms like *the cup* and *fruit of the vine* as they are used in Matthew 26, Mark 14, and Luke 22 can only have one meaning, unless otherwise specified, and that meaning is wine. In First Corinthians 11, Paul complained that the believers were so careless about their communion celebrations that they were becoming drunk, yet he did not urge them to use non-alcoholic materials, only better manners. In John 2, the narrative is quite explicit that Jesus changed water into wine, not juice. And one of the most common charges lodged against Jesus by the religious authorities of the day was that he was a shameless winebibber. The Christian churches taught this without exception well past the time of the Reformation.

The very same deficits apply to those who would defend the use of individual servings of bread and juice. Without exception, the symbolism of the gospel accounts and the discussion in First Corinthians 10 and 11 both presuppose and make explicit the notion of one loaf and one cup in the service. "Is not the cup of thanksgiving for which we give thanks a participation in the blood of Christ? And is not the bread that we break a participation in the body of Christ? Because there is one loaf, we, who are many, are one body, for we all partake of the one loaf" (1 Cor. 10:16-17). It is simply not possible to make a case for prohibiting the use of either wine or the common cup in the communion service that is grounded in the Word of God, much less to absolutize such a prohibition to the point where we would judge those who continue the ancient practice.

On the other hand, many denominations offer their communion services with grape juice instead of wine. And in most cases, these same churches provide individual servings of the communion elements. The most common reasons given for departing from traditional norms are concerns about alcoholism and prevention of contagious disease. Dare we sit in judgment on them at the expense of the Lord's prayer, which tells us to love one another and come together in His name?

From the standpoint of history, there is no question that both of these practices are fairly recent innovations. But nowhere in Scripture is the point made explicit that only wine and only the common cup may be used. Although the communion service is the normative activity of the gathered people from the Book of Acts on, there is no serious effort to so much as describe the service and its conduct until it has been going on every Sunday, and in many places every day, for more than a century! That is how little concern there was for uniformity of practice during the inaugural period of the Body of Christ.

A QUESTION OF ATTITUDE

To return again to First Corinthians, the only book of the Bible containing an extended discussion of Holy Communion, we find that the reason for the discussion is Paul's passionate concern over how the Corinthians are making a sacrilegious hash of the sacred service. However, Paul's concern is always directed not to the Corinthian practice, but to the attitude with which they practice. In the midst of his lecture on communion that begins in Chapter 10 and spans Chapter 11, Paul wrote, "'Everything is permissible'—but not everything is beneficial. 'Everything is permissible'—but not everything is constructive. Nobody should seek his own good, but the good of others" (1 Cor. 10:23-24). Granted, the next verse makes it clear that Paul is continuing his teaching about eating meat that has been sacrificed to idols, but he moves seamlessly from that point back into the Chapter 11 communion material. It is clear that he is trying to say that it is the heart we bring to our spiritual exercises that is the heart of the matter.

Again, within that broader discussion, he wrote, "...For why should my freedom be judged by another's conscience? If I take part in the meal with thankfulness, why am I denounced because of something I thank God for? So whether you eat or drink or whatever you do, do it all for the glory of God. Do not cause anyone to stumble..." (1 Cor. 10:29-32). It is simply not possible for Christians to sit in judgment over one another for their conscientious use of non-alcoholic fruits of the vine or for individually packaging the elements, at least not if we would stand on the Word of God. The Son of God calls on us to imitate what He has done—in the Spirit in which He walks—as often as we do it at all. He implies, and Paul makes it explicit, that the Communion service should always be an exercise in fine dining rather than fast food, a time of deep sharing and not of gluttony. If that is our sincere intent, He is going to be fine with it.

Once again, agreement in all points is not a necessary feature of the Body of Christ. Love, honest respect, and lightening up on one another, as we submit to Christ, is what we cannot live without.

The question of women in leadership has been a nest of hornets since the beginning of the Body. The Council of Elvira, held in A.D. 308, went so far as to forbid women to preside at Holy Communion or to function as priests in any other way. But the urging to prohibit these activities shows that women were functioning in leadership positions from the time of the apostles until the fourth century. Scripture is ambivalent on the issue.

Certainly the Jewish priesthood of the Old Testament was an all male fellowship. Although women such as Deborah functioned as judges, and women like Ruth and Esther played pivotal leadership roles (not to mention Sarah, Rebecca, and Rachel) the Old Testament is quite explicit that only men (and only men of the tribe of Levi) could function in the sacred ministry of altar and temple. However, even in the face of their exclusion from presiding at occasions of corporate worship, the presence of women such as Deborah (see Judg. 4) at the very pinnacle of the cultic pyramid demonstrates that God at no time commanded the exclusion of women from Kingdom leadership altogether.

In the New Testament, the situation becomes much more complicated. Acts 1 is clear that the apostolic fellowship was much larger than the band of eleven that became twelve with the casting of lots just prior to Pentecost. "They all joined together constantly in prayer, along with the women and

Mary the mother of James, and with his brothers" (Acts 1:14). The congregation numbered about one hundred and twenty when the Holy Spirit fell at the beginning of Acts 2, and that is where the proverbial rubber meets the road. Although the Twelve occupied a special place at all times, and they were admittedly all male, it is just as clear that the Holy Spirit in all fullness fell on all of the gathered ones, male and female as He created them.

It is just as clear that the first witnesses of the Resurrection were women (see John 20:1-16) and that the first exercise of leadership in the primary task of proclamation was theirs (see John 20:17-18), as all of the Gospel accounts bear witness.

Paul is reputed to be the New Testament author most clearly opposed to women in leadership because of statements he made to the effect that women need to keep silent in church and receive necessary instruction from their husbands at home (see 1 Cor. 14:34-35). But the Book of Acts records the congregation (founded by Paul himself) that met in the home of Lydia, a woman in the dye business who was clearly the leader in her household (see Acts 16:11-15). And Paul is the one who went out of his way to greet women as his co-laborers at the close of his letters to the Romans, the Corinthians, the Colossians, and in the second letter to Timothy. Sometimes he greeted women as co-leaders with their husbands, such as Priscilla or Junia. Other times, it is just as apparent that the women were the primary pastors of their flocks, as in the case of Phoebe, Tryphena and Tryphosa, Persis, and Julia, all of whom were leaders of congregations in Rome. Nympha clearly led her flock in Colossae.

For Paul, there was no higher accolade or acknowledgement of apostolic primacy than to address someone as a co-laborer. In Galatians 3:28, he said that in Christ there is neither male nor female, and in Hebrews 7:12, he made explicit reference to the abolishing of the Levitical priesthood in favor of the priesthood of Melchizedek when he said, "For when there is a change in the priesthood, there must also be a change of the law." Paul had no problem with women in leadership, for worship or in any other way.

On the other hand, it is obvious from reading the New Testament that seeing women in positions of leadership is the exception rather than the rule. The vast majority of leaders in the churches Paul founded were male. We know of no women who led congregations of the Jerusalem Church, and we find no women who stood out of the larger tapestry in the sense that specific stories were told of them as we find of Peter, Paul, Stephen, and Philip.

For the most part, where women are mentioned in the New Testament, the context is like that of Ephesians 5 and Colossians 3, in which women were called to stand behind the leadership of men, even as both genders are called to mutual submission in Christ. It is the case that there were no women included in the inner circle of the apostles that we know as the Twelve. It is true that Paul stated in First Corinthians 11:3 that, "the head of every man is Christ and the head of the woman is man," and in First Timothy 2:12, "I do not permit a woman to teach or to have authority over a man; she must be silent." He wrote in First Corinthians 14:34-35 that "women should remain silent in the churches," and even that their questions were to be answered at home by their husbands.

I will not try to defend the idea that women are at all times to be subordinate to men in the Body of Christ because, frankly, my convictions are on the other side of the aisle. But I have to say that, as in the other issues that we looked at in this chapter, a credible case can be made for both including and excluding women from leadership in the New Testament Church. If we are to be ambassadors of reconciliation, we need to begin by respecting the right of denominations and congregations to order their corporate life as they (not we) read the Scriptures. We need to lighten up on one another as we work out our own salvation with fear and trembling, submitting our minds to the Mind of Christ as best He enables us (see Phil. 2:12-13). We need to let the Spirit of Jesus adjust our attitudes toward one another before we presume to appraise their practices.

What about spiritual gifts? What about tongues? What about the doctrine that these things were imparted to the Church in the beginning and, having served their inaugural purpose, they passed away a long time ago?

In their climactic verses, the books of Ezekiel and Revelation both show forth the image of a river of God that begins as a spring from beneath His own throne and becomes a mighty torrent watering all the world. For the past century, that river, the Body of Christ, has divided itself into three principal streams. Widely known as the charismatics, the evangelicals, and the liturgical or mainline churches, all three tend to cross-pollinate in some areas and differentiate in others with frequent instances of two having more in common than the third and a regular pattern of shifting alliances within that economy. In one of these, the charismatic churches tend to celebrate and uphold the presence of spiritual gifts, and especially tongues, as normative for Church life in the current age while the others are less likely to see and proclaim this kind of dynamism as a contemporary reality, at least one that is rooted in the life of God.

Jesus told His disciples on the night before His death that signs and wonders would be a feature of their life together. In John 14:12-14, He said, "I tell you the truth, anyone who has faith in me will do what I have been doing. He will do even greater things than these, because I am going to the Father. And I will do whatever you ask in my name, so that the Son may bring glory to the Father. You may ask me for anything in my name, and I will do it." His statement contains no qualifiers that might lead us to interpret it as transitory; it rings of permanence!

In the first Christian sermon, found in Acts 2, Peter quoted the prophet Joel to the effect that God will pour out His spirit on all men and women during the last days. Ordinary people of all kinds will speak extraordinary prophecies and share visions while God Himself shows signs and wonders that will shatter our imaginations. Peter was declaring Pentecost to be the first outpouring of that revelation, but the three thousand souls welcomed into the Kingdom of Heaven on that day hardly constitutes all men and women. There are hundreds of millions of people today who have never heard of the gospel or of Jesus Christ much less experienced the promised outpouring of God's Holy Spirit. Yet as the good news spreads over our planet, the leaders chorus the signs that precede it, including creative miracles and people raised from the dead. This prophecy can scarcely be said to have run its course.

It is a truism that revivals throughout history are accompanied by signs and wonders that authenticate the Kingdom in the midst of the believers. The signs defy prediction or predication. Healing miracles characterized the charismatic renewal of the 1960s and gave prominence to such healing ministries as those of Agnes Sanford and Francis MacNutt, and such miracles have been typical of the revival launched in my own region of northern California in the 1990s. Yet the type of sign so common to the first and second Great Awakenings, which were so formative of the American nation, featured thousands of people falling to the ground in an agony of conviction over their sins that led seamlessly into ecstatic joy over their newfound relationship with the Savior. Often such grassroots outbursts of grace do not fit into existing denominational structures. The general outpouring of the gifts of tongues and prophecy that typified the Azusa Street Revival of the early twentieth century gave rise to two new denominations. In all cases, the miracles defy our stereotypes of cause and effect and even neighborhood in the Body!

For example, the most common healing miracle of the Jesus Movement of the 1970s was dramatic release from drug addictions. Francis MacNutt was a Catholic and Agnes

Sanford an Episcopalian, and the man generally credited with triggering the charismatic revival of the 1960s was fellow Episcopalian Dennis Bennett—hardly your typical background for the more flamboyant ministries of signs and wonders. The dramatic convictions of sin so typical of the Great Awakenings are more akin to the Brownsville Revival of the 1990s than to our imagination of church life in the mid eighteenth century. The ecstatic outbursts of laughter and tears are reminiscent of the Toronto Blessing Movement. But God was necessarily the source then, as now, unless we wish to attribute the phenomena to a nearsighted preacher with a reedy voice who read his sermons in manuscript form named Jonathan Edwards.

It is Paul who wrote, in First Corinthians 4:20, that the Kingdom of God is founded not on words but on power, not at this or that stage of development, but now and forever. Yet this same Paul was used as an anchor for theories that deny that dynamic power working in the Body today because he said in First Corinthians 13:8-13 that prophecy, knowledge, and tongues will pass away when the Kingdom is fully established and that only love will remain. Of course, this is ultimately true. What would be the use of prophetic utterance, supernaturally charged knowledge, and language we do not comprehend when the Kingdom is fully established? But when two thirds of the world's population does not yet know Jesus, how can anyone imagine the Kingdom has indeed come, as evangelicals and mainliners imply when they contend that the gifts have ceased?

On the other hand, how can anyone seriously argue that tongues is the litmus test of Holy Spirit in-filling, as many charismatics would claim? Tongues is labeled by Paul as one of the lesser gifts in First Corinthians 14. "I thank God that I speak in tongues more than all of you. But in the church I would rather speak five intelligible words to instruct others than ten thousand words in a tongue" (1 Cor. 14:18-19). I witnessed my first healing miracle a decade before I ever uttered a word in tongues. I have seen astounding miracles, ranging from the dousing of a wildfire to the raising of a woman from the dead, all without resort to tongues. I have seen and heard the utterance of many wonderful prophecies from the lips of people who do not pray in tongues, just as Caiaphas prophesied that one man would die for the Jewish nation (see John 11:49-51). I have heard messages delivered in a language not of this world that, after a vernacular interpretation, were most edifying to the gathering. I have heard my own wife praise God and offer comfort and assurance in Hawaiian and Spanish, neither of which she can speak or understand in the natural, in settings that could only build up the faith of those fluent and native speakers who were present and who knew that Diana was acting outside of her ability.

And is the laying on of hands as a gift limited to setting apart the clergy? Let's cut to the chase on this one and simply point out that Acts 1 numbers the company in the upper room to be about one hundred and twenty. The Holy Spirit, in His fullness, fell on all of them. When members of the Body created in that manner traveled to other cities, the typical method of passing membership on to other gatherings of people who hungered for God was through the laying on of hands—by any of those filled with the Holy Spirit—on all who were willing to be filled with the Holy Spirit.

Reality is that God both uses and orders spiritual gifts to authenticate His presence and His plans in the midst of His people and to benefit those who do not yet know Him. He is not limited to the lists and manifestations of gifts that we have in Scripture, but they do provide a template for recognizing Him in action, and that template is as useful today as it ever was. Tongues, whether as celestial languages or human languages employed for heavenly purposes, are a gift from the Holy Spirit. But they are by no means a pre-requisite to dynamic activity in the Spirit. As they did in the beginning, we all need to lighten up on one another and focus on obeying God as He comes to gift us, however that may be, rather than focusing on whether or not our brother and sister churches have the same understanding of how the Spirit works as we do.

A LEGITIMATE LITMUS TEST

So is there a litmus test for doctrine and practice? Is there a lowest common denominator that enables us to identify orthodox Christianity in the faces of Christians who do not do the faith the way we do? Like the Word of God itself, the standard is very near to us.

The Council of Nicea met in the city of that name from A.D. 323 to 325. The gathering was the broadest cross section of church leaders ever assembled, called together by the Emperor Constantine in order to hammer out the irreducible bedrock of belief that must be held in common if Christians are even to discuss God through a common frame of reference. They produced what we call the doctrine of the Trinity—that God the Father, Son, and Holy Spirit are co-equal Persons and one God. They also produced a summary of the teaching of the Bible that we call the Nicene Creed.

The creed is as simple as it is elegant. It reads:

We believe in one God, The Father, the Almighty, Maker of Heaven and earth, of all that is, seen and unseen.

We believe in the Lord Jesus Christ, The only Son of God, Eternally begotten of the Father, God from God, Light from Light, true God from true God, begotten, not made, of one Being with the Father. Through Him all things were made. For us and for our salvation He came down from Heaven: by the power of the Holy Spirit He became incarnate from the Virgin Mary, and was made man. For our sake He was crucified under Pontius Pilate; He suffered death and was buried. On the third day He rose again in accordance with the Scriptures; He ascended into Heaven and is seated at the right hand of the Father. He will come again in glory to judge the living and the dead, and His kingdom will have no end.

We believe in the Holy Spirit, the Lord, the Giver of life, who proceeds from the Father. With the Father and the Son He is worshipped and glorified. He has spoken through the prophets. We believe in one holy, universal, and apostolic Church. We acknowledge one baptism for the forgiveness of sins. We look for the resurrection of the dead, and the life of the world to come.

The Nicene Creed is all the litmus test we need to identify an orthodox gathering of the Body of Christ, at least according to the witness of the historic and undivided Church of Jesus Christ.

Take the first section, for example. The Father is clearly identified as the Creator and Sole Proprietor of everything that is. The language calls us to realize that creation is a personal and purposeful event. It rules out any possibility of the universe as some sort of perpetually birthing entity on the one hand, and it just as clearly cancels theories of accidental or internally conceived evolution on the other hand. God clearly states, in Scripture and the creed, that He brings forth out of personal purpose and preference, and that He begins with nothing else.

The middle section is an unambiguous statement concerning who Jesus is and what He has done. It is irreducible if we would pray to a personal Lord, yet it calls on us to lighten up on such matters as when and how to expect miracles, what Jesus thinks about national health care, and a host of other things on which the Lord has not unequivocally revealed His mind. It is, however, quite clear on one divisive issue—the authority of Scripture. When we say that Jesus rose again, "in accordance with the Scriptures," we are saying that all has been exactly what the Word of God said it would be. We are confessing that the Scriptures contain all things necessary for salvation, even as we affirm that what is not contained in them cannot match their value—whatever other credentials may be claimed for it.

The last section deals with the Holy Spirit and the Church—God's bodily presence in the world. As clearly and concisely as the earlier sections, it says that the Spirit is God. God speaks through the prophets, and the Church is both universal and consistent with its earliest witness. Baptism is necessary, and resurrection is promised to the baptized. There are many other things that the Spirit seeks to teach to the Church, but none of them are required for membership in the Body of Christ. To the contrary, John 16:13 states clearly that the Spirit comes to lead the Church into all truth, not to find us already there.

In Romans 10:9, we learn that *all* that is required for full membership in the authentic Body of Christ is to confess with our lips and believe with our hearts that Jesus is Lord, wholly and with unadulterated heart. In Acts 15, the assembled council of the apostles dealt quickly and cleanly, after much debate, with the doctrinal and practical anomalies of a Gentile Church that had sprung from the heart of the Father and the Son through a brief letter (see Acts 15:1-31). "I have other sheep that are not of this sheep pen. I must bring them also...," is what He said about it in John 10:16. The letter is recorded in Acts 15:23-29. The council promised to send ambassadors of reconciliation in the persons of Judas and Silas. They ask that the new branch of the olive tree keep itself from food sacrificed to idols, from strangled or blood curdled meat, and from sexual immorality. In all other matters, they pledge to lighten up on the one hand and embrace their new brothers and sisters on the other. We should ask no more of one another today, and demand no less of ourselves.

And here it needs to be stressed that lightening up is not enough; nothing short of embracing our brothers and sisters of other Christian denominations (any who can confess the Nicene Creed) as co-laborers for the Kingdom will satisfy King Jesus. What Paul taught by the Holy Spirit, that we are many members of one Body, is as true for the churches of that Body as it is for the member of any local church congregation.

The eye cannot say to the hand, "I do not need you!" And the head cannot say to the feet, "I do not need you!" On the contrary, those parts of the body that seem to be weaker are indispensable. And the parts that we think are less honorable we treat with special honor. And the parts that are unpresentable are treated with special modesty, while our presentable parts need no special treatment. But God has combined the members of the body and has given greater honor to the parts that lacked it, so that there should be no division in the body, but that its parts should have equal concern for each other. If one part suffers, every part suffers with it; if one part is honored every part rejoices with it (1 Corinthians 12:21-26).

There is nothing of toleration in Paul's words, no passive acceptance of what we inwardly despise. There is only the most passionate engagement with the other for the good of the whole and the glory of God. The reality is that we need each other; God has ordained that we cannot make it without each other into the fullness of the life He has created for us.

This is nowhere drawn into sharper clarity, as an issue, than in the ongoing conflict between the so-called catholic and protestant factions over the place of Mary in the hearts of the faithful. Many Christians of the Roman Catholic wing of the Church commit idolatry with the figure of Mary—although this is nowhere accepted as official teaching in the Church of Rome. They venerate her statues and offer prayers directly to her, as though she were herself divine. And, of course, that is nonsense to any Christian who knows and reveres the Word of God. Just as untenable is the notion that Mary was somehow born outside of the reach of original sin, and just as horrifying are the dark rumors (and they are only rumors) of an embryonic movement to officially elevate her to the Godhead as co-equal with Father, Son, and Holy Spirit. But in how many of the denominations who decry Roman error do we see clear teaching on the biblically explicit reality of Mary as *theotokos*—the mother of God? To the contrary, attitudes in these regions tend to ignore her altogether except when they fulminate against those who dare to pray the Hail Mary.

Reality is that Mary is a redeemed sinner, just like the rest of us. She revealed herself as such when she, along with Jesus' brothers, came to fetch Him as though He were a mad relative needing to be brought home and kept out of trouble (see Luke 8:19-21). But reality is also that she, while yet a virgin, was chosen by the Father from all of the women in the world to bear His Child in her body. She accepted this mission, which is eternal, despite her youth and the risks of being shunned or even stoned for being found with child out of wedlock. And the Hail Mary prayer is as biblical as the Our Father—it is found in Luke 1. But Mary runs the same risks today as she ran then—along with the added risk of being made into an idol. If the divided parties of Christendom could develop a proper attitude toward her on their own, they would surely have done it in the past two millennia. Catholics and Protestants need to consult with and respect one another if they are to achieve balance in their attitudes toward this remarkable woman.

The reality of our need for one another is cast in a much more positive light on any mission field in the world or in the first book to emerge from the Iraq war. In the pages of *A Table in the Presence,* Lieutenant Cary Cash, a chaplain with the Fifth Marine Division, recounts miracle after miracle attending the toppling of the Saddam Hussein regime and the liberation of twenty-five million Iraqis. Rocket propelled grenades were stopped on impact with a military backpack, and the soldier wearing the pack was uninjured. Marines walked into ambushes and the enemy troops surrendered instead of opening fire. Humvees without armor were ripped and riddled with bullets but the men riding inside were not hit and were unharmed. A sandstorm raged for days, stalling the advance and providing fodder for the commentators back home who had prophesied failure, but when it died down, all of the tank traps left in the desert were exposed and the troops were able to drive around them safely. But the greatest miracle recorded by Lieutenant Cash is the baptism of half of the men in the company he served—and his own conviction that God spared the lives of those who had committed their lives to Him as a witness.

This evangelical chaplain recorded miracles that his leaders back home believe ceased after the close of the apostolic era. He brings the Holy Communion with him wherever he goes because he and his men have come to have no doubt that Jesus is somehow present with them in the sacrament. They simply leave wide open the question of how He does it even though Cash's denomination believes the supper is only a memorial of what happened in Jerusalem once upon a time. And he teaches his men from the Bible, chapter and verse, as only his denomination knows how to do because of their great and abiding reverence for the Word just as it is.[2]

What Cash discovered in Iraq is what missionaries of all backgrounds discover all over the world when they get down to it, they work in an environment that hates what they stand for. We can and should act with integrity toward our respective doctrines and practices when we are at home. When we are out and about the business of the Kingdom in our communities, we act with integrity to respect the doctrines and practices of our brothers and sisters of the other flocks—those we recognize as serving the one master shepherd who is revealed in creed and Scripture. Benjamin Franklin said it best, "We must all hang together or we shall all hang separately."

There is a wonderful Jewish story about two brothers who lived on opposite sides of Mount Gilboa. The elder brother had twelve children and worried about who would care for the other brother, who had no family, in his old age. The younger brother was obsessed with how the hard-working family man would support a family of 14. Both were farmers. Both knew that neither would accept a gift that might jeopardize the security of the other.

The brother with no family hit upon a brilliant plan for the aid of the other. In the dead of night, he loaded all of his grain and made the trek over Mount Gilboa to deposit the harvest in his brother's barn before dawn. He knew that the Lord would provide more grain for his needs, and he chose to depend on it. The other brother conceived an equally brilliant plan for the aid of his sibling. On that same night, he loaded all of his grain and made the journey around the base of the mountain to deposit it into his brothers' barn before dawn.

When the first brother saw the abundance that had come into his barn upon his return home, he praised God and decided that he would make a second gift to his brother from the abundance that God has presented to him. The other brother made the same discovery and the same decision. The process unfolded for some weeks with the brothers praising God and giving abundantly to one another night after night until the younger decided to take the route over the mountain one night for a change of scenery. Around midnight, the two brothers meet one another at the top of the mountain and fall laughing into one another's arms. They give God all of the glory for what had happened to them, they marveled at the improvement in their physical condition from all of the exercise they had taken in the past weeks, and they vowed to always care for one another no matter what the circumstances may be.

To our fleshly minds, this is a useless exercise. We can see no benefit to the exchange of the same grain. It looks like an emotionally satisfying fable that does nobody any real good. But God says to the denominations, and to the congregations within the denominations, "My thoughts are not your thoughts and My ways are not your ways. Seek first My Kingdom and all of your other needs will be met with abundance" (see Isa. 55:8; Matt. 6:33). We can and should hold each other accountable for the irreducible bedrock of doctrine contained in the Nicene Creed. Beyond that, we need to lighten up on sheep from other Christian folds while we actively love and learn from them. We need to shout, as Peter did in Acts 10:34-35, "I now realize how true it is that God does not show favoritism but accepts men from every nation who fear Him and do what is right." The account goes on to say that while Peter was speaking, the Holy Spirit fell on all who were present and Peter ordered that all should be baptized and welcomed into the communion of the redeemed (see Acts 10:44-48).

We should ask no more of one another—and expect no less of ourselves.

ENDNOTES

1. Quote from American Indian leaders Red Jacket of the Iroquois (in 1805) and Spotted Tail of the Brule Sioux (in 1876). Richard Twiss, *One Nation Many Tribes,* (Regal, 2000), 84-88.

2. Lt. Cary H. Cash, *A Table in the Presence: The Dramatic Account of How a U.S. Marine Battalion Experienced God's Presence Amidst the Chaos of the War in Iraq* (Nashville, TN: Thomas Nelson Publishers, 2004).

Chapter 4

INCORPORATING THE GENERATIONS

THE young man was a poster child for what we called the generation gap back in the sixties. He came down to answer the altar call at a Promise Keepers meeting in San Diego. Brought by friends, he responded to the offer of abundant life, not just hereafter but right here and right now, in Christ Jesus. It was an offer he had not heard before, and the only thing in his life that resembled the unconditional love of God in Christ was the love he had shared with his wife of the past eight years. When he met the older man on the infield of San Diego Jack Murphy Stadium and accepted the man's offer to pray with him to receive Jesus, he found himself excited and peaceful, at the same time, in a way he had never known before.

It was a random encounter, if such there be. Promise Keepers organizers always have volunteer prayer counselors lining the field to pray with those who would receive Jesus that night. The volunteers are always planning to ask the newest disciples if there is anything else to pray over once the prayer of faith is completed, and this older man did the job for which he had been commissioned. "Yes," the young man answered, "there is something else I want to pray for. You see, my wife is the most wonderful woman in the world. I love her with all my heart and all my being, and I see only now what real love is."

"When we planned to get married, my wife was a believer and I was not. She was raised in a very religious family, and her father wouldn't hear of her marrying an unbeliever like me. He wouldn't even meet me, and he told her that if she went through with the wedding he would never speak to her again. She gave up her family for me, but she never bailed on Jesus. I know in this moment what it means that she has been praying for me—and for her family—every moment of the last eight years. And I want to ask God to make it so that her father will know what has happened to me tonight and that my love can be re-united to her family. I never knew before tonight what sacrifice really means; and I want it to be for something and not for nothing."

The older man standing before the younger man began to tremble as he asked the young man for the name of his wife. When he named her, the older man began to weep as he gasped out the words, "Young man, I am your father-in-law. Can you ever forgive me?"

Reconciliation with God in Christ had led to reconciliation across the generations. Any member of that family, on either side of the divide, would gladly testify that the reconciliation with God was not complete until reconciliation within the family had been achieved. For some, this is an academic concept; for that family, it is simply where they live. In the grace of God they can now live there together.

Unfortunately, the grace of God is stretched thin across the generations in our world today, and it has been for some time. I was raised in the fifties and sixties; terms like generation gap came into popular usage while I was coming of age. It was a time of reform that was revolutionary in scope (and sometimes just plain revolutionary), in civil rights for minorities, sexual mores across the society, acceptance of mind-altering drugs, and new boundaries for acceptable speech and artistic expression. The Vietnam War brought a renewed focus to America's traditional distrust of government and its structures. But this focus was applied through the lens of my generation, preparing to enter into leadership, as the generation of our parents, the ones who fought World War II, prepared to pass the baton. As things were wrung out, that baton was never really passed. The effects of the generational conflict that erupted are still reverberating throughout the land. We see them in the ever escalating polarization of political parties and movements, the balkanization of reality that characterizes the post-modern era, and the increasing tribalism of interest groups large and small in an era supposedly devoted to becoming a global village. We see them in the social chaos and complete lack of moral consensus that finds its most lurid expression in the trial of a married president for perjuring himself about having oral sex with an oval office intern.

What are the historical roots of this generational conflict?

OF ROOTS AND REBELLION

At the very least, it goes back two generations before the generation of the baby boomers. War has been a feature of human life ever since Cain killed Abel. But no war had ever been seen with the scope of World War I; that is why it was known as the Great War.

World War I was a classic clash of empires—the British, the French, and the Russian forming one side while the German, the Austro-Hungarian, and the Turkish formed the other. There was no moral high ground at stake beyond the desire of the major powers to dominate whatever they could reach and reduce the power of their rivals. Emerging nationalistic movements were a threat to all of the colonial powers, whether their governments were elected or monarchical. When the triple entente defeated the triple alliance, they proceeded to carve up the enemy territories and plunder the enemy resources. American diplomats led by President Woodrow Wilson largely failed when they attempted to broker a peace that would not engender such bitterness as to make another war inevitable. The utter humiliation of Germany, coupled with the devastating reparations the Germans were forced to pay, made the rise of someone like Hitler almost axiomatic.

There *were* great moral issues at stake in the second world war, fought a short two decades after the close of the first. Totalitarian regimes bent on world domination attacked societies grounded in republican and democratic principles. But those principles were applied primarily to the citizens of the republics under attack. A major aim of the wartime partners in the West was the retention of colonial empires in which nationalistic movements were emerging and contending for their own freedom. The World War I generation of leaders passed the baton to a new generation, a generation that today knows itself as the greatest generation because it fought and won World War II and ushered in an era of unprecedented prosperity for America and Western Europe. But this generation failed to anoint and bless for leadership the generation that followed it.

The America of the 1960s witnessed the Civil Rights Movement and the Vietnam War. There were many other movements of that era, and beyond it, such as the revolution in sexual mores, the rise of feminism, and the environmental movement. But it was the ferment over civil rights and American participation in what many Americans came to see as a war against the very values for which we fought in World War II that pitted the generations against one another. While it would be simplistic and silly to say that all older people supported the racial status quo and the unpopular war while all young people fought for change, it is a matter of history to say that political and moral leadership was wrested from the older generation in the streets of the cities when it should have been passed down to the new generation in an orderly fashion. Two presidents were brought down in the turmoil—and the post-modern era in which truth is relative and everyone does whatever he thinks best was birthed.

The era of the sixties made leadership accountable to constituents in new ways and swept aside institutions that had become only the skeletons of the vision of America they were intended to safeguard. But that era also gave us abortion on demand and all of the other features of a society in which an individual's perceived needs and wants are the highest authority.

Great social movements tend to become visible and comprehensible when they can be viewed through the lens of family life. In my own family, there was always tension that revolved around my mother's addiction to prescription drugs. One of the dynamics of my dysfunctional family was that I, the older brother of two, was usually held responsible for my brother's behavior although I was given neither the authority nor the power to hold him accountable. In other words, if I failed to stop his misbehavior, I was in trouble, and if I made any effort to coerce him into good behavior, I was in trouble. By the time I entered high school, I had begun to rebel against the economy of my family.

In the same way, young Americans were sent off to fight a war in Southeast Asia that was planned and orchestrated by people of an older generation who had no will to win that war. Those who fought and died in this war had neither the power nor the authority to set the terms of engagement; they were only permitted to bear the burden and shed the blood.

Two incidents in my teen years stand out as watersheds in which my own attitude of rebellion crystallized. The first was during the presidential election of 1964. There was on the ballot in California that year a referendum of a state law that forbade racial discrimination in the sales of residential real estate. My parents had always taught me that a person should be judged on the content of his character rather than on the color of his skin (to steal a phrase from Martin Luther King). As the election approached, I recall asking my mother if she would be willing to sell our home to a black family since one of the terms of my parents' divorce required the sale when my brother turned eighteen. She looked at the floor and said she would have to consider the feelings of the neighbors, shorthand for "not very likely." I was shocked and disgusted at such a complete reversal of what she had always taught me when the conversation was academic.

The second concerned a bump between our car and another in a supermarket parking lot. The damage to the other car was negligible but visible; as the driver, I began to write a note to the owner giving our name, address, and phone number and accepting responsibility (as I had been taught to do all of my life by both of my parents). My mother forbade me to do this, and as a dutiful son, I obeyed. But the disillusionment in my heart over this act of hypocrisy was the fatal blow to any moral authority my parents held over me.

In the same way, my generation became disillusioned with the World War II generation over its general failure to stand for the ideals of a society of equal opportunity that we had been taught in the very schools they had set up for us. Whatever moral authority that generation held over us was squandered on the battlefields of Vietnam, the streets of Selma, Alabama, and in all of the venues where Watergate played itself out.

From that time on, I made up the rules for my life as I went along. I did not know Jesus Christ, my parents and teachers had never introduced us, and the only moral compass I carried had proven itself progressively bankrupt. I had received no training for leading my own family and career other than to be told to watch my parents and do what they did. But they had dissolved our family, and they stood against the very values they had preached. In my rebellion, I knew what I was *against* but had no idea what I could be *for*. I felt perfectly free to experiment with sex and drugs and to lie my way into a new construction of reality because I saw nothing to lose and hoped I might find something to gain along the way. My friends were the only anchor I had, and they were as drifty as I had become.

The generation of the sixties made pretty much the same corporate decision on the macro level as I made on a personal or micro level. It was not a good decision, and the fruit has not been good; the fruit of rebellion never is. But even after more than thirty years of repentance into the abundant life of Jesus who is Christ, I would have to say that we came by our dilemma honestly. A house divided against itself simply cannot stand.

Our Houses Long Divided

The Bible is full of cross-generational conflicts. The conflict between King David and his son, Absalom, is often cited as the textbook case of a son who rebels against his good-hearted father and brings about nothing but war and death (see 2 Sam. 15-18). David is, of course, on the other end of a cross-generational feud with King Saul that toppled a dynasty before it was well underway (see 1 Sam. 15-31). There is the famous injunction of Paul to Timothy that he should permit no one to despise his youth as he led and instructed the church entrusted to him (see 1 Tim. 4:12). (There would have been no charge needed had not someone already been despising Timothy's youth.) And there is the famous quarrel between Paul and John Mark that fractured a mission team but that was resolved and redeemed by the time Paul made his famous charge to Timothy (see Acts 15:36-40).

Jesus says plainly, in Luke 12:51-53, that He came to bring about generational division—between those who decide to take up their crosses and follow Him and those who refuse. This call for decision will come between fathers and sons and mothers and daughters—but it is by the will of the people concerned and not by the will of God. For the very Greek word we translate as "division" is more accurately rendered "decision." The work of God is to give spiritual gifts for the up-building and uniting of the Body of Christ (see Eph. 4:11-16) because the will of God is that none should perish and that none should remain separate from His Body. But we alone have the power to decide to adhere to His will as though it were our own.

In the case of Absalom and David, there is an event that both precedes and precipitates the rebellion of the son. The relational dynamics echo down the centuries to the nineteen sixties when I came of age and right into the present moment. Absalom had a sister named Tamar and a half-brother named Amnon. Amnon had fallen in love with his half-sister, Tamar, and had lured her into his home with the help of a mutual friend. When she resisted his advances, he raped her. With the rape an accomplished fact, she begged him to honor her with a marriage covenant, but he had already grown tired of a prize possessed, and he sent her away in disgrace. Absalom insisted that his father, King David, take appropriate punitive action. But David wimped out, and Absalom responded with the rebellion that cost his own life and great grief to David and the kingdom (see 2 Sam. 13).

There are no stars on either David or Absalom, no accolades awaiting either of them. David was absolutely wrong to fail to bring justice to the situation in his own family. He provoked Absalom to further outrage over the failure of the father he trusted to do the right thing (because that is what dads are for). Yet Absalom was just as wrong to attempt to wrest the kingdom from his father's hand before his time had come. There is no way that two wrongs can make a right— and that is no mere platitude, but rather a description of how God's world is structured by the God who created it. David's family is a symbolic representative of the covenant, and covenants do not work unless all parties obey their provisions. Absalom's attempt to work the covenant unilaterally was futile at best and arrogantly sinful at worst. He paid with his life, and David never did get a clue.

The cross generational conflict between David and Saul had a much happier ending, though Saul paid with his life finally, as did Absalom. Saul had lost the authority to be king of Israel, though not the political and military power of that office. Most of the people knew that David had received an anointing; there was no claiming of the throne, but his bearing proclaimed his identity in God. Saul did whatever he could to discredit David, and when that failed, he did whatever he could to kill David. David operated like a Robin Hood sort of character, except that he would not permit himself or his men to attack King Saul or his family. David resisted Saul's injustice, but he refused to rebel against the man who was there before him, even when Saul was at his mercy in a cave one afternoon.

David waited in faithfulness for some two decades, knowing that whatever he gained without God's sanction would be but powder in his hands. David saw his life frequently at risk; he endured many hardships, and often the crown seems further away than when he was first promised it by Samuel, the messenger of God. When things were as bad as they could possibly be, when his wife and children have been kidnapped, his city stronghold burnt to the ground, and his own men were plotting to take his life, he worshiped God and led his men out once again to recover their families and their goods. At that very moment, Saul and Jonathan were falling in battle on Mount Gilboa and God was giving new poignancy to the old saying that it is always darkest before the dawn.

Saul, the unfaithful one, was dead. David, the faithful one, was king. But one has to wonder why David could not have remembered that faithfulness, that integrity before God, when Absalom first begged justice for his sister?

What if I and my generation, not to mention my parents' generation, had been steeped in these stories and had committed to an intimate relationship with the Lord Jesus Christ during the sixties? Would the abortive passing of the leadership baton between generations have played out differently in an atmosphere where repentance, reconciliation, and revival were normative to our national life?

There is no necessity for cross-generational conflict to result in evil, although it invariably comes from evil. The book of Acts tells how Paul and Barnabas took John Mark with them on a mission trip to Cyprus. The younger man, who would later write the Gospel of Mark, was acting as a sort of apprentice to the older apostles. When the company arrived in the city of Perga, John Mark left to return to Jerusalem (see Acts 12:35-13:13). He apparently left without permission of Paul, because Paul refuses to take him along on a later leg of the journey due to what Paul calls his desertion. Another quarrel erupts between Paul and Barnabas – over the inclusion of Mark – and the mission team splits up over it (see Acts 15:36-40). We don't know the details of why Mark left or what provocations there may have been on either side, but we do know that God's redeeming hand was accepted by all parties at some point.

By the time of Paul's imprisonment in Rome, Mark is so close to his mentor that Paul included his greetings with Paul's own in Colossians 4:10. He even added an unambiguous endorsement of Mark's ministry for any who might read the letter, and he asked Timothy to bring Mark to him for the help he could give to Paul's ministry. Paul was, incidentally, so able to let go of leadership at that point in his ministry that he told the young Timothy repeatedly of his confidence in him and exhorted him to accept no condescension from older

members of the church he led on the basis of Paul's appointment of leaders.

This is a long way from the Paul who could not share leadership even with his contemporary, Barnabas, when they
split up in Antioch. It is also a long way from the John Mark
who bailed out when the going got tough. Had there been
repentance on both sides, just as there was between the men
at the San Diego Promise Keeper's meeting? Was that repentance likewise enabled by supernatural grace poured onto the
two men? Does it matter from which end of the relationship
the grace began to be poured so long as both men took up the
fresh opportunity that God provided in their lives? Reality is
that resurrection is a holistic re-creation of our lives. God
needs to have it all from us in order to give it all to us. But it
is a process rather than an event.

The most time-honored story of generational conflict
and what God is prepared to do about it is the parable of the
prodigal son. Jesus' wonderful tale of a father who loved
both of his sons, even though only one seemed to deserve
it, is recounted in Luke 15:11-31. The younger, instead of
returning devotion for devotion, demanded his share of the
father's estate so that he could go and live his own life. The
clear message was that the father had no value to him other
than as a source of funding. The father's response was to
give the boy what he asked. And the consequence of this
giving was what anyone might expect: the empty-hearted
(empty-headed, too) son wasted his property and soon
found himself so broke that he commited a symbolically ulti-

mate abandonment of his Jewish faith and identity. He became a keeper of pigs on starvation wages.

Jesus says of the young man:

He longed to fill his stomach with the pods that the pigs were eating, but no one gave him anything. When he came to his senses, he said, "How many of my father's hired men have food and to spare, and here I am starving to death! I will set out and go back to my father and say to him: Father, I have sinned against Heaven and against you. I am no longer worthy to be called your son; make me like one of your hired men." So he got up and went to his father... (Luke 15:16-20).

It should be stipulated (for the benefit of any legalists reading this book) that the son has not yet really had a change of heart. He has had a disastrous change of circumstances and he had the good sense to see that his pitiful condition was not his only option. He knows that he can humble himself (perhaps not a lot of fun but definitely better than starving) and expect at least decent treatment from his father. Yet a sincere appreciation of his circumstances and the remedy for them is enough to begin the process of repentance. And that process is more than encouraged by the father. "But while he was still a long way off, his father saw him and was filled with compassion for him; he ran to his son, threw his arms around him and kissed him" (Luke 15:20).

In traditional Jewish culture, it is considered horribly undignified, to the point of humiliation, for an older man of substantial means to run anywhere for any reason. Yet this Jewish father runs to his son the moment he sees him coming on the horizon. His compassion for the child of his own body is so full that he has no place in his heart or his mind for a sense of humiliation. His insistence on engagement with the other who is his son fills the space between them, not because he is too dull to know that the son did not care for him but because he doesn't care about anything beyond that compassionate identification with the son. In such a context, compassion begins walking the road toward mutual repentance and full reconciliation. The slightest hint of reciprocity forms a basis for closing the connection and that connection, once renewed, does not care who made the first move.

But it is significant that New Testament stories of cross-generational conflict seem to always work out well, impregnated as they are with the resurrection presence of the crucified Son of God in the power of the Holy Spirit. That good prognosis attaches to contemporary stories in the same way, whenever they are impregnated in the same way.

IMPREGNATED WITH THE SPIRIT

Roger Craig, longtime manager of baseball's San Francisco Giants and a former world-class pitcher in his own right, tells a wonderful story of how his father dealt with a prodigal Roger. The younger Craig found himself resenting the rock and hard place between which he was stuck on a sunny summer vacation day when his father had ordered him to clean the garage before going out anywhere. Roger cleaned the garage, but he gave it the two minute version instead of the two hour project his father had in mind. Then he went to do what he wanted to do.

Craig's father was a fair man, but he was one who did not accept excuses and one who expected his orders carried out in spirit as well as in letter. When Roger arrived home to see his father's car in the driveway and the old man disappearing into the garage, he knew that he was in a world of trouble. His main concern was the punishment he expected to fall short-ly. But he also understood at that moment that he had traded all of the day fishing for what could have been most of the day fishing plus his father's respect and trust.

When he entered the garage, he found his father with his coat off and in the process of rolling up his sleeves. Bracing himself for what he expected to be some very physical disci-pline, he heard his father say, "I am going to have to show you what it means to clean a garage."

For the next two hours, the elder Craig did not speak. He simply cleaned the garage while his son watched. He then indicated that the boy should accompany him into the house for a long- delayed supper. He never said another word about the incident to the end of his life. And Roger Craig never for-got the sight of his father after a long and exhausting day at the job he worked for the support of his family, redeeming the time and the responsibility that the son had betrayed. It was indeed physical discipline, and it set up a cross-genera-tional reconciliation as surely as did the running father of the parable.

So what can the Baby Boomers and the Greatest Generation do at this point to seek the reconciliation that is at the very core of the Kingdom of God? We can all choose to recognize that our adversaries in this conflict have much that is admirable in their resumes. We can also recognize that all have sinned and fallen far short of the glory of God (see Rom. 3:23). These twin recognitions are a seamless garment, a big canopy under which we can gather in mutual repentance and restoration of the respect and love to which we are called. It makes no difference who steps forward first, chicken or egg.

ACCOLADES AND ACCUSATIONS

For example, it is true that the generation of World War II fought the greatest conflagration in history. Without their sacrifice, the freedom and prosperity we Americans know and share with the world to an unprecedented degree would be unimaginable. Not even the Civil War mounted an effort that so touched every square foot and every heart of the nation (military and civilian) as this war. No other chapter in American history produced the unity of mind and purpose that emerged from this one. After defeating the most aggressive enemies of freedom and democracy around the world, they gave lavishly of their time and treasure through the Marshall Plan to rebuild the very nations they had reduced to rubble in the campaign called World War II. They achieved this in the wake of their own mind-numbing and ultimately unsuccessful (until the war came) effort to resolve the Great Depression that was the legacy of their parents' generation.

This is not all that they achieved. This generation led America into space and onto the moon. All of the pioneering astronauts, as well as the rest of the NASA leadership, was drawn from their ranks. They had the vision, and they guided the process that led to the communications revolution, the new hardware, and what we refer to today as space age technology. It has enabled cleaner burning fuels, multiple medical breakthroughs, and a transportation and distribution system that is the envy of the world. The developers of so many wonders from cell phones to the modern football helmet stand on the shoulders of this generation.

The core of the American dream has always been the prospect that all families could live in a home that they themselves owned. This generation made that dream a reality across the land in the 1950s. They did this not simply by growing the most robust economy on the planet, but by standardizing construction and materials to reduce the price of a family home into an affordable range for untold millions.

At the same time, they invented the concept of leisure as we know it so that the average American could barbecue in his own backyard and watch the game on his own TV. Or he could save for a vacation and take the family to an affordable home away of reliable quality, like the Holiday Inns that were invented by Kemmons Wilson in the fifties and were followed by so many other chain businesses devoted solely to providing a comfortable getaway for the unwealthy but hardworking. The McDonald brothers developed the *sine qua non* of food industry efficiency while Ray Krock perfected the standards and techniques that spread it nationwide.

The modern missions movement is a post-war phenomenon of American invention, and more people have heard and received the gospel in the past half century than in all of the other centuries preceding it. This generation did more than any generation before it to spread the gospel, as a small sample of their activities will demonstrate. Retired members of it travel the country in their recreational vehicles to spend weeks camping at one location, building churches if they belong to MAPS, or building homes if they affiliate with Habitat for Humanity. They propelled the Gospel around the world through the creation of Youth With A Mission (YWAM) as they revitalized the Body of Christ at home through the Jesus Movement, both of which are fabulously God-blessed cooperative efforts birthed by the older generation and bequeathed to the younger.

They created uniform standards for educating children. And they put college within reach of middle and even poverty class people through the GI Bill, which greatly expanded student loan and scholarship opportunities, and through the explosive growth of state college and university campuses.

However, the news of the World War II generation is a mixed bag at best. Just as the generation that fought World War I gave us the post war settlement that created, as much as it allowed, the totalitarian dictatorships we fought in the 1940s, so the so-called Greatest Generation left the world with the Cold War, the Korean War, and the Vietnam War. All of these conflicts came about as a result of accommodating the expansionism of Soviet Communism on the one hand, and the bankrupt ambitions of defeated (in 1940) western colonial powers to recover their lost Asian empires on the other. They came to pass because this generation claimed victory in 1945 for a conflict that would truly end only with the tumbling of the Berlin wall, in 1989, when the greatest opponent of freedom in this war of ideology finally gave it up. It was the power of the human spirit, fed by the Holy Spirit, that gained the final victory.

This generation understood the limits of political and military power in a world exhausted by many years of total warfare, but they did not understand the power of prayer and of the very gospel they were so effective in spreading.

It would be this Kingdom power, supported by the last of the World War II era presidents, Ronald Reagan and George H. W. Bush, that brought down almost all of the Communist world hegemony. But the legacy of my parents' generation in this arena is one of forty-five more years of worldwide suffering and the holocaust of war throughout Southeast Asia and Africa that ended and followed colonialist rule in those regions. Reagan and Bush were faithful watchmen, stewards if you will, of the resolution of the decades long confrontation. But it was my generation of Baby Boomers who laid their lives on the line over the years at the same time that they shouted from the rooftops that something was dreadfully amiss in our republic and in our culture.

Reality is that Baby Boomers both fought the Vietnam War and fought against it. It is a well-documented historical fact that the Korean and Vietnam conflicts were wars our leaders never intended to win. Without attempting to sort out the dynamics of community-of-nations and cold war politics, it must be said that American troops were sent to risk and give their lives for the advance of those political considerations instead of a military victory. They never had a chance to succeed; they only had a roll of the dice over whether they might survive. And their elders, seeing a generation pitted against itself in terms of support or opposition to the war, simply presided over the butchery of our young warriors while criticizing and condemning those other young warriors who said no to it.

The Civil Rights Movement began in the 1950s and was entirely the product of Christians who hungered and thirsted for justice in the land. (Later the movement was co-opted by people with only a political vision.) These were the same people, in spirit, as those who produced the abolition of slavery in the previous century out of reverence for their creation in the image of almighty God. But the unfortunate reality of this movement is that the acceleration of results came about largely as Boomers, people from my generation, with a secular worldview brought the movement to optimum strength. The older generation of leaders in government, education, and society did everything in their power to slow down and stop this movement – from those leaders who blocked the school house door to those in the congress and the executive and judicial branches who said the desire of minorities to be the equal of the majority was too much and too soon.

The generation of our parents invented the three-martini lunch and the valium culture while they roundly condemned those of their children who saw no moral difference in lighting a joint or dropping (into their mouths) anything from acid to speed to cocaine. The hypocrisy was overwhelming.

This older generation was also the generation who largely forgot that the practical import of the fifth commandment, "Honor your father and your mother..." (Exod. 20:12), was to enable and ensure that the younger generation received knowledge of the covenant relationship with God from the elders. Mainstream American society had little interest in passing along spiritual knowledge of any kind, although church attendance rose to unprecedented heights during the fifties. In all too many American homes, God was invoked only as an expletive, and in too many others, He was only the inspiration behind all good manners. Our parents largely failed to give us our spiritual birthright and then became outraged when we rejected polite substitutes for it.

The World War II generation congratulated itself for giving their children the best life, in terms of material prosperity, that the world has ever seen while at the same time accusing them of having no moral compass, a moral compass that it was the chief responsibility of the elders to provide. Instead, they provided abortion on demand, made divorce a socially acceptable phenomenon, and created the first generation of latch-key children from families in which both parents worked for the almighty dollar. At the same time, they accused Boomers of lacking gratitude for the material things and the freedom from restraint that they were given.

The problem with the generation that preceded my own is really pretty simple at its heart. They left a world with at least as many problems as the one they inherited. They did not know how to resolve them. But instead of passing the leadership baton to those who came behind in the ordinary course of events, they clung to their leadership prerogatives and tried to force the Baby Boomers to be just like themselves. They refused to part with the inheritance, even when it was timely and proper to do so. And they rationalized their greatest failure by calling the heirs unworthy.

There is much that is good to be said about the generation of the Boomers. This generation, which is so often accused of having everything given to it with no gratitude in return, is the generation that staffed the Peace Corps and VISTA (Volunteers In Service to America). This is the generation that went out with missionary groups like YWAM, New Tribes, and many other mission organizations that brought the gospel to even more people than their parents' generation.

The Boomers are the Christians who have brought our own nation to the doorstep of a national revival and produced the most faith-filled president in more than a century. They are the people who brought reform, faith-based reform, to a welfare system that was out of control and doing no good for anyone. They are the generation that has begun, at last, to seek healing and reconciliation across the boundaries of tribe, culture, and denomination.

The Boomers fought the war in Vietnam as they fought against it. They provided the elbow grease and much of the theory behind the Reagan Revolution and the effort to bring down the Berlin Wall that their parents allowed to be built.

They rode the buses into the American South to bring the vote to black people, and they launched the modern substance abuse recovery movement. They commanded and orchestrated the fight in the Gulf War and the more recent war to liberate Iraq. They have stood by Israel as has no generation before them.

The Boomers, men and women in their twenties, manned the control rooms and solved the problems confronted in the space race as they ushered in the modern era of high technology and the internet society. They achieved breakthroughs in education, including the home school and charter school movements. They have matched their parents in charitable giving, and they have become more involved in their communities than those who came before ever thought of being.

But like the generation of their parents, the news of the Baby Boomer generation is a mixed bag. If the generation that fought World War II gave us abortion on demand, then my generation embraced it to the tune of forty million dead. We have made pornography into one of the most lucrative industries in the world, and we permit our children to watch TV programs that would have been considered pornographic when we were growing up. We divorce, commit adultery, and engage in domestic violence at far higher rates than did the previous generation, and we have embraced the occult and the New Age to a greater extent than our elders would have dreamed possible. We have made an idol of spirituality for its own sake. We use more drugs and more alcohol than our parents did, and we admit to lying when the truth is inconvenient, as though that were a good thing. We have all too often failed to respect the good things our parents accomplished, and we have an almost non-existent sense of history. We say that we respect women and embrace children, but we tolerate music that advocates their deaths by violence. We have made a dirty word of repentance, and we have made tolerance of what is perverse and life destroying, so long as the parties are volunteers, the ultimate virtue.

We have difficulty telling the God and Father of our Lord Jesus Christ from the God and Father of Mohammed or the Dalai Lama; and when we recognize the difference, we prefer not to offend anyone by mentioning it. We insist that any and all speech, however vile, must be protected and made available, even to children, if restricting access would impact adults. Yet our colleges and universities are among the most censor-dominated places on the planet.

The problem with the generation of the Baby Boomers is that we had a fine grasp of what we were against and no clue about what we ought to be for. Possessed of a deficient education in leadership, we forged ahead anyway and wrested leadership from the hands of our parents. We played Absalom to our parents' King David, and much suffering has been the fruit.

THE ONES WHO BLESS THE MOST WIN

Let's face it—"all have sinned and fallen short of the glory of God" (Rom. 3:23). All of us need to repent and lighten up on one another, unless one generation can figure out how it is without sin before casting the first stone (see John 8:3-11). My generation needs to see the face of Absalom in the mirror and recognize that only death and destruction come from rebellion as a lifestyle, regardless of the provocation. My parents' generation needs to see the face of King David in the mirror and decide that justice delayed is better than justice denied, if the time of delay is over at last.

It doesn't matter who makes the first move any more than it did in the story of the Prodigal, but somebody needs to say that this war has gone on long enough and that God has wept over His warring children long enough. We need to forgive and start again by the grace of God. And we need to do this before the last of our parents' generation dies off and before the generation of our children is so hopelessly alienated from us that there is no going back. For we are doing to our children what was done to us—and as David and Absalom show us—no one benefits.

When I was growing up, I saw in my father nothing but a writhing bundle of unreasonable expectations. He was a man for whom personal loyalty in the context of personal integrity (to family, friends, and employers) was the principal value by which he lived his life. He was an authoritarian parent because he could conceive of no better way to prepare his sons for a harsh and unforgiving world. He expected that loyalty and integrity to be mirrored in his sons but (it seemed to me) in the arena of conviction rather than in relationship. We frequently clashed during my teen years, but even more frequently, I simply avoided his company.

Yet when I was twenty, I went to him (out of desperation) for help with college expenses even though his help could place him in defiance of a court order regarding my parents' divorce settlement. I expected nothing but to find him obeying the rules at all costs, but I asked him for help anyway. His response was that he would help his son no matter what it would cost and no matter what a judge or anybody else might say about it. From that day on, we began to have a relationship.

Over the next few years, we became best friends; and I hungrily absorbed whatever he could teach me about being a man, a husband, and a father. He taught just by being who he was, and we laughed together as we never had before.

The proudest moment of my life came on the day of my marriage to Diana. Dad invited me back to his hotel room a couple of hours before the wedding was to take place. He poured us both a glass of scotch whiskey—because that was his way. He toasted me and gave me his blessing for the rest of my life. He said that he had waited for years for this opportunity to tell me that he was proud of the man I had become. It was not just a blessing—it was a sacrament of blessing—because it put the seal to my relationship with God the Father.

My father died and went to be with the Lord less than four years after that day. I miss him every day, to this day. But no one can ever take from me what he gave to me—his blessing. No one can ever take from him the fact that I humbled myself and went to him when I was twenty. And no one can take from either of us, in Heaven or on earth, the reality of our reconciliation and subsequent relationship in the name of the Lord Jesus Christ.

Both of us had to let go of what we thought belonged to us. He surrendered control, and I surrendered rebellion. We had ten years of the fruit of that act, and I would not trade it even for having him back on earth. Let those who have ears to hear, in each of the generations, listen up. And let the generation that follows us, even as we speak, be blessed and taught to avoid the pit into which their parents and grandparents toppled once upon a time. Let us all compete with one another to be the more extravagant in giving out the blessing that is our heritage in God our Father. The last word of God to His people in the Old Testament, that incredible history whose whole purpose was to prepare the people of the Father for the coming of the Son, is found in Malachi 4:6. "He will turn the hearts of the fathers to their children and the hearts of the children to their fathers; or else I will come and strike the land with a curse."

Chapter 5

RECONNECTING THE REGIONS

O NE of my favorite pieces of history emerges from the Civil War. The story of the Great Locomotive Chase documents the efforts of a federal spy named James J. Andrews who loved the union and hated the war. Andrews attempted to smuggle a score of union soldiers into Georgia, steal a train from the confederates, and burn the bridges between Atlanta and Chattanooga in the Spring of 1862. By destroying the Western and Atlantic Railroad line, he hoped to shorten or even end the bloody conflict between Americans divided by politics and regional loyalties. He got his train and would have gotten clean away with his plans but for two seemingly insignificant factors. One was that he changed his plan to allow for a rainy day. The union commander with whom he was working did not hear of the change and continued on schedule with the seizure of Chattanooga. The resulting logjam on the railway, as the secessionist forces escaped south from the union attack, so delayed Andrews that he was caught and ultimately hanged.

The other factor was the courage and devotion of the train's conductor, William A. Fuller, a man as devoted to his cause and his duty as Andrews was to his. Fuller, virtually unarmed and unaided, chased the raiders on foot, on a hand-car, and on a succession of commandeered engines. He pursued them so closely that they never guessed how easily they could have overpowered him. He finally caught up with them when they ran out of fuel after some eight hours and the local militia took them into custody. The raid so captured the imagination of the nation that the first recipients of the Congressional Medal of Honor were members of this raiding party, and Walt Disney made one of many movies commemorating it.

It is this movie that teaches a great lesson about reconciliation, despite its alteration of some of the facts. Sometimes myth is truer than history, and certainly this is so when it arrives at the same destination while painting a clearer and simpler picture of the reality it represents. A climactic moment in Walt Disney's rendering of the history shows Andrews asking for and receiving reconciliation with Fuller just before his execution. That particular vignette did not occur, but there can be no doubt that Andrews, whose genuine love for his enemies contributed materially to his success as a secret agent, deeply desired such a reconciliation. Just as clear is Fuller's heart, for he gave his daughter in marriage to one of the raiders after the war. As the incident is presented on film, Andrews asks for Fuller to visit him in prison. He tells the conductor how much he respects him and how much he regrets having deceived him. He confirms that both have fought with heart and conviction for what they believed in, and he points out that "one day this terrible war is gonna end and both sides will have to shake hands. I won't live to see that day. Couldn't we shake hands now? I'd be glad if you would, Sir." Fuller reaches across the bars and the scene fades on the clasped hands of one who will live to make the peace for which the other has died. I have watched this film many times and this scene never fails to bring me to tears of joy for what God ordains and tears of grief for how rarely we permit it to happen.[1]

What can we learn about reconciliation from this poetic reconstruction of reality? One thing we learn is that men who are fully convicted of the righteousness of their cause are more amenable to reconciliation than those who act in the double-mindedness of mixed motives. What Fuller and Andrews had in common was unswerving devotion to their respective causes and the courage and ingenuity that is born of such devotion. They sensed the wholeness of commitment in each other, and they responded to that with mutual admiration and respect, despite what they may have felt about the cause of the other and the actions taken to advance it. God is forever asking of us, and offering to us, this wholeness of conviction as the foundation for abundant life in us. "To the Jews who had believed him Jesus said, 'If you hold to my teaching, you are really my disciples. Then you will know the truth, and the truth will set you free" (John 8:31-32). To our minds, it seems as though people who can entertain conflicting loyalties might more easily turn from the one to the other, to forgive and embrace the former enemy. But Jesus tells us, "My thoughts are not your thoughts. You need to learn to think like Me, and the way to do that is to begin to act like Me—concerned only with what you see the Father doing and speaking. Only then will your life become real" (see Isa. 55:8; John 5:19).

Mitsuo Fuchida was a hero to the Japanese people during World War II because of his utter embrace of the Japanese cause. I include his story in a chapter on regional reconciliation because it would be difficult to overstate the hatred that existed between Fuchida's people and the American people— a hatred that is usually reserved for conflicts between people of natural kinship separated by regional differences. The cultural code by which Japanese and American warriors lived, the Samurai and frontier traditions we share, and the sense of manifest destiny that is common to our peoples, made the conflict between us almost a war between brothers.

Fuchida led the attack on Pearl Harbor, which he believed was absolutely necessary if his people were to survive what he saw as American imperialism. He commanded the air forces in the Battle of Midway and in many other Pacific engagements, and when the war ended in defeat for Japan, he was a broken man. His spiritual life revolved around Bushido, the Japanese warrior's code, and he assumed the Americans had won only because their bushido was stronger than his. Yet he continued to hate these Americans who—to him— expected him to be soft and in love with their comforts. The world of late 1945 made no sense to this man.

Shortly after the war, Fuchida met two people who were obviously as convicted in their single-minded loyalties as he was in his. Peggy Covell was a nurse, the daughter of missionaries to the Philippines who had been executed by the

Japanese. When Fuchida met her, she was caring for wounded Japanese. She told him that she knew her parents, as servants of the Lord Jesus, had forgiven their murderers even before the bullets smashed into their heads, and she could do no less. She also told him that there was nothing passive about forgiveness; if she could not embrace those she had forgiven, there was no point in pretending she had forgiven at all.

Fuchida met the other one in 1946 after reading the pamphlet he had written under the title *I Was A Prisoner of Japan.* Jacob DeShazer was the bombardier on one of the planes of the Dolittle raid on Tokyo. He was captured in China and held in brutal captivity until the war ended. His hatred of the Japanese was profound when he enlisted in the army; it was exponentially multiplied during his years at the mercy of their vengeance for his part in the bombing of their cities. He had never broken, and Fuchida recognized in him a man of the same warrior code as his own, a man he could respect.

DeShazer tells of how he had been on the edge of insanity when a copy of the Bible found its way to the prisoners. He was permitted ten days with the only reading material he had seen in years before having to pass it on to another. He concentrated on memorizing passages to give himself something to think about instead of dwelling on his hopeless situation— for his captors constantly reminded him that he would never leave prison alive. Something in the Gospel of Luke grabbed hold of him, for the Lord seems always to do His best work when there are no distractions or alternatives to paying Him attention, and DeShazer gave his life to Jesus in the prison cell. But then something just as remarkable happened; he began to forgive and even to love the guards who beat and humiliated him. By the time he was released, Jacob DeShazer was as committed to bringing the gospel to the Japanese people as St. Patrick had been to the Irish fifteen hundred years earlier.

Mitsuo Fuchida, at last overwhelmed with the love of Jesus in and through his encounters with DeShazer and Covell, became just as committed to reconciliation with the Americans as he became to sharing in the effort to lead his own people to new life in Jesus Christ. And there has never been a more effective missionary to Japan than Mitsuo Fuchida, warrior ambassador of reconciliation.

That sounds wonderful for nations who never lived together under one cultural roof, but can regional reconciliation come about in the same way? Is it possible for brothers convinced of betrayal by the other to return to communion with one another?

RECASTING MYTH TO REALITY

There are other incidents from the Civil War that express the truth of our calling to regional reconciliation as clearly as does the film about the Andrews Raid (with no need for recasting the realities to fit the time constraints of a motion picture). The story of George Washington Dame, the founding pastor of a congregation I led for a time in Danville, Virginia, is one such story.

Dr. Dame was so thoroughly Southern in his sympathies during the war that he caused the bells of Epiphany Church to be melted down and given to the confederate army to be made into a cannon. Yet his love for the Lord Jesus and the people for whom Jesus died was such that he cared for the wounded on both sides with the same skill and commitment. When federal forces eventually occupied Danville, their commander sent for Dame. He told him that he was well aware of Dame's commitment to the secessionist cause but that he was equally aware of his selfless service of compassion to the union wounded. He was so impressed, he said, that he was happy to present Dame with anything for which he might ask at any time during the occupation.

At the same time, there was a local hothead named Smith breathing fire and threats against the northern aggressors and all of their works. Smith could not be called a Christian hypocrite, because he was not a Christian at all. Likewise, he had never served in the military, but now that his service would be academic at best, he shot and killed a federal officer in the street one night. Quickly captured, he was tried and condemned to hang for the cold-blooded murder. When Dr. Dame heard of it, he went at once to see the union commander.

When he was ushered into the commander's office, he said that he had come to collect on the promise the commander had made to him. He said that he wanted Smith remanded into his custody, permanently. When the officer asked if Smith were a member of Dame's flock, the pastor admitted that he was not, while insisting that Smith was indeed one of those for whom Jesus had given His life on the cross. But the commander could only spread his hands in resignation. It was out of his hands, he explained, for the man had already been tried and condemned by the military tribunal. (There was, of course, no question of his guilt.) Dr. Dame also spread his hands in resignation. He said, "You are the commander, and what you say is true. However, it is just as true that you told me I could have whatever I asked of you, and I am asking for custody of this man."

The commander gathered his officers for a brief conference in an inner room. When he returned, he spoke in measured tones to the clergyman. "I have already explained to you that it is impossible to give you what you are asking. I would be in defiance of my orders and answerable to the officers above me. Having said that, I tell you that my officers and I, all of them, are required in another part of town for the next hour. I cannot spare anyone to guard this facility, and I am asking you to take charge while we are gone. The keys to the cells are in this desk, and I am holding you responsible to see to the prisoners' welfare while I am gone. Good day to you, Sir."

As soon as the officers were gone, Dr. Dame took the keys and released Mr. Smith. He took him to his home and reminded him of what they both knew, that this was the only house in town that the federals would not search and that to leave it guaranteed that he would be shot on sight. Smith remained in the home of Dr. Dame until the incident blew over, some months later. But that was only the beginning. He received Jesus Christ as his personal savior and was a thoroughly changed man until the day of his death at a ripe old age.

This story of a faithful pastor and a man condemned to live on the wages of mercy teaches two things about reconciliation, regional or otherwise. The commitment to becoming an ambassador of reconciliation is jump-started by the commitment to Jesus Christ, through obedience to the Great Commandment and the Great Commission, one person at a time. Just as crucial is the reality that such a commitment is initiated by Jesus Christ and no other. That is, unless we believe that Dr. Dame behaved as he did and the commander as he did because they remained such nice people after four years of war that ravaged the community of one and destroyed many close friends of the other at the hands of people representing them both in a fight to the death.

The history of Israel includes a thousand and more years of regional rivalry and hatred between the northern and southern kingdoms of the covenant with Yahweh. Even the kingdom unified under Saul, David, and Solomon was born out of the sinful longing of the people to be like other kingdoms. These kingdoms all had gods they worshipped, but never in human history had a people lived in the intimate communion with their god that Yahweh had lavished on His people. As the Lord Himself explained in First Samuel 8:7, it was this very communion that the people rejected when they demanded a human king. And just as it is with denominations, ruptured communion inevitably leads to more rupture, disengagement leads to more disengagement, as we keep discovering new ways in which our brothers have sinned against us in all of our supposed innocence.

Samuel gave the Israelites a king who turned out badly. David was much better, although himself not without sin; and his son, Solomon, re-introduced the idolatry that was never wholly absent in the life of the nation, from Abraham to the time of the Babylonian conquest. But the prophets decided that things had gone far enough, even before Solomon's death and even though the Lord had promised that a son of David would always reign in Israel. One of their number, Ahijah, recalling the Lord's declaration to Solomon that He would take all but one of the tribes from the rule of his son and give them to a subordinate, met Jeroboam, son of Nebat, on the road and told him that he was the chosen one (see 1 Kings 11:26-40). The transfer was not to occur until after Solomon was dead, and we have no indication in First Kings 11 that Jeroboam was the actual choice of the Lord. But Jeroboam began his rebellion at once, and the stage was set for centuries of intermittent war between the kingdoms.

Doing God's work for Him instead of with Him never seems to work out. The dynasty in the northern kingdom changed more than once, but the kings of Israel were a pretty sorry lot of idolaters right up until the Assyrians burned them out more than two hundred years later. There was the occasional glimmer of reconciliation, as when the two kingdoms made common cause against Moab in 2 Kings 3. But the truth is that this kind of conflict is so intimately tied in with our original sin of betrayal and disengagement that its healing can only originate with an act of God; this is the second necessary feature of regional reconciliation. The longer the regions remain in rivalry and enmity, the longer grows the list of outrages on both sides, and reunion becomes less and less likely. By the time Jesus appeared on the scene, the Jews had fully justified their rejection of their northern brethren for rejecting the Mosaic Covenant, and the Samaritans had retaliated by accusing the Jews of adding to the covenant all of the prophetic writings as manufactured additions. Like all of the authentic work of the covenant, human participation and sacrifice are required, but the healing must originate in God.

WHAT THE GOSPELS SAY

How important to God is the reconciliation of the regions? There are at least four episodes in the Gospels that deal specifically with this issue.

The first is found in Matthew 15:21-28 and tells of a Canaanite woman from the territory of the tribe of Asher that is within the boundaries of ancient Samaria. Canaanites were the lowest of the low inasmuch as they worshipped idols and even (once upon a time) sacrificed their children to them. This one came to the Lord begging Him to free her daughter from the grip of a demon. She made no effort to hide her origin; she was as fully committed to her Samaritan identity as William Fuller was committed to the secessionist, slave-owning cause two thousand years later. Jesus gave a standard

Jewish response to the effect that there was no communion between them. She begged again, and he dismissed her with the famous statement, "I was sent only to the lost sheep of Israel" (Matt. 15:24). She could have taken the implied hint that she was not of that house (even though historically she was one of the sojourners who was to be included), but instead she made a groveling oblation of herself before Him. "Yes, Lord," she said, "but even the dogs eat the crumbs that fall from their master's table" (Matt. 15:27). Translation: "Call me what you like, Lord, for I may be a dog, but I know that even dogs are considered part of the family at mealtimes, and I will accept your grace any way I can get it." Jesus, of course, was overjoyed because she had just supplied the third and final necessary piece of the process in which reconciliation can occur.

The woman had demonstrated that she was every bit as committed to seeking the face of God as she ever was to being a person of Samaria. That fulfills Matthew 6:33, which says that those seeking first God's Kingdom will have all of the other things that they need as well. "Then Jesus answered, 'Woman you have great faith! Your request is granted.' And her daughter was healed from that very hour" (Matt. 15:28). But more than that, the One sent only to the lost sheep of the House of Israel had demonstrated that He wants all of the sheep, from whatever portion of the House, restored to their rightful home in the Kingdom.

The second episode is found in Mark 7:24-30 and is very similar to the first. In this case, the woman was of Syro-Phoenician stock, and they were the sworn enemies of even the Canaanites and Samaritans. The dialogue between the woman and the Lord is much like that of the other story except that it takes place right after an incident in which Jesus had been upbraiding some Pharisees for putting greater focus on the outward appearance than on the inward core of the heart. He had told them that what goes into the body can never defile it, but that only what comes out defiles a person since the emission emerges from the heart (see Mark 7:15). In that context, as we read the passage, He was clearly stating that including this woman from the wrong region and the wrong tribe in the Body could in no way defile it since she came out of the faithfulness of a heart seeking His face.

The third episode makes the identical point (only in spades, just in case the listeners think Jesus was only making an exception for a desperate foreigners in Matthew and Mark). Samaritans were considered especially vile in Jewish society precisely because they shared their ethnic and cultural heritage with the people of Zion. To Jews, the Samaritans had been heirs to all of the abundant life of the Mosaic Covenant and had thrown it all away in a series of massive acts of betrayal and depravity that made Adam's act in the Garden almost an academic case. Foreigners might claim ignorance of the enormity of their sin, but the Samaritans knew what they were doing when they practiced every reprobate behavior, from worshipping the Baals to ritual prostitution (both heterosexual and homosexual), to outright cannibalism when under siege (see 2 Kings 6:26-29). Surely, the Jews would reason, there was no redemption for these people.

The parable of the Good Samaritan is found in Luke 10:25-37 and tells of a Jewish man who was beaten and left for dead by highway robbers. A priest and a Levite passed the man by for the understandable (to Jewish listeners) reason that to touch a man near death could defile them and leave them unfit to participate in the sacrifices at the Temple in Jerusalem. Then a Samaritan man found the Jewish man, bandaged the man's wounds, and paid for his expenses while recovering at an inn. When Jesus commended the Samaritan, He was commending the compassion that comes from a heart after God as being more important than ceremonial piety; and He was calling that compassion the stuff of the Kingdom. But He also laid the basis for regional reconciliation, demonstrating that it comes between people of like hearts rather than of like accents and favorite foods.

My favorite of the four (the most detailed account of the process) is the story of the woman at the well of Sychar, recounted in John 4:1-42. Again the story concerns redemption for and reconciliation with Samaritans, only this time it is not a parable. Jesus walked out every detail in His incarnate majesty.

Jesus began the encounter by breaking a social taboo about talking with an un-attached woman at a well. His reasoning was as practical as it gets; He was thirsty and she was drawing water. This Lord—who was always scrupulous to observe the strictures of the Covenant—was openly contemptuous of those laws tacked onto it by men for their own convenience or self-aggrandizement. The woman, of course, pointed out the impropriety of a Jew conversing with a

Samaritan. (Like the others, she made no apology for being who she was.) But Jesus merely stuck to His point that conversation with the Messiah was a privilege that transcended the requirements of a first century Emily Post. With the dialogue opened, He did two things. He told her everything about her that might cause a holy person to stay away from her (such as the fact that she was a multiple divorcee and was currently living in conjugal relations outside of wedlock), and He offered her abundant life just for acknowledging Him as the source of all holiness.

Jesus' sole concern was building the Kingdom of God. That is why He stated in Matthew 11:6 that the Kingdom is populated by those who take no offense at Him. He is not concerned with history (regional, cultural, or denominational) except insofar as history makes it easier for us to recognize Him as the embodiment of the progressive revelation of His Father over all the years of the Covenant. (He knew, for example, but was willing to forgive even the fact that both Jews and Samaritans had practiced occasional human sacrifice of their own children and that the Jews continued the practice for some decades after the destruction of Samaria, according to Second Kings 23:8-20.) He only wanted to know if they were ready to give up their ways and take up His from that moment onward. The same is still true today. But He is acutely aware that if we are unwilling to enter the Kingdom in the company of people we see as more notorious sinners than us, then we are not ready to enter it at all. And so a commitment to be reconciled to fallen brothers and neighbors must take center stage.

The woman at the well more than justified the investment Jesus had made in her. She ran back into her village and brought out the whole community to "Come, see a man who told me everything I ever did…" (John 4:29). She was committed to being who she was, which is why she had not repented of her sexual sin before this meeting. Her redemption and reconciliation was initiated by God. And she was eager enough to seek His face that she did not hold onto her sinful identity when it was exposed to daylight. Instead, she grabbed eagerly for the real life that was offered to her. And Jesus demonstrated (once again) that being a member of a despised and rejected wing of one's own community (and apostate wing) does not in and of itself disqualify one from citizenship in the Kingdom. But continued rejection of those people whom Jesus has accepted just might.

Jesus laid the framework for regional reconciliation in the Gospel passages, but it remains for the Church to act on what He clearly intended. It will take more than Jesus' resurrection, more even than the coming of the Holy Spirit on Pentecost, to bring this about.

COMPELLED BY CIRCUMSTANCE

One feature of the necessity for genuine reconciliation to begin in God is the simple fact that we won't do it unless we are compelled by our circumstances. The Apostles were perfectly content to remain in Jerusalem, even though Jesus made it clear in the Great Commission that His gospel was to be preached in all the earth, until they were scattered abroad by the first great wave of persecution. That event is recorded in Acts 8:1-2, and it was triggered by the death of Stephen.

The religious authorities in Jerusalem had become sick and tired of the upstart apostles healing beggars and proclaiming the name of a dead messianic figure who they claimed was the source of it all. They were so committed to their own self-righteousness (recall that their high priest had prophesied the death of Jesus as being for the good of the nation) that the signs and wonders accompanying the apostolic ministry were only seen as further proof of the danger they presented. Recall that the plot to kill Jesus dated from the raising of Lazarus from the dead (see John 11:45-53); it never occurred to the authorities that raising the dead might actually authenticate the ministry. (One need not be a member of the Jewish hierarchy to be this self-righteous. Think of the McCarthy era or of the politically correct thought, police on our nation's university campuses today.) When Stephen delivered an especially blistering analysis of their historic rejection of everyone that God had ever sent, and he an Hellenic Jew from another region at that, they stoned him to death for blasphemy; then it really got wild in the city.

The authorities begin hunting and lynching every Christian they could identify. The people were scattered into the Judean countryside and as far away as Samaria, compelled by the persecution to do what God always intended. (As it says in Romans 8:28, He makes all things come together for good for those who believe. What the enemy meant for evil, God meant for good.) Wherever they went, the apostles began to share the great events, and the great opportunity that they had witnessed.

The preaching was not limited to the re-constituted band of twelve; in fact, they appear to have remained in Jerusalem. A deacon named Phillip was particularly effective in one of the Samaritan cities, and demons fled whenever he came near. He baptized large numbers of Samaritan people and healed their sick. When Peter and the rest of the Twelve heard the stories, they went to the city themselves, and inasmuch as the Holy Spirit has not yet fallen on the Samaritans, they asked for the baptism of the Spirit, and there was a renewed explosion of abundant life in the city.

But wait! In the popular wisdom, this was not possible. Everybody in Judea knew that the Samaritans were the most unholy reprobates in the world. They were renegades to the covenant with Yahweh! Yet, when they received Jesus, the Holy Spirit and the whole life of Christ was made available to them; indeed, it had been available to them all along.

The point here is that the apostles had not simply happened on a city and found God to be there ahead of them. They came from Jerusalem, bringing the Spirit with them, as their Lord had commanded them even before His death and most certainly after His resurrection. For this to occur, it would first be necessary for the apostles to become committed to reconciliation with their regional opponents. Their commitment to reconciliation would have had, of necessity, to be part and parcel of their post-resurrection repentance on the shore of Lake Tiberias (see John 21), or they would have been unwilling to believe God had visited Samaria, just as the

Jewish authorities were unwilling to see God in the miracles performed through the apostles in Jerusalem.

The same three dynamics were operating in this Samaritan reconciliation as in the Gospel accounts mentioned earlier. The people in question were utterly committed to the rightness of their cause; they walked in integrity to the degree that had been revealed to them. (If the religious authorities could claim that same integrity, they would hardly have been making arrests by night or using mobs as instruments of policy.) God initiated the circumstances leading to an opportunity for reconciliation. And the people in question, the apostolic band and those others who adhered to the Way, were just as committed to allowing God to re-write their worldview and their sense of identity as they were to the identity they already possessed. The process of reconciliation for them was both symptom and trigger for what God had in mind.

I live in California where there is a long history of rivalry and hostility between the northern and southern regions. People from the respective regions do not shoot each other on sight, but the South considers itself to be more culturally enlightened and more spiritually dynamic than the North. For the last century, beginning with the discovery of oil, the birth of the entertainment industry in Hollywood, and the consequent building of the Los Angeles Aqueduct, the South has felt pretty free to help itself to northern resources, which in their minds were at once more needed and more deserved. These resources include water that is piped south, even when doing so drains northern watersheds, tax money that is collected in the north and spent on southern roadways, and facilities in the north that are used to warehouse paroled criminals. At the same time, the South has exercised political clout coupled with environmentalist zeal to effectively cancel the timber industry, which was the principal anchor of the northern regional economy. (The center of the state depends on agriculture and has remained relatively untouched by this rivalry.) The southerners tend to see themselves as constituting the real California, which they tend to think of as ending around San Francisco on the coast and at Sacramento inland.

The North, for its part, tends to live in splendid isolation. Northerners take a perverse pride in their reputation as country cousins. They resent the southerners as people who are foolish enough to build their cities on land that cannot support their enormous population and who are, therefore, reduced to forcing the more sensible northerners to support them. They tend to be more politically conservative than the southerners and congratulate themselves on not being responsible for all that gives California a reputation for flakiness (even though the North recently voted three billion dollars in bond money for embryonic stem cell research by nearly as wide a margin as the southern counties). They express the hope that the southerners won't become more aware of the northern region, as more of them might want to move north and ruin the neighborhoods. They pride themselves on being able to live without the race riots and racial tensions that have plagued the South, forgetting that the ethnic tensions of the nineteenth century (in the North) were solved by massacre and forced relocation.

Truth is that the South is the usual aggressor in the current regional rivalry. But just as true is the fact that in confiscating northern resources for southern needs without regard to how the northern environment is diminished, the southerners are treating the northern region pretty much as the northerners themselves treated it during the Gold Rush days when most of the original inhabitants of the land did not survive to complain about it. Truth is also that, while northerners consider themselves as a group to be more likely to be Christian in thought and deed, almost all of the great revivals of the last century that have swept the nation have originated in the Los Angeles Basin.

Neither side can truly claim the high ground of righteousness. We need one another to be a whole state. God is not going to let us avoid the reality that He has established in our midst any more than He was willing to allow Joseph and his brothers to permanently avoid reunion. But is there any basis for reconciliation? How then shall we learn to live together and with God?

There is, of course, the same triune basis for reconciliation that appears in the Scriptures that we have looked at in this chapter. Reconcilers must be genuinely in love with the constituency they represent, whether it is denomination, generation, or region. God must initiate the movement (though this is no excuse for passive waiting until some by and by time when the Lord might move). He is passionate about reconciliation—passionate enough to have sacrificed the life of His Son for that cause—and He will move quickly as soon as He has people ready to respond to Him, any people. The third piece is our participation, our own passionate love for Him that will leave us as committed to the changes that He wants to make in our hearts and environs as we are committed to the loyalties that were already there. This third piece moves us into the realm of what is called identificational repentance.

STANDING IN THE GAP

Identificational or representational repentance is one of the more controversial moves of God to take a prominent place in the contemporary Church. It is nothing more, nor less, than what happens when a person or group of people plant themselves in the place of a larger group in need of reconciliation. It is the process of seeking God's face and/or the forgiveness of an injured party on behalf of, in identification with, as the representative of, another. It is what the actors portraying James Andrews and William Fuller did when they shook hands in the movie about the Great Locomotive Chase. It is what I do when I come before the face of the Lord on behalf of my generation or when I represent my denomination in seeking the re-unification of the Body of Christ or in prayer-walking churches, as we did in Chapter 3. More importantly, it is what the heroes of the Bible did over and over again in the pages of Scripture as they responded to the call of God from Ezekiel 22:30, which tells us that He seeks one to stand in the gap for the nation.

Nehemiah engaged in this process in the first chapter of his book when he prayed, "I confess the sins we Israelites, including myself and my father's house, have committed against you. We have acted very wickedly toward you. We have not obeyed the commands, decrees and laws you gave your servant Moses" (Neh. 1:6-7). Isaiah identified with his people and repented on his own and their behalf when he said, "Woe to me!...I am ruined. For I am a man of unclean lips, and I live among a people of unclean lips, and my eyes have seen the King, the Lord Almighty" (Isa. 6:5). Daniel represented his people as himself in when he prayed, "O Lord, the great and awesome God, who keeps His covenant of love with all who love Him and obey His commands, we have sinned and done wrong. We have been wicked and have rebelled; we have turned away from your commands and laws" (Dan. 9:4-6). And, of course, the greatest example of identificational repentance in history is the example of King Jesus, who took our sins onto His cross with Him although He had never sinned in His life. This is the One who said that we would do the things that He did, and greater things, after He went to the Father (see John 14:12).

Is it possible to be an actor of repentance on behalf of others who perhaps do not even know or care that we act on their behalf? Jesus reminded us that what is impossible for men and women, is more than possible for God (see Matt. 19:26). By their fruits we will know them.

God began a major push toward molding California into a state after His heart (a whole state after His heart) with the establishment of the Pray California ministry in late 2002. Coming into being as a response to the City Transformation phenomenon that has now been felt in more than five hundred communities worldwide and that is chronicled in the series of Transformation Videos produced by George Otis' Sentinel Group, Pray California is a fellowship of prayer and reconciliation leaders from many cities across the state. The ministry is devoted to identificational or representative repentance for and over the state of California. The ministry hosted the first ever statewide pastors' prayer summit at the Oakhurst Conference Center, in the southern gateway to Yosemite, in late October 2003 as a kickoff event. In that same week, the devastating wildfires that burned tens of thousands of acres in many parts of Southern California broke out. And the southerners who planned to come had the chance to choose to give up life in order to win it.

Of the 125 or so pastors and intercessors coming from all over California for three days of prayer and worship together, some 40 percent were from communities threatened by the fires. They had to choose between remaining at home and caring for the immediate needs and safety of their homes and families and keeping a commitment that they had made months earlier to come before the Lord. To a man and to a woman, they chose to attend the summit. And to a man and to a woman, the rest of us decided in the Spirit of the Living God to devote the summit to lifting these faithful ones and their homes and families before the face of God. That meant that we claimed them, not as distant relations for whom we would intercede, but as intimate siblings the way the King of Israel claimed the King of Judah in 2 Kings 3:7 when he said, "I am as you are, my people as your people, my horses as your horses."

It also meant that we prayed the prophecy together. We had in our possession a written transcript of a prophetic word given by a nationally known modern day prophet named Chuck Pierce. The word had been issued some months earlier and it foretold the very fires that were raging across the southern part of the state. It stated that God would send a wind from the west to put out the fires and that He would then send a great flood of rain during the months of December, January, and February. Although drought had been predicted by the meteorologists and flooding would be a danger if the rains came in the wake of the fires, the Body did not need to fear any of these things if we prayed faithfully. Pierce had said that the tide, for the fires, would turn on October 28.

We prayed for that west wind over the three days of the summit, even though we knew that such a wind could easily re-stoke the fires that thousands of firefighters were slowly bringing under control. We prayed, and a friend of mine who loves to watch the weather patterns on the internet told me later that he watched as a weather front bearing lots of water came down off of the west coast on a course to miss the land altogether. It had already passed southern California and was continuing south when the tail of the front, on the evening of October 28, turned east to come over the land. At midnight that night, this front deposited rain on the fire lines and broke the back of the fires.

Just as huge (from the standpoint of our witness) were the events of the next several months as intercessors from all over the state continued to pray over the prophecy. December looked very much like the lead-in month to a season of drought, just as predicted, until the rains came. They were indeed torrential; it was one of the rainiest seasons on record. There was some flooding in the southern fire areas, but in light of the fire devastation and the subsequent vulnerability of the land, it was minimal. And the intercessors of the state continued to pray together. But the biggest miracles, from the standpoint of regional reconciliation, were yet to come.

The statewide prayer summit proved to be the first in a series of concerted prayer efforts, including what came to be known as the I-5 Project, in which hundreds of intercessors were deployed in a single day on the overpasses intersecting Interstate 5 from the Oregon line to the Mexican border. The intercessors prayed the Kingdom description from Matthew 11:4-6 over the state, and they prayed it together. Numbers of signs and wonders were witnessed all over the state, but the biggest miracle was that warriors of prayer from all over the state blessed one another from wherever they happened to be deployed. Many journeyed from one region to another just to be a blessing to the people of the region they visited.

At the end of January 2004, I was one of a dozen or more invited to speak at a prayer meeting at the Hollywood Presbyterian Church. We were each invited to simply share our testimony of what God had been doing up and down the state in the context of these concerted prayer efforts, especially the I-5 Project. When it was my turn, the Lord prompted me to begin by identifying myself as a prayer facilitator from northern California. I said that we were all aware of the history of resentment and hostility between our regions and that I wanted to preface my testimony by lavishly bestowing the blessing of the region I represent on the region that was good enough to host me. I gave my testimony and took my seat while another went to the podium.

I was astounded, and filled with joy, to see one of the pastors from the host church take the microphone after the last speaker had finished. His tears flowed as he referred back to "that man from northern California who blessed us on behalf of his region." He then led the congregation in prayers of repentance for their treatment of the northern region and expressed his personal hope for the full reconciliation of the regions in this state that we both call both home and the place of our calling.

As I write this, another two years have passed. PrayNorthstate and similar ministries from all parts of California continue to mobilize prayer all over the state to seek God's face for the blessing of the whole state. We continue to pray for and bless and walk out reconciliation activities in the state. We are networking with each other and sending teams of intercessors into each others' regions, always by local invitation, to bless one another at various installations. We are training each other and sending teachers south to sow into the southern region what God is teaching us up north that they don't yet know about in the South. We are sending teachers north to impart in the same way what God is birthing in the southern region that has not yet appeared in power in the North. Most importantly, we are choosing each day to bless one another in the Name of the Lord, and we are crying out to Him to bless the region that we once eyed with suspicion and old grievances.

ENDOTE

1. *The Great Locomotive Chase,* DVD, directed by Francis D. Lyon (Burbank, CA: Walt Disney Pictures, 1956).

Chapter 6

His Peace to the Nations

I n April 1998, Diana and I flew to Hawaii on the generosity of a good friend and longtime supporter of our ministry. He believed we needed a rest, and he was willing to pay for it, but (as always) God had bigger fish to fry, even in the act of providing us with the rest we needed through the gift of a friend. The moment we landed in Oahu, we were overwhelmingly aware of a peace in the air that we had never experienced before in Hawaii.

The first divine appointment took place in the commuter terminal of Honolulu's International Airport. While we waited to board our flight to Maui, we noticed a dark-skinned man wearing a windbreaker lettered with something like "Warriors for Christ" who was seeing some people off. We picked up right away that the Holy Spirit was fairly dripping off of this man, and I had a strong impulse to walk over, introduce myself, and bless the man. As I began to rise from my seat, God spoke audibly to me. "Sit down. You will meet this man. But it will be when I say and where I say." I shared what had happened with Diana and we simply committed ourselves to pray for "the man at the airport" until God would bring us together.

The next time God reached into our lives (visibly) was a few days later on Maui. I was out swimming, and Diana had remained in our hotel room. God came to her and told her to take out a pencil and paper because He was going to give her the bust of the angel who guarded Maui. He had told her some time back that He wanted her to paint this angel, but until that moment, He had not revealed anything of what the angel looked like. When I returned to the room, she had finished a drawing of the angel's head, face, and shoulders. Everywhere and every time we have had opportunity to show this drawing to ethnic Hawaiian people, they have immediately responded with something like, "Yes, that's him," while they marveled that God would reveal his appearance to a non-Hawaiian first.

The last time God intervened in our lives during that visit was on our last day in Maui. We had gone to a local mall to look for some souvenirs for our children, and while we shopped, I heard the sounds of praise music floating over this commercial shopping mall. I ran out of the bookstore I was browsing, and there, in full regalia, was a group of Hawaiians dancing hula and praising the Lord for all to see. We went over to them and, when they were ready to take a break, introduced ourselves to them. The sense of family and belonging that swept over us and them was instantaneous. Eight weeks later, they would visit us in California and we would be introduced to Hawaii's Spiritual Warfare Project or, as it was known in Maui, the 'Io Project.

The Spiritual Warfare Project was the vision of a teacher and scholar named Daniel Kikawa. Over the course of several years he and a small group of people dedicated to the Kingdom of God in Hawaii gathered ten thousand intercessors to pray for the coming of the Kingdom to Hawaii. They prayed with special intentionality from 1996 to 1998 while they waited for God to give them the word to go out. On March 14, 1998, they received the word, and they visited each of the more than seven hundred *heiaus* (places of pagan worship) in the Hawaiian islands. They observed proper and respectful protocol at all times, asking permission of the landowners to visit these sites on which human beings had been sacrificed to volcanic deities. They fought a war of the spirit, using only the weapons and authorities that God has given to His people. That is to say, they blessed the land—for the Body of Christ has unlimited authority to bless, and we are even commanded in Romans 12:14 to bless and not curse. They forgave the sins committed in those places because Jesus came as one with authority to forgive sins, and He commanded us to do likewise in John 20:23. They celebrated communion together, knowing that Jesus commanded His followers to do this for the remembrance of Him whenever they gathered to celebrate His presence in their midst (see Luke 22:19).

There were many signs and wonders that accompanied this massive cleansing operation, not the least of which was the lifting of a drought that had hung over the islands for the previous two years. But the phenomenon that must have impressed the Lord Jesus was that many thousands throughout the islands came to know, love, and serve Him over the next few months. The bondage of the islands to their pagan past had been broken. It had been broken by a united Body of Christ under the leadership of indigenous Christians.

Diana, my bride without a drop of Hawaiian blood in her veins, was one of the ten thousand who prayed daily for this harvest in Hawaii. The Lord enlisted her for service with a word given in California in 1996, although she had never even heard of the 'Io Project until we met the Tahauri family on Maui in 1998.

What did we learn from our immersion in the lives of these people of a very different ethnic and cultural stock from our own, an immersion that was as progressive as it was spontaneous on our part and steeped in the plans and purposes of God for us and for the islands? Just one thing—God really meant it when He said through the mouth of the prophet Isaiah, "Their burnt offerings and sacrifices will be accepted on My altar; for My house will be called a house of prayer for all nations" (Isa. 56:7). He really means to bring every tribe and nation together around His hearth to dwell together with Him in His dwelling place. The very language employed in Isaiah 56:7-8 indicates that God means for the tribes and nations to come together as they are, rather than as we would like them to be. He says that their burnt offerings will be accepted, not that their offerings will be accepted when they cannot be distinguished from our burnt offerings.

What does it mean to be an ambassador of reconciliation to tribes (ethnic communities) other than our own? What does it mean, as Isaiah puts it, to call nations we know not? (See Isaiah 55:5.) Is the reciprocal proposition just as true, that nations who do not know us are calling us into the family of God? One thing of which we can be certain is that the God who calls us, in the Great Commission, to teach one another to observe all that He has commanded also expects us to both respect and cherish one another in the differing incarnations of our humanity within which He has called us to Himself. He has left His fingerprints on each and every culture. Just as the Old Testament exists primarily to call a people to become the family of God in such a way that they are prepared to recognize their Messiah when He comes, so to a lesser extent, the Father has prepared the signposts by which He could be recognized in the person of His Son in each of the cultures of the world (see Rom. 1:20). In our sin, we have obscured and papered over those fingerprints, in every culture, but we cannot and have not blotted them out.

Hawaii has never been the peaceful paradise of racial harmony and simple beauty that is depicted in the tourist brochures. The kingdom founded by Kamehameha the Great was birthed in a war of extermination of his enemies, and the native people living prior to the coming of American missionaries lived in fear of an ugly death if they transgressed any part of the kapu system, a social and religious set of rules instituted in the fourteenth century by an invading Tahitian people who wiped out the indigenous culture and most of its people. The Hawaiians of modern times have seethed with understandable resentment over the theft of their kingdom by American business interests in the late nineteenth century. This final loss followed nearly a century of fierce tug-of-war between competing national and economic interests who lusted after the natural resources and strategic assets of the islands in which the Hawaiian government fought a losing battle to maintain independence for itself.

IMPREGNATED WITH THE WORD

In spite of all of this, the Hawaiian culture was impregnated with the Word of God from the moment the first settlers landed in the islands. These sea voyagers worshipped a God they called 'Io in the language they developed for their new home. 'Io translates into English as a synonym to the Hebrew Yahweh or Jehovah, I am that I am. 'Io was understood as a Father who loved His people. The prophets of 'Io said that this God of blessing had one and only one Son. The name of the Son was not revealed to the prophets, but 'Io did say that His Son had given His life up for the sins of the people. He also revealed that one day men and women representing the Son would come to Hawaii and usher the people into relation with the Son so that they could have eternal life in His name. These representatives would be known by the fact that they would arrive in a canoe of gigantic proportions bearing square white sails. (Hawaiian vessels used triangular sails that were the same beige color as the beaten tarot fibers from which they were made.) The canoes of the missionaries would anchor at a specially designated rock in Kailua Bay, on the island of Oahu, and the missionaries would carry the words of 'Io for His people ashore in a wooden box.

When the missionaries arrived in 1820, they traveled on a square-rigged schooner. They anchored at the rock in Kailua Bay, and they carried the Bible ashore in a wooden box to protect it from water damage. The people, as many as still worshipped 'Io, greeted them with the word *aloha*, a Hawaiian word that has been in their language since about A.D. 500. It is made from three Hawaiian phonemes which mean in succession the Father, the Son, and the Holy Spirit. Its traditional meaning is, "May the Spirit of the Living God be all over you."[1]

The meaning of *aloha* will not be found in a Hawaiian language dictionary. It is revealed by Hawaiian people to those they trust enough to take into their confidence. This revelation is not the fruit of research, but of relationship.

This seeding of culture with the tools necessary for recognizing Him is not unique to the Hawaiian culture. It is typical of how God prepares people from their foundation for the living out of their destiny. It is just as typical that He sends people from outside of the culture to trigger His revelation in its fullness. This is one way for God to walk out the reality that He presents in First Corinthians 12, the wonderful essay about the neediness of the parts of the Body of Christ for one another.

Now the body is not made up of one part but of many. If the foot should say, "Because I am not a hand, I do not belong to the body," it would not for that reason cease to be part of the body. And if the ear should say, "Because I am not an eye, I do not belong to the body," it would not for that reason cease to be part of the body. If the whole body were an eye, where would the sense of hearing be? If the whole body were an ear, where would the sense of smell be? But in fact God has arranged the parts of the body, every one of them, just as He wanted them to be (1 Corinthians 12:14-18).

When God sends people from outside of a culture to introduce the abundant life that only faith in His Son can bring, it is not because of any inherent superiority of the missionary culture. No culture is inherently superior to any other for all have sinned, and Jesus died equally for all to redeem us all. When God sends ambassadors of His reconciliation, instead of growing them within the home culture, it is simply His way of dealing with the delusion of self-sufficiency that all cultures share. It is His way of making certain that we know how desperately we need the revelation that only the other can bring.

And who was the man we saw in the airport who we were not allowed to meet at that time? His name is Suuqiina, and he is an Inuit man from Alaska. He is a scholar and missionary in his own right. He and his wife, Qaumaniq, have become dear friends of Diana's and mine. They have brought many revelations of the God who loves us that our own culture was somehow unable to supply, and we have returned the favor as many times. It was three years from that day in the airport before God enabled us to meet in a location more than twenty-five hundred miles away. And He used the time to teach the four of us about walking with Him just one step at a time by declining to show us two steps at once. He brought us closer to that meeting by introducing us to many other people who knew both couples until He finally closed the circle in another airport. But it was a mutual friend named Lynda Prince, born in yet another culture ,who facilitated that closing.

The Inuit people of Alaska worshipped a God they called Sila before the coming of the missionaries to their land. The name means, "He who creates all things without Himself being created," and so the correspondence to the God we know as Yahweh is unmistakable. Sila also had His own prophets among the Inuit, the most notable being the nineteenth century seer called Manilaq. This man of God prophesied that Sila had a Son whose name would be revealed by men from another tribe who would visit some time in the future. (The people of King Island, where Manilaq lived, had no contact with people of European descent before the twentieth century.) They would tell of how the Son had died for the sins of the Inuit and of all mankind, and they would offer the opportunity for eternal life in His name. They would be recognized because they would come in a flying canoe that would land on the river. They would be dressed in black from head to toe, and they too would bring the words of Sila ashore in a wooden box.

The most startling facet of this revelation was that the foreigners would also bring the body and blood of Sila and invite the people to eat and drink of it. Nothing was more abhorrent to the Inuit than the specter of cannibalism, yet they were assured that they would honor Sila by eating in this way, and many of them chose to believe it.

Sila also called the people, through the ministry of Manilaq, to prepare their hearts for the coming of His son. He told them that He had prepared one mate for them so that they could become one flesh with another. Although their polygamy was undertaken for survival reasons, many children were a hedge against the extinction of a family name, Sila wanted them to live in His will rather than to merely survive in their own. He likewise ordered that one day was to be kept as a Sabbath, despite the reality that theirs was a subsistence culture of people who needed to be out hunting and gathering each day in order to survive. Their God called them to choose abundant life in Him instead of mere survival in themselves. Although the words were different, Sila could not have issued a clearer call to seek first His Kingdom and trust Him that all they needed would be added to them as well.

When the missionaries did come, they arrived in a flying boat. They were Roman Catholic monks, dressed in black head-to-toe cassocks. They brought in their hands a wooden box holding the Bible and the bread and wine of the Holy Communion, which they identified as the body and blood of the Son of Sila. Although Manilak did not live to see that day, the people who remembered Sila and the prophecies said, "Welcome. We have been waiting for you for a long time."[2]

God's Fingerprints on His Family

The first eight verses of Isaiah 56 deal with the makings of a true Israelite. They make clear that anyone who does justice, anticipates the Lord's salvation, and keeps the Sabbath is one of the Lord's people. They go on to specify that foreigners who practice righteousness are no longer foreigners; they are full members of the family of God. They are Israelites. The Father says, "These I will bring to my holy mountain and give them joy in my house of prayer. Their burnt offerings and sacrifices will be accepted on my altar; for my house will be called a house of prayer for all nations" (Isa. 56:7). Jesus referred to these verses in Mark 11:17 when, after clearing the false worshippers from the temple, he said, "My house will be called a house of prayer for all nations, but you have made it a den of robbers." When we reject the God who made us by rejecting the people that He has made, and then retreat to the temple for an exercise in piety, we make the temple not the scene of the robbery but the den of the robbers.

Jesus' parable of the Good Samaritan follows the same set of principles. He commended the member of a despised tribe in Luke 10:25-37. But it was not because the Samaritans were intrinsically of higher quality than the Jews had imagined; they were corporately guilty of the charges leveled against them throughout their history. Jesus held up the Samaritan who went out of his way to care for the wounded traveler as an example of good character precisely because his behavior transcended his ethnicity. For Jesus, ethnicity neither commends nor condemns. The determining factor is the degree to which a man walks out the declaration of Micah 6:8, "He has showed you, O man, what is good. And what does the Lord require of you? To act justly and to love mercy and to walk humbly with your God," not the degree to which his background has prepared him to know about it. But it ought to be newsworthy that Jesus did not expect the Samaritan to shed his culture before he could be worthy of the good deed that he did. Obviously his culture, as corrupt as it was, contained enough of God's fingerprints to enable the Samaritan to act in the image of God in which he was made.

In Acts 10, Peter was summoned to the home of Cornelius the centurion. By this time in history, the culture of Imperial Rome had already descended far into the decadence and debauchery that would ultimately destroy it. Rulers of the known world, they feared neither God nor man. They took the service of captured peoples as their due rather than appreciating the hardiness born of service, piety, and patriotism that made the Romans themselves the envy of the peoples they supplanted, such as the decadent Greeks. But Cornelius had retained enough of what made Rome great to recognize greatness in the high ethics and exquisite simplicity of the gospel. He could see the apostolic revelation as the fulfillment of those same qualities in the Old Testament revelation. His culture, as debased as it may have been, carried enough of the likeness of the Creator of all cultures to enable him to recognize his redeemer. When Peter came in response to the cry of the centurion's heart, he shared the recognizable truth and baptized everyone in the household into the new faith.

But Peter needed to hear from Cornelius as much as Cornelius needed to hear from Peter. It is in the exchange that God comes over Peter in His Holy Spirit to point out that what He had named clean (in the vision of the animals let down from Heaven on a sheet) was clean indeed. Jesus had made this clear in Mark 7:1-23, but Peter needed to hear it in a new context in order for him to get the message. We need each other; it is a First Corinthians 12 world in which God has called us to live.

The best example of cross-cultural ministry I have ever known is found in Acts 17:16-34. Paul was in Athens when he was confronted by the hundreds of gods worshipped and served in that city. He knew that he had the best news anyone had ever heard in the gospel of Jesus Christ; he knew that his message was for the people of Athens. But he also knew enough of Athenian history to recognize how God had primed the pump for His revelation six hundred years earlier. The Athenians had an altar to an unknown god in the midst of the statuary honoring all of the deities whose names they know. The altar was erected during an ancient plague when the people had offered sacrifices to every conceivable god in hopes of getting relief. A poet and prophet from the island of Crete by the name of Epimenedes told the people that a god whose name he did not know had said that he would end the plague if the people offered sacrifice to him. This god had also declared that he wanted no statues—he did not resemble any created being and would not tolerate idolatry. The people erected the altar and offered the sacrifice and this unknown god healed their city. (Unfortunately, the people did not take the hint and tear down their statues to other gods at this point, but they did include the new god in their sacrificial system right down to the day Paul stood on Mars Hill.)[3] Taking full advantage of what he knew of God's existing fingerprints on the culture, Paul began his statement by praising them for their evident piety. He moved on to declaring that he would reveal the name of their unknown God to them. He then told them what Jesus Christ had done for them in His life, death, and resurrection.

Paul saw what God had been doing in Athens to prepare the people for His coming in the apostolic proclamation. He respected what he saw, even as he realized that the vision of God in the Athenian heart was incomplete without the explicit message of the gospel. And he presented Christ as a revelation of transformation and resurrection of the culture, not as its replacement. Through the boldness and the humility of Paul, God won the day in Athens.

The common denominator—whether of the biblical stories I recount or of the people of 'Io or Sila—is that God had left His fingerprints on each of these cultures and when Jesus came onto the scene, there were enough of them left to enable the people to recognize Him from within their culture. There is always a need for repentance on both individual and corporate levels, but there is never a need to renounce what God has planted in our hearts as culture, or the way in which our community makes sense of the created world. What God has made, we must call good.

Even though God seeded Himself into the cultures, I would not presume to say that all traditions of God refer to the same God—they do not. The Canaanites of the Bible sacrificed their children to Molech in fire; there was nothing of the loving Father we serve in that atrocity, and there was nothing like God's call to cross cultural reconciliation when the Hebrew people allowed themselves to be seduced into that cult. Allah is a deity who demands works in place of simple faith, a god who never sacrificed himself for the people he supposedly loves, but a lord who loves only those who please him. And he does not guarantee heaven even to these! He specifically denies that he would ever have a son in his holy book, the Quran. This is not the God we know, who created Heaven and earth out of his unmerited love and who gave His own life in the life of His Son as a ransom for many.

The revelation of God attributed to Buddha calls for the obliteration of the self (if ever that self achieves nirvana), and it is a far cry from the everlasting personality we are offered in the Lord Jesus Christ. Yet even when a religious tradition is found to be demonstrably false, the Lord Jesus asks no more than the Apostolic Council of Acts 15 required of the first Gentile converts, that idolatry, sexual immorality, and the eating of blood or the products of strangulation be abandoned and that Jesus be proclaimed as the sole way, truth, and life. God reaches out to Muslim people especially with dreams and visions that remind them of the truth of their heritage as children of Abraham. He connects to Buddhist people by revealing to them the embodiment of their traditions of self denial in Jesus Christ, and He occasionally reminds them that their founder believed in a Trinitarian godhead because Yahweh had given him that revelation.

The people who lived in darkness and have at last seen a great light are asked only to let go of those facets of their own cultures that spit in the eye of Jesus, not those that point to Him or even those that run on a parallel track. They are no different (and are under no greater obligation) than those of us who need to repent of our conviction that our good works will land us in Heaven or that God helps those who help themselves. We are all guilty of syncretism, of mixing our pagan traditions with the true history of the living God in our midst, and we have equal need to repent of it as we forgive one another.

Romans 3:23 reminds us that all have sinned, individually and corporately. No culture can say, "We have carried the image of God before us; we have been true and worthy of imitation." Yet Paul says earlier in the same epistle, "For since the creation of the world God's invisible qualities—his eternal power and divine nature—have been clearly seen, being understood from what has been made, so that men are without excuse" (Rom. 1:20). Although the Jews are in a unique relationship to Yahweh (since He has more fully revealed Himself to them in the Old Testament than to any other people), we have all received the proper equipping necessary to recognize our God when He comes to us, if we believe the Scriptures. No tribe can say they had no way of knowing. And none can say that their culture is so superior to the others in godliness that people of other tribes should become like them before they can be acceptable to God.

UNITED IN THE NEED TO REPENT

Yet more often than not, when one culture discovers another, the first impulse of the discoverers is to conquer and dominate. And all too often, the infusion of faith into the conquering peoples makes little or no difference when it comes to the exercise of mercy or understanding. In my own state of California, the discovery of gold only accelerated the process of subjugation and near extermination of the native peoples that had begun decades before. The Spanish, and the Mexicans after them, practiced the forced enslavement of any natives who crossed their paths. American Indians were forced to work the ranchos and to provide sexual companions for the land owners. Those who refused were tortured and often killed; those who escaped captivity were likewise brutalized. Between 1770 and 1850, a mere eighty years, the American Indian population of California was reduced from about seven hundred thousand to about two hundred thousand because of those who were murdered and those who succumbed to disease and the destruction of their settlements and environment. When California passed to American rule, the gold miners simply wiped out bands who angered them or stood in their path.

One of the most infamous atrocities occurred in what is now Trinity County. A party of four Nor-rel-muk men had demanded food from a white trader. When the trader refused to give them the food, they killed him and took what they wanted. When word of the killing reached Weaverville, a posse set out to avenge the crime. Coming upon a group of some one hundred and fifty Nor-rel-muk women and children at the site of what is now called Natural Bridges, near the town of Hayfork, the posse systematically wiped out the entire band. No effort was made to identify the killers, who were long gone by then, and only one child survived the massacre.

The white settlers of Eureka had not even this slim provocation to justify the 1860 massacre of the Wiyot People on Indian Island in Humboldt Bay. They simply rowed out to the island at night, while the American Indians were sleeping, and hacked and clubbed the entire band to death. Not even the youngest child was spared. And not even the local newspaper could imagine a reason why.

The most treacherous incident in this history of horrors occurred in the Jones Valley near the Oregon border in 1851. The Shasta People had just concluded a treaty of peace with the immigrants, and a great barbecue feast was planned to celebrate the event. The beef was impregnated with strychnine and more than three thousand Shastas died that day. Those who recognized their peril before eating the poisoned meat were shot as they tried to escape. This incident, recorded in newspapers of that day, is denied by the federal government to this day.

Does the Church fare better in this sad chronicle? Not much. While incidents such as Colorado's 1864 massacre at Sand Creek, in which militia led by a Protestant minister named John Chivington wiped out a peaceful Cheyenne village living under the American flag (because, in Chivington's words, "I live to kill Indians"), are rare, the forced conversion of American Indians under the Spanish missionaries (using torture if necessary) was policy.

American missionaries operated mission schools in which native children were whipped with leather thongs if they spoke a word of their native language, and this is not just ancient history. Lynda Prince, founder and president of First Nations of North America, Honorary Grand Chief for Life of the Carrier-Sakani Nation of British Columbia, and a personal friend of mine, was educated in such a school after having been kidnapped from her family's home. Dr. Suuqiina, grandson of an Inuit king and the man of God whom God brought to encounter Diana and me in the Honolulu airport, was threatened with commitment to an asylum when he began to think and speak of himself as a man of his people. The indigenous peoples of Hawaii and mainland North America are told in many of their churches, even today, that there is nothing of God in their traditional cultures and that they must dress, speak, and act like people of Northern European heritage if they would live godly lives. Such things as the hula and the 'awa ceremony, with which Hawaiians honored 'Io for centuries, are considered an abomination in many of the churches of God. This is so even though we immigrant peoples worship God with music formerly used in drinking songs, such as the tune for *A Mighty Fortress Is Our God,* and even though we use the rite of baptism, which was originally a pagan rite for initiation into the tribe. Do we truly believe that what God has redeemed, by dedicating it to Himself, may not be called unclean (as Jesus said in Mark 7), or do we only use the vessels that we ourselves have declared clean? Jesus says that by their fruits we shall know them (see Matt. 7:16), but we seem to say that by their roots we shall know them. It has been that way more often than not. How do we become this way?

In my own life, Lucas was the best excuse I could ask for the practice of racism. He was Hispanic and a year older than me, and we both attended Van Nuys Junior High School in the early 1960s. We knew each other by name, and little else of each other. One day, we passed each other in the school quad. Without warning or provocation, he punched me— hard. Before I could recover—or retaliate—he was gone, and the incident was history. It became an indelible piece of my history; I did not forget the humiliation I felt at receiving his abuse and being unable to respond. Even when I met the Lord Jesus in 1970, I held onto this piece of my pre-Jesus identity.

Truthfully, it is not true to say that I remembered. The history lurked in the backwaters of my soul, unremembered and unhealed. I had plenty of Hispanic friends in high school and college, although none were close. I liked and respected my friends, but if you asked me what I thought of Hispanics in general, I would tell you that, while likable enough as indi-viduals, they tended to be violent and unpredictable. I was not comfortable going into their neighborhoods; you never knew what might happen. On the other hand, when we were on my turf, when I felt like I had some control over the conditions, I was perfectly happy to be among the people as one who served. In other words, as long as Hispanic people were will-ing to become like me, I was happy to love and accept them— as long as they were willing to become like me.

I remained, blind and unaware, in this attitude until God convicted me and brought me to repentance and healing of the shame out of which I had been operating. Fear and shame, unsubmitted to Jesus, make for a life unsubmitted to Jesus. People who know themselves called to fulfill the Great Commission in other cultures and who have not submitted their fears and their shames to Jesus will treat even the people they mean to serve the way I treated people who looked like Lucas. They will treat them like so many Euro-American missionaries treated the Hawaiians and the American Indians, insisting they adopt western dress, manners, and even housing, before their profession of faith in Christ Jesus could be acceptable in Heaven and on earth.

The other way we become like that is even less complimentary than the first. I still remember how, as a young high school teacher, I read the classic study, *Bury My Heart at Wounded Knee*.[4] I found this history of the American Indian wars along the American frontier as fascinating as it was heartbreaking. The book offered copious documentation of the aggression and cruelty with which my people had pursued and nearly obliterated the native peoples of the continent we share. But I did not choose to permit my heart to be broken, even though I serve a Lord who says, "Blessed are those who mourn" (Matt. 5:4). I did not choose to risk my self-understanding as a member of a people who do only good to others, even though I am bonded to a Savior who says, "Whoever wants to save his life will lose it, but whoever loses his life for Me and for the gospel will save it" (Mark 8:35).

I said, "Hey, it's really sad that all of those things happened. But it was a clash of cultures. We won; they lost. Move on." It was not until I met people like the Tahauris (Hawaiian) and the Suuqiinas (American Indian) and engaged them heart-to-heart that the Lord convicted me of the hardness of heart I had displayed when I viewed these people as simply characters in a book. Entering into relationship became the basis of reconciliation and of major growth for me as an ambassador of reconciliation. To do otherwise is to leave wide open the doorway to that cultural imperialism that all cultures practice to a greater or lesser extent, and that makes reconciliation more necessary than it has been at any time since the meltdown at the Tower of Babel.

Reality is that most of us have treated the rest of us badly. Euro-Americans, white people, have barged into many of the cultures of the world asserting a racial and cultural superiority that is grounded in technology and what we pridefully call our "work ethic." But the indigenous peoples have differed from us only in the level of atrocity that they have been able to perform; their attitudes have not been much different. As my friend, Dr. Suuqiina, likes to say, "If we had owned your guns, we would have done it to you."

The Hawaii of the fourteenth century was brutally transformed by invaders from Tahiti led by a priest named Pa'ao. They wiped out the indigenous culture and the religion of 'Io worship, substituting in its place the dreaded *kapu* system that included human sacrifice to the gods of volcano and sea and meant death to any commoner who so much as walked on a king's shadow. They became the dominant culture that was similarly destroyed by Europeans following the first visit of Captain Cook in the late eighteenth century. Kamehameha the Great consolidated his rule over all of the islands with the help of European munitions for which he traded sandalwood and other Hawaiian products. He thought he was using the foreigners for his ends, and there is no question that the *haoles*, as the Hawaiians called them, were using the succeeding governments of the islands to establish their own purposes in them. It is true that all have sinned and fallen short of the glory of God.

The native peoples of the American mainland have been brutalized and displaced by immigrant peoples from Europe, and genocide is not too strong a word to use in describing the situation. But it is just as true to recount how the woodland tribes fought and clawed at each other for supremacy in the forests of Kentucky and Tennessee before white people taught them new levels of ferocity. The tribes of the great plains displaced one another as they moved onto hunting lands that had long been occupied by people more indigenous than them. They stole horses and took captives into slavery for centuries before Americans with cannon and repeating rifles came along. Their ideas of warfare were limited, in that they rarely destroyed whole communities. They took what they needed for subsistence and dominance and would often break off an attack as soon as they themselves began to take casualties. But no tribe on earth can take second place to another when it comes to declaring that they are the favorite of God.

The names that most of the peoples of the earth give to themselves, and indigenous peoples are no exception, when translated literally mean that they are the authentic people of the land. Hawaiians, as one example, refer to themselves as *kanaka moili* – the "real human beings." *Lakota*, the name of the people we know as the *Sioux*, means simply "the people" in their language. The name Sioux was simply a term applied by the plains tribes they had oppressed and it means "enemy." (The Sioux were seen by their neighbors as *that* aggressive.) In our own majority culture, the name we use for ourselves, *Americans*, names us as the authentic people of America—North, South, and Central.

The irony here is that we are all right as far as we go—God really does love each of us as though we were His special favorite. Jesus really meant it when He said, "I have other sheep that are not of this sheep pen. I must bring them also. They too will listen to My voice and there shall be one flock and one shepherd" (John 10:16). As adamant as He is about there being one shepherd leading what is ultimately one flock, He is just as clear about the multiple cultures sharing His unearned love when He quotes Isaiah 56:7, "These I will bring to My holy mountain and give them joy in My house of prayer. Their burnt offerings and sacrifices will be accepted on My altar; for My house will be called a house of prayer for all nations."

Reality is that each of us is marked with the unique and authentic imprint of our common Creator, and each of us has tarnished the image in which we are made. But God, in His mercy, and with His incomparable sense of humor, has made it so that we cannot get along without one another.

American Indian scholar and theologian, Terry LeBlanc, points out that one trait that indigenous peoples seem to have in common is a cultural paradigm for what might be called living toward subsistence.[5] In other words, their traditions tend toward work that is designed to remove from nature just enough to take families from one seasonal cycle to another with a little extra reserved for winter. The upside of this way is that the creation and its ecological balance receive a high degree of respect and the people reserve enough time and energy to enjoy the fruit of their labors and God's creation. As an early Texas settler of Native American extraction wrote, before giving his life for Texas at the Alamo,

"Of food we had not overmuch—chili and beans, beans and chili... but there was time to eat and sleep and look at growing plants."[6]

The downside was that the tribes were never far from starvation and a miscalculation of the weather patterns or the availability of pasture for the animals often spelled catastrophe. They were never very close to fulfillment of the commandment to be fruitful and multiply under such a mindset; that is one reason why they were overcome by strangers who came into their land from another world.

The immigrant peoples, Euros (as some natives call us), have a very different orientation. LeBlanc calls it a paradigm of surplus.[7] We take the commandment to be fruitful and multiply, and its corollary about establishing dominion over nature, very seriously. We are ever willing to devise ways to produce more and more, and better and better. We invented the storage barns and the methods to keep them fuller and fuller. We built the ships and planes and trains that would carry our extra goods and people to every corner of the earth so we could be ever expanding, and we built the weapons to ensure our hegemony wherever we went. We have not had to be concerned about starvation since the days of the Pilgrims. Even the Great Depression was not to be compared, for devastation, to one bad winter in a Plains Indians village. This horn of plenty that we have made is what gives us the security to build a culture the depth and breadth of which is the envy of the whole world, and that is the upside.

The downside, of course, is that we and the nations who follow our lead, the so-called developed world, have more divorce and more crime and more war and more suicide than can even be imagined in indigenous communities that are not cut off from their spiritual roots as we have cut ourselves off from ours. We imagine that God said He would help those who helped themselves and that survival is only for the fittest among us, although His Word teaches the opposite on both counts. We have forgotten what Jesus revealed in Luke 12:20 when God spoke to the rich fool who had spent his life working for tomorrow instead of walking with God today. When he finally decided that he had gotten far enough ahead that he could afford to relax, God spoke to him, saying, "You fool! This very night your life will be required of you. Then who will get what you have prepared for yourself?"

If we Euros cannot be sufficient in our paradigm to walk out the opportunities and obligations God has planted in our midst, and if the indigenous peoples cannot do it solely in terms of theirs, what would happen if we began to praise God for what He has planted in each of the cultures? What would happen if we took seriously the Great Commission instruction to "teach one another all things that I have commanded you"? What if we began to rejoice that it really is a First Corinthians 12 world that we have been given? If we did these things under the lordship of Him who is the way and the truth and the life, we could begin to walk together, not into subsistence and not into surplus, but into the sufficiency of abundant life right here and right now.

I am a mixed bag of Norse, Celtic, Germanic, and Jewish. Each of the tribes that lives in me makes its voice heard in my life. When I see movies like *The Vikings* or *Exodus* they feel like home movies, and they have since I was far too small a boy to have rationalized anything like the concept of biological memory. It is the same when I hear the Celtic harp or the pipes playing or when I look at a painting of a German castle or river. If so many tribes can live in peace in my body, surely the Church can make room in her Body for all of the tribes that the Lord has raised from the dead. Surely we can praise Him for making us need the unique contributions He has drawn from us without attempting to belittle, dominate, or retaliate against one another. It should be enough that all of us are prince-heirs to the King, all of us are called as priests, and all of us began as publicans.

It begins with a choice to respect one another out of respect for God. It makes no difference whether it begins on one side or the other of the ethnic divide, except that God has a special appreciation for the peacemakers. "He has shown you, O man, what is good. And what does the Lord require of you? To act justly and to love mercy and to walk humbly with your God" (Mic. 6:8). There is no better formula for cross-cultural evangelism—or any other kind.

ENDNOTES

1. Interviews with Jill Tahauri, George Kaimiola and Daniel Kikawa conducted from 2000 to 2003; *Perpetuated In Righteousness,* Daniel Kikawa (Aloha Ke Akua Publishing, 1994), 134.

2. Interview with Dr. Suuqinna, June 2, 2001.

3. Don Richardson, *Eternity In Their Hearts* (Regal, 1981), 9-25.

4. Dee Brown, *Bury My Heart at Wounded Knee: An Indian History of the American West* (Austin, TX: Holt, Reinhart and Winston, 1970).

5. Terry LeBlanc, Lectures delivered at 4th World Christian Gathering on Indigenous Peoples, October 2002, Honolulu, Hawaii

6. Lon Tinkle, *The Alamo,* (McGraw-Hill, 1958), 141

7. Terry LeBlanc, Lectures, see Note 5 above

Chapter 7

LIBERALS AND CONSERVATIVES

A friend of mine tells a hair-raising story of a day on a highway in Kansas when he stopped to change a tire. As he finished the job and looked back up the road, he saw a car approaching at about sixty miles an hour. There was no time to step away, but he thought he was perfectly safe hugging the side of his car, which was already on the shoulder and well off of the road. He thought he was safe until the very moment the car struck him.

He was hurled into the air with such force that the shoes were exploded off of his feet, and he landed on his back in the roadway. The driver stopped her car and came back to examine the victim, and both were amazed to find that with his many bruises he had no broken bones and no serious bleeding. He thanked her for coming back to care for him, but then he asked her the obvious question: "Why did you hit me?" She thought about it for a moment and answered, "To tell you the truth, I was so obsessed with avoiding you that, before I knew it, I was steering right into you."

Liberals and conservatives are like that. They tend to focus so intently on the problems they are convinced have been created by the other side that they expend all of their creative and dynamic energy on defeating the other side, leaving little or none of it for actually achieving a solution to the problem. There is a fatal flaw in the focus of political people of all stripes on the heat of the competition. Intent on frustrating the designs of their opponents, they can easily forget to develop a design of their own. In the Church, we would call that letting the devil determine the rules of engagement.

This was absurdly evident during the 2004 election cycle. During the presidential debates, for example, both candidates made repeated references to the "real issues" that they were certain their opponent had no plan for dealing with. These "real" issues were concerns such as health care, education, and national security. Each candidate lambasted the other on his record of deficiencies in these areas but rarely provided insight on how he (the speaker) would deal with the issues. The same pattern held for the state and local elections. We heard a great deal about how socialistic or narcissistic the respective candidates were accused of being and even more about the unsavory characters who were endorsing them, but we heard little about how they would guide the electorate through the next term if elected.

The men and women in the street, and the political operatives who masquerade as ordinary citizens, were far more over the top than the candidates themselves. If one believed all of the propaganda of the Democrats, a vote for George Bush was a vote to cancel all medical research and prevent people from leaving the wheel chairs that would certainly go on the scrap heap if only John Kerry were the next president. But following the implications of some of the Republican rhetoric would lead one to believe that the United Nations would be annexing Washington DC shortly after the inauguration of any president but Bush. Likewise, President Bush was depicted as deliberately leaving Osama Bin Laden at large just so that people would fear a Kerry presidency, while Kerry was pictured as the walking death knell of the American family.

I have never seen the nation so polarized in the more than half a century that I have lived on this planet. The height of the Vietnam War did not see such sharply drawn partisan lines or such a thorough demonization of those who disagreed with the politics of one side or the other. The days of the Weather Underground and the Symbionese Liberation Army did not produce so much seemingly random violence and gross paranoia connected to an election. Yes, the liberal party seemed to be altogether fixated on bringing anyone to the White House who was not the hated George Bush (and Richard Nixon in the middle of Watergate was not hated to the degree that these people hate Bush). But the conservative party made, literally, a religious crusade out of beating the liberals at their own game. Even a number of Christian leaders joined in with alleged prophecies naming the president "the burning bush" as they compared him to Moses and the prophets.

In the aftermath of the election, I have never seen such bitterness, depression, and jihad-like hatred of the foe from the defeated. Media pundits, most of whom probably do not believe in such a thing literally, were actually predicting that the rapture would soon come and that only liberal democrats would go to Heaven. Hundreds of thousands of liberal Americans looked into emigrating to Canada, and psychotherapists were doing a land office business dealing with cases of what they called post election trauma stress disorder. And conservatives are having their turn with this stuff as the Kingdom of Heaven does not come marching in behind the inauguration of George Bush—a man they elected but who cannot possibly bear the spiritual expectations that some are placing on him, including the turning back of Roe vs. Wade, the re-introduction of prayer in every school, and a pro-family curriculum in every classroom. With that kind of attention paid to the man at the side of the road instead of to the road itself, it is not surprising to find the man a magnet for the hurtling machine.

Peter and the other disciples found themselves in a situation of similar dynamics in Matthew 14. After Jesus feeds the five thousand on the shore of the Galilean sea, He struck off on His own for awhile, leaving the band of twelve to cross to the other side in a boat. When a storm came up, the only thing more alarming than the prospect of sinking was the sight of Jesus walking toward them on the surface of the water. Suspecting that they were seeing a ghost, they demanded that the Messiah identify Himself. When He did,

Peter called out, "Lord, if it's you, tell me to come to you on the water" (Matt. 14:28).

Peter obviously had not learned the lesson about being careful what you ask for; when Jesus told him to come ahead, he was at the sticking point. In an act more of bravado than of actual faith, Peter stepped out of the boat and began to walk. He was doing fine as long as he had his attention on Jesus. But when he looked down and realized that his problem (men cannot walk on water) was frothing and churning around his feet, he immediately began to sink. At this point, he did display real faith, the kind born of desperation that the Lord makes such good and consistent use of. He called out, "Lord, save me!" (Matt. 14:30) and Jesus, taking his hand, escorted him back into the boat. Hand in hand, they were both capable of walking on the water. With his eye on the solution (Jesus), Peter was quite able to walk on the water.

When our eyes are on the problem, that is all we tend to see. Likewise, when our eyes are on the solution, that is all we tend to see. Adding insult to injury, when we focus on the problem, we rarely see all of it at the same time.

Both liberals and conservatives in this country have it right when they say that we are at war, and they have it wrong when they think we are fighting simultaneous wars against terror and for the cultural template that each side favors. Reality is that we are engaged in one war; it is a world-wide war, and it is the third of its kind in the past hundred years.

A War of Ultimate Concern

World War I was fought from 1914 to 1918; it was a war of imperialism, a war fought between competing empires to see who would control the most territory and thus the greatest commercial empire. Imperialism, which seeks political and military hegemony leading to economic prosperity for the winners, is not an ultimate value, and World War I ended with little but the players changing. It planted the seeds for a larger and longer conflict in the bitterness of the so-called peace it brokered. Under the mask of national self-determination for defeated enemies and formerly colonized regions, it simply changed masters while creating hopes that could not be later suppressed. The Russian Revolution, civil war in China, the rise of Imperial Japan and Nazi Germany, and the Spanish Civil War were all predictable precursors to the next worldwide conflagration.

World War II was fought from 1939 to 1989, when the Berlin Wall finally came tumbling down. It was a war of ideology. Competing cultures fought to determine whether governments, in principal, existed to serve the people they governed or to be served by those same people. Nazi Germany, Fascist Italy, and Imperial Japan had fallen by 1945, but the greatest threat to secular concepts of freedom, because of its imperialist drive settling down over the centuries coupled with a national paranoia about the western republics, remained in the Soviet Union. Even the world of today, which features military dictatorships and the juggernaut of Communist China that is only beginning to flex its economic muscle, does not hold the secular expansionist tendencies that marked Soviet Russia. The dismantling of that empire began in 1989 and ended the second world war. But that war also failed to plant the seeds of peace because it ended in political terms. There is only one source of peace in the world and only one ultimate issue that seeks to engage it. Ideology is not that issue.

Today the United States is embroiled in World War III, a war of idolatry. This war, at least the parts that end up on the evening news, is also being fought in political and military terms so far. But it is a war of the spirit. This is the third and last of the world wars.

The Middle East is a land of dictatorships. Only Israel emerges as an exception to this rule. (Our president and his advisers are attempting to leave a democracy in Iraq when American forces depart, and the jury is still out on whether they will succeed. But there is no doubt of the brutality of the totalitarian state they found when they arrived and even less about what sort of government the insurgent terrorists are seeking to re-establish.) But each of these dictatorships is grounded in spiritual values that share in one form or another of the Muslim religion, a religion whose founder alone launched twenty-seven so-called holy wars.

Muslim people are not the enemy in this, and I would not want anyone to construe that they are. But Islam, the religion founded by Muhammad in the seventh century, is a religion of idolatry alongside all of the other idolatries of history. That is to say that, like all of the alternatives to the covenant with Yahweh that was established on Sinai and transformed on

Calvary, it is a religion of works earning salvation rather than relationship gaining a free gift of salvation. And to speak ill of the human founder is considered blasphemy, just as it is in any other cult.

It is not necessary for an American Christian to make the claim that World War III is a war of spiritual dimensions and values. The terrorists and the governments that support them have been saying for half a century that they are embarked on a holy crusade to destroy Israel and the American satan who is her most reliable ally. When a nation, such as Iran, transitions from a secular dictatorship into an Islamic dictatorship, the first nations put on the national enemies list are always the United States and Israel. Every attack on U.S. installations in the past two decades has been motivated by a self-proclaimed desire to serve the god Allah and to promote the perpetrators into the Muslim idea of paradise. The terrorists themselves have made it clear that the war they have launched against our nation is a war of their religion against what they consider to be our religion.

The attacks launched in this war are not limited to military adventures. Idolaters who serve the Dali Lama make annual forays into the cities and waterways of various states, attempting to introduce spiritually inhabited works of art called sand mandalas into these places in a declared effort to exercise spiritual dominion over the land. Idolaters who practice Wicca and other forms of witchcraft pray regularly at national conventions and gatherings; they have been doing so for a long time. They pray against anyone they perceive as calling the nation back to a Christ-like vision for America, and they are not respecters of one party or another.

With respect to political liberals and conservatives jockeying for power in the American government and culture, one side claims it is the decadence of our consumer driven society and our sense of entitlement on the world scene that drives the conflict while the other asserts that it is this implacable terrorist enemy and hater of all that is decent and good in our society who threatens our very existence. Liberals declare that the Bush administration attempted to do what cannot be done: manufacturing a just and humane government in a region with no cultural framework for it, invading a nation that had not yet attacked us while lacking an exit strategy for when we got there, engaging unilaterally and contrarily (to international opinion) in what can become a Vietnam-type quagmire as America becomes once again the policeman of the world and the lightning rod for nationalistic hatreds of the impulse to colonize. Conservatives hold that we addressed the untenable risk of attack with our pre-emptive strike at Saddam Hussein after assessing the well-documented evidence of his ferocity, his use of weapons of mass destruction, and his arrogant disregard of the risks of attacking even more powerful neighbors. They rehearse the decade-long history of consensus on both sides of the political aisle, in the U.S. and in the United Nations, about these facts. And they trumpet that they and only they had the courage to act on their convictions. They point out, with accuracy, that in all but three of the Iraqi provinces there is now peace and stability, that elections and the formation of a democratic republican government are on schedule, and that other rogue states in the region, such as Libya, have demonstrably backed away from their aggressions since the United States entered the picture.

Both sides are correct, as far as they go. The United States did invade Iraq without a clear strategy for disengagement. And those whose lives are defined by their hatred of Jesus Christ and those they believe are a corporate representation of Him are more filled with the bile of that hatred than ever before. We have brought a large and dangerous boil to a head. Yet all of the claims of the administration to have succeeded in most of their aims for our security and the betterment of the region are backed up with solid reality. Never have I witnessed a more altruistic approach to international relations than what is embodied by the sacrificial service of so many young men and women of our nation. Our nation is embroiled in a world war, but we need to recognize that the Iraqi, Afghan, and Israeli/Palestinian war zones, along with the international airports of our land, are just the tips of the iceberg. The divide between liberal and conservative loyalists is far deeper than differences over foreign policy reveal, and the primary battle fronts are in our houses of worship and in the privacy of our hearts. Wars over idolatry have always been fought in these personal places, from Bible times to the present moment. What we do in the Middle East is nowhere near as crucial as what we do on these primary fronts.

What we do on the primary fronts decides our ultimate loyalty. It is either to Jesus, who is called Christ (including the implication that if He is truly Lord then we need not only to support His claims, but also His methods and agenda), or it is to some sanitized shortcut or substitute for the radical dependency on Him that He demonstrates in His own radical dependency on His Father and His equally radical devotion to every point of the revelation of His Father. It means that when we fight as the principal soldiers in the war on idolatry, and this in no way precludes the current actions of our military forces, that we are charged to use only the weapons He provides. These weapons are at all times connected to and derived from seeking first His Kingdom and His righteousness and doing only what we see Him doing (and doing all of it, regardless of the cost).

THE LOGIC OF HEAVEN

In Mark 8:14-21, Jesus and the disciples, at least the core group of twelve, were crossing the Sea of Galilee shortly after Jesus fed four thousand on a few loaves and fishes and just prior to the healing of a blind man in Bethsaida. The disciples were discussing among themselves that they had no means with which to sustain their lives, let alone their vision, because they had forgotten to bring some bread along on the boat. Jesus then made the apparently cryptic statement that they should beware the yeast of both Herod and the Pharisees. They talked it over, concluding that He was criticizing their lack of preparedness in having no supplies on board. Then He asked them, with some exasperation, why they continued the inane discussion of bread.

"Do you still not see or understand? Are your hearts hardened? Do you have eyes but fail to see, and ears but fail to hear? And don't you remember? When I broke the five loaves for the five thousand, how many basketfuls of pieces did you pick up?"

"Twelve," they replied.

"And when I broke the seven loaves for the four thousand, how many basketfuls of pieces did you pick up?"

They answered, "Seven."

He said to them, "Do you still not understand?" (Mark 8:17-21).

There is really nothing cryptic about Jesus' approach for those who have truly invited Him into the lordship of their lives without conditioning their allegiance upon whether or not His performance meets their specifications. Yeast was often used in His parables to represent the living core of a thing; it is the stuff that makes the bread dough rise and become truly bread. The yeast of Herod, or that of the Pharisees, would be what made them tick, and Jesus told His friends to avoid that deadening yeast at all costs. But what is it?

Herod was one of the most successful kings Judea ever had. He was a master at playing one powerbroker against another in order to get what he wanted for his country and for his own personal glory. The palaces, the aqueducts, and a completely refurbished temple were mute testimony to his ability to wring concessions and cooperation from the Roman overlords who often wondered why they bothered with what they considered to be a rebellious backwater in their colonial empire. He managed to hold the various nationalistic forces in Judea at bay as well, and he got them to sign off on the taxes needed to finance his projects. He was completely unscrupulous in his methods, even ordering the slaughter of every boy baby in Bethlehem on the off chance that there could actually be something to this messiah talk. His was a can-do spirit, but on his terms alone and in terms of his understanding of *realpolitick*. He got the job done if there was a way in human capacity to get the job done, and he never wondered if the cure might be worse than the disease. Jesus, on the other hand, said, "I tell you the truth, the Son can do nothing by Himself; He can do only what He sees His Father doing..." (John 5:19). He warned His disciples to go and do likewise.

The Pharisees were the acknowledged defenders of the Jewish culture. They were the ones who scrupulously kept the Law during the good and the hard times (and keeping the Law is a hard thing to do). They did not sign off on the agenda of Herod and company, although they lacked the political muscle to prevent his activities. They were the bastions of Jewish integrity, the ones who sacrificed in order to remain pure, the ones who did not give in to the vagaries and vulgarities of the modern world. The revelation of Yahweh in the desert was eternally normative for their lives, although they were often baffled at what that revelation meant in a given situation. No matter, they would discuss and analyze until they found a way to adapt their behavior to what they thought God might have meant, and they would strain a gnat through a needle hole in their efforts to get it right. Legalism didn't bother them; they gloried in it. Theirs was the spirit of cannot-do, don't look, don't touch, and don't risk your purity for anything like a transformative vision. But Jesus addressed them in the opposite spirit; He intended to do all that He saw His Father doing. When they attacked Him for ministering on the Sabbath, He responded that His Father continued to work and therefore so must He. He warned His disciples to go and do likewise.

Back on the boat, Jesus was pointing out that it is not possible to comprehend Him or what He does with the math of the world. Beyond the stark reality of the fact that He had just created a banquet from virtual thin air is the additional reality of the leftovers. If there was any earthly logic in the cause and effect they had witnessed, there should have been more crumbs and pieces from the seven loaves used to feed four thousand than from the five loaves used to feed five thousand. But that is precisely the point—the logic of the thing is not earthly; it is Heavenly. Jesus did not come to make things in Heaven as they are on earth, but to make things on earth, a fallen earth at that, as they are in Heaven (see Matt. 6:10). The disciples could only hope to understand what was going on from inside relationship with Jesus. The fact that they had brought Jesus with them was of infinitely greater significance than whether or not they had brought bread. And the fact that their next stop, after healing the blind man, was where Jesus received the confession of Peter that He was indeed the Christ, the Son of the Living God, was of infinitely greater value than a chance to limp back and forth between the spirits of can-do and can't-do.

If there is ever to be authentic reconciliation between the liberals and conservatives of our nation and in our day, it can only come about in these terms. But the stakes are much higher than that; we are talking about reconciliation between who we are and the vision of God that established our nation as one under Him.

WHAT THEY BELIEVE OF THEMSELVES

Conservatives say of themselves that they are fiercely proud of electing a president who, most of the time, acts on principle instead of political calculation, seeking the face of the Lord his God before he does anything. If they are social conservatives, they tend to believe that he has acted in the name of the Lord in his efforts to put faith-based ministries on an equal public footing with their secular counterparts, to pursue an unpopular but wildly successful reform of public education accountability, and to demonstrate a genuine yet risky compassion for sufferers from AIDS around the world while identifying the lifestyle causes of its transmission. He has called the nation to prayer like one who means it.

Conservatives believe that private individuals are generally better equipped to raise and spend their material resources for both private and public good than is the government, and the contrast becomes increasingly stark the more large-scale and centralized that government becomes. There are obvious exceptions to such a philosophy enshrined in our constitution (the conduct of foreign affairs, inter-community relations, public works, and the criminal justice system come to mind), but these exceptions are envisioned in our constitution in order to make possible that very private decision-making norm. These conservatives believe that government is a necessary evil, because it places limits on the freedom for which Christ set us free and usually tends to want to increase those limits through some inherent quality, that exists in order to ensure a level playing field in the conduct of human affairs. They recognize that God, after man's expulsion from the Garden, instituted governments in order to reward good and punish evil.

They hold that the United States, while never a perfect or even an adequate image of what God called for when He dispatched a bunch of European Christians to establish a community in the wilderness of New England, is indeed a chosen nation called to become a city on a hill in the sense in which Jesus spoke (see Matt. 5:14). Our political and social institutions were forged in that crucible, which was a spiritual enterprise with commercial overtones, as opposed to the Virginia colony, which was a commercial enterprise with spiritual overtones. They would say that people who call themselves fiscal or economic or *laissez-faire* conservatives forget that bit of well-documented history.

Conservatives tend to believe that freedom is only worth having if we see in it the opportunity to establish a succession of healthy families in the lives of our children and grandchildren. That means that what we sometimes call traditional family values—the need to pass on to our children their heritage as created people; to protect them from exposure to drugs, pornography, violence, and a value system that says all family structures are equally life-inducing; and to give them an education that draws from them their God-given best regardless of whether or not it offends some groups lobbying for an artificial equality of conditions—are crucial to the maintenance and growth of authentic community. It also means that social structures or programs that threaten those values, and are indicated to be threats in the studies that examine them, are viewed as things to be opposed at every turn, regardless of how many people might vote to support them.

Many conservatives believe that the political left at this time (in the very vehemence of its identification of all of the forces that prevailed in first national elections of a new century with the evil beast they call evangelical or fundamentalist Christianity) has shown itself to be in total moral and political bankruptcy. And it is true that many in that camp have spewed great hatred on anyone publicly identifying with Christ in repeated statements since the election campaigns of 2000, 2002, 2004, and 2006. But if this is true, is it the whole truth?

Liberals tend to say of themselves that they call on government to fight the evils of a sinful world that private parties cannot or will not address. Their roots in America are certainly within the Body of Christ, as anyone looking at the abolitionist movement of the nineteenth century (for one example) would have to admit. They can counter conservative claims that social reform is best done privately by simply asking, "Did a strong Church end hunger, slavery, the exploitation and massacre of Native Americans, or illiteracy?" Reality is that it took a massive effort of the government to address these issues at all, imperfect though that address may have been. In our time, it has been liberals, citing the biblical concept of the inherent dignity of all persons, who have pressed the government to deal with sexual harassment in the workplace, violence in the home, and destructive actions in the environment. Although many large corporations point with pride to their policies for dealing with these evils, it was liberals pushing government that pushed these corporations to do the right thing. And it was governmental action inspired by liberal leaders that pressed home family values so that now parents are more and more able to take leave time with pay when their families need them, whether a new baby needs bonding or a health crisis needs presence. Some studies indicate that productivity even improves when compassion is shown to employees in these circumstances. It was liberals who fought for and established the right of employees to bargain with employers from a position of political and economic power through trade unions.

On the international front, it tends to be liberals who have called attention to issues of genocide in places like Darfur, the historic oppression of the apartheid system in South Africa, and the deaths of countless third world infants from drinking baby formula contaminated by local water after some corporations conducted advertising campaigns claiming that their formula was more nutritious than their mothers' natural milk. Many of these prophetic people, in the sense that Amos and John the Baptist are prophetic, are avowed

Christians. Certainly, they are as motivated by the compassion of Christ as they are by His sense of justice and fair play.

In politics, as in everything else, there is good news and challenging news; there is enough to blame and enough to learn from in each of the principal political camps.

AMERICAN POLITICAL HISTORY

The political dimension of the spiritual conflict in which we are presently engaged around the world and in our most personal spaces has its roots at least as far back as our own Civil War. Prior to that defining contest in our history, most Americans saw government as principally an entity that required restraint. It was tolerated as a necessary but most dangerous instrument that had little power to improve human life yet was needfully invoked under emergency conditions to do for us what we could not do for ourselves without the enforced cohesion of government. It was not considered useful for making social change; individuals and the Church were available, and were much less dangerous to social health, for that purpose. But the great issue of slavery changed all of that. It was an issue that threatened to tear the country apart, and the framers of the constitution had dodged it from the beginning.

Whatever we may believe about the changing economy in the North and the dependency in the South on cotton, reality is that the abolitionist movement began in the North because men and women under Christian conviction could no longer live with themselves and tolerate the institution of slavery at the same time. Many Christians in the South held similar beliefs, but they were unwilling to challenge what seemed to be a core of their community values; they chose instead to rationalize their cowardice by doing violence to the interpretation of the Bible. When it became increasingly clear that the Body of Christ would not address the issue in a unitary manner, war became inevitable. Equally inevitable was the coming paradigm shift over the role of government in both public and private life.

When government was revealed as the only social institution capable of addressing the issue of slavery, it established for itself a new identity for Americans as a maker of positive social change that surpassed the Body of Christ in both power and ethical virtue. That new identity was strengthened when it took the government to reign in the power of the post war robber barons, to address conditions in tenements, and to bring about an eight hour workday, child labor laws, and the regulation of many other conditions in the workplace. In our own generation, government has made itself the arbiter of access for all to education and (more recently) to a well conducted childhood. It mattered little that many of the reformers were moved by Christian zeal to do the work they have done; it mattered less that government is better at making things happen than it is at determining whether they ought to happen and what the unintended consequences might be. The Body of Christ left a vacuum in the wake of its divisions, and government stepped in happily.

In the America of today, liberals tend to seek a greater role for government in addressing whatever evils they identify, and they have achieved some things that surely needed to be achieved. It was, for example, liberals who would not accept the status quo of race relations in this country prior to the landmark Supreme Court decision known as Brown v. Kansas Board of Education, the case that desegregated the public schools and set in motion all that we now consider to be the modern civil rights movement. They drove the drive to end the exploitation of women and children in labor, brought about the modern trade union movement, and enshrined the right to participate in it. They pioneered anti-trust legislation, which in theory is nothing more than a guarantee of a level playing field in commerce and which is, thus, dear to the heart of conservatives. They fostered concern and awareness of the damage being done to our environment and ecological balance when others did not care about the death of Lake Erie and a number of the rivers of our land. And it was the nation's artists, liberals for the most part, who called our national conscience to account for the gaps between our national vision and practice in the areas of equal opportunity.

Liberals came to recognize, although a liberal administration engaged American troops in the Vietnam War, the political and moral bankruptcy of going to war not to win but to preserve a status quo in which the successive governments we backed in South Vietnam (from the Diem to the Ky to the Thieu regimes) were as totalitarian as their communist counterparts and a good deal less competent.

Finally, it was people we call liberals who conceived a vision to eliminate poverty and make the American dream truly accessible to all.

Despite their general hostility toward Jesus and His Church today, many historical liberals (and certainly all of the early civil rights activists) were pulsed forward by their faith in the One who died for us. The dreams and visions for social engineering to the betterment of mankind were born in the hearts of men and women who loved Jesus as their Lord. But when the Church failed to champion their causes, or simply stood impotent before the issues they tried to address, the secularists turned to the government and cause was transformed into program. The results were in some cases promising but in most cases (finally) grisly. In fact, they were the very essence of the leaven of Herod.

Equal opportunity gave way to affirmative action (with its incipient racism against majority and minority groups alike) and a culture of entitlement. The so-called war on poverty has created far more poverty (and falling down public housing projects) than it ever eliminated. Abortion on demand and no-fault divorce have led to an epidemic of (relationally) unfathered children and millions of unborn baby deaths. A *laissez faire* attitude toward pornography, media-portrayed violence, and defining family in whatever way suits us at the moment has led to epidemics of youthful suicide, attention deficit disorder, and a culture of rampant self-medication through drugs and other unhealthy habits. The debate over what constitutes viable life now ranges from the experimental cloning of human beings to the question of who is entitled to life support and who makes such decisions for those who cannot speak for themselves. Our schools have often been reduced to places of social experimentation, and our universities are no longer bastions of free speech. To the contrary, they are now notorious for the censorship they practice against both students and faculty in the name of the politically correct.

Untold forests have burned and thousands of families have been reduced to unemployment and chaos because an environmental movement run amok has valued snails and small birds above human need, seeking to govern even nature with management practices that fail to account for long-term environmental needs in favor the limited vision of activists. And, while liberal protests did result in bringing the troops home from Vietnam, they also enabled a predicted bloodbath throughout Southeast Asia and led to nearly thirty years of American self-doubt and timidity that was only partially offset by the Reagan years and the triumphal end of the second world war. These attitudes, which valued pulling back militarily, also environmentally weakened the nation's ability to protect ourselves and our allies and diluted our efforts at energy self-sufficiency. It partakes of the very heart of pharisaism.

But conservatives dare not say, "Aha! See what those liberal policies brought us." Yes, these conditions were wrought during a time when a liberal agenda became the national agenda, and yes, that agenda consumed the leaven of Herod and the pharisees. But the truth is that God never destroys a city over the wickedness in it; only the inaction of the righteous brings such retribution, and this has been true since Sodom and Gomorrah (see Gen. 18:16-33). Prayer was removed from the public schools because people were not praying in the public square, not because of some shadowy liberal conspirators. The Judeo-Christian values we hold dear have atrophied because we did not hold them anywhere dear enough. Cults and idols tend to be the unpaid bills of the Church, and the liberal vision was a substitute for what should have been the rallying cry of the Body of Christ to let justice roll like a mighty river for all Americans, and the cry for a city on a hill called the United States!

Just as liberals achieved positive things, so conservatives can boast of their own accomplishments in the past half-century. The incredible economic growth for all kinds of people, minorities included, that characterized this nation (from affordable housing developments springing up from coast to coast to the rise of the leisure and vacation industries that began with the Holiday Inn chain, from the PC revolution and the internet and its cafes to the McDonald's phenomenon, from the greatest medical breakthroughs of all time to Disney World and Magic Mountain) has resulted from permitting entrepreneurs relatively untrammeled and unprotected (whatever their personal politics) opportunities to pursue their dreams. It may have been government that funded men on the moon, but it was private individuals like Jerry Vultee, Jack Northrop, and Howard Hughes who built the modern aerospace industry that built the hardware foundation, on speculation, that took them there.

It is conservative business people who have hired and promoted minorities and women at a much faster pace than have their liberal counterparts once they realized that stonewalling was counterproductive to their own interests. (President Bush's cabinet and court appointments serve as an icon of this reality, and his background is in business.) These are the same people who have developed the environment-friendly technology and energy alternatives coming on line today, not to mention the revolutionary methods of production that use less fuel and do less damage to ecosystems. These same people have designed weapons of war that do the same job as their World War II counterparts but with far fewer casualties on all sides.

It was conservative political and spiritual leaders Ronald Reagan, Margaret Thatcher, and Pope John Paul II who ended World War II by standing strong against the adversaries of freedom while liberals counseled that the cold war could not be won.

It is conservative faith-based movements that are doing the research and putting in the labor that is revealing what really makes children thrive in schools, and what is coming out is exactly what the Bible has always taught. The mantra of the movement is that the best guarantee against poverty and social chaos is having heterosexual parents who are married to each other, who graduated high school, and who love their children more than their achievements. Hard research shows that people who practice their faith in Jesus Christ on a regular basis live happier, more stable, and more healthful lives. (People who are Christians in name only are actually more likely to divorce than are non-believers.) And it is conservative Christians who have been shown in multiple studies to be more personally engaging, accepting, and helpful to those who are different or less fortunate than are people who are more liberal and less faith-directed.

On the other hand, it was conservatives who dragged their feet during nearly every wave of positive social change from the trade union movement to the civil and voting rights movements to the environmental movement. Thus, they paved the way for the liberal excesses they decry because these excesses were simply reactive to that foot dragging. In these arenas of necessary social change, conservatives partook of the worst sort of pharisaism. We expected those who were bereft of opportunity to attain what we defined as the American dream to just accept the status quo and be silent, whether they were ethnic, gender or sectarian minorities. Conservatives too have partaken of the leaven of the Pharisees.

It was conservatives who established the web of relationships with repressive regimes who had nothing to recommend them but that they professed to be anti-communist (the aforementioned South Vietnamese governments, the Cuban government of Batista, and the Philippine government of Marcos are but a few examples). This caused millions of people to embrace communism due to the hopelessness of their situation, and the world groaned in travail. It was conservatives who urged the people of Hungary to cast off Soviet rule and then looked the other way when Soviet tanks entered Budapest. It was conservatives who promised freedom and air cover to the Cuban fighters who would try to drive Castro from Havana soon after John Kennedy took his oath of office. We did what we did out of a concern for so-called real-politick, the misguided (in terms of Christian faith) notion that our ability to broker a genuine peace in the world was limited and that we had to do the best we could with what we had to work with. This conservative position was a textbook definition of the leaven of Herod.

RACING AGAINST HORSES

One of the chapters of Scripture that God keeps drawing back across my sight is Jeremiah 12. The chapter begins with the prophet asking the Lord to account for the fact that the wicked both live and prosper. He acknowledged God's omniscience and His goodness, but he wondered then why those evil ones seem to be doing so well. And God answered with a question of His own, as He so often does, that put the light right back on the servant himself. He said, "If you have raced with men on foot and they have worn you out, how can you compete with horses? If you stumble in safe country, how will you manage in the thickets by the Jordan" (Jer. 12:5).

We want to know when God is going to realize how valuable we are to Him and when He is going to begin to take better care of us; God wants to know when we are going to realize that our thoughts are not His thoughts nor our ways His ways (see Isa. 55:9). He wonders when we will ask Him to transform us into His likeness instead of thinking Him too slow to adopt our agenda, however praiseworthy it may be.

He is passionately curious as to when we will stop asking Him to bless what we are doing and begin to make a lifestyle of blessing whatever we see Him doing.

The followers of Herod are bankrupt; there is nothing the Lord can do with them because there is no recognition that they have done whatever they want in the serene knowledge that there is no Lord to see or hear or intervene. They are grimly determined to make the world better than it is, to the limit of their abilities, and in their minds, the noble end justifies any means they care to employ. There are both liberals and conservatives in the party of the Herodians.

The followers of the Pharisees sense that they have taken the moral high ground because they have acknowledged the Lord as their God. They are just as bankrupt as the Herodians because they acknowledge where God was, they are far better students of history than are their counterparts, but they are too busy looking at the water to look at the Messiah who beckons. They hate and fear the chaos of new creation. Rather than going in radical obedience where He calls them when He calls them to a strange destination, they cling to what they can recall of the Lord's plans, grimly determined to protect Him from the new things that He is planning and doing. They are the political counterparts of the Christians who teach that God's miracles in the Bible are actual historical events that do not occur in our time, companions of those who have seen and participated in a miraculous and revival-producing move of God and are quite certain that the style He revealed then is the only authentic way of His manifestation. There are both liberals and conservatives in the party of the Pharisees.

The Lord goes on to speak through the mouth of Jeremiah that all, even his own family, have betrayed the prophet. He says that He is sick and tired of the evil done by all parties to the debate and of the lack of radical faith. He promises to uproot the entire vineyard (see Jer. 12:6-14). "But after I uproot them, I will again have compassion and will bring each of them back to his own inheritance and his own country. And if they learn well the ways of my people... then they will be established among my people" (Jer. 12:15-16).

There is right and wrong in the world today, and it has a political dimension at its very heart. But alignment with what is right comes from knowing and walking every moment with a God who is radically not us or our image. It does not come from what we know about Him and much less from what we believe He would be doing if He were actually in our midst. Political health is a product of a spiritual hunger that never ceases.

If we would fight in the war of idolatry, we will have to limit ourselves to the weapons He makes available, weapons of faithfulness, witness, and relationship-building in Him, for fighting the principal battles. We will have to permit our thoughts to become His thoughts and our ways His ways. We are going to have to become so obsessed with seeking God that we have neither time nor opportunity to so obsess over our enemies that we steer into them even as we seek to avoid them. That is what God means when He says, "If my people, who are called by My name, will humble themselves and pray and seek My face and turn from their wicked ways, then will I hear from Heaven and will forgive their sin and will heal their land" (2 Chron. 7:14).

A good place to start with one another is in the recognition that while our vision and our practice may take us in very different directions, we do indeed spring from the same spiritual stock. It is the highest quality stock in the inventory of the Lord our God. It is the stuff from which cities on the hill are made. And while competing in the marketplace of ideas and elections is healthy and creative, demonizing our opponents when we run out of ideas is stagnation on the hoof. "For Christ's love compels us, because we are convinced that One died for all...that those who live should no longer live for themselves but for Him who died for them and was raised again. So from now on we regard no one from a worldly point of view..." (2 Cor. 5:14-16). At least that is what God says, and it works for me.

Chapter 8

RESTORING THE SEXUALLY BROKEN

S HORTLY after taking my first pastoral post, I was called to a recovery facility for chemically dependent people. Ed had asked for a pastor to come and hear his fifth step, a confession of everything he had done or failed to do as an addict that is a standard point in any twelve-step recovery program. When I arrived at the facility, I was taken to meet Ed, who promptly told me there had been some mistake. He had asked for a pastor alright, but I was the wrong denomination, and he was nowhere near ready to do his fifth step!

I apologized for the misunderstanding and got up to leave. He asked me to wait; as long as I was there, we might as well talk and perhaps he would let me pray for him. He told me that Jesus had saved his life in an auto accident some years earlier and that he had often felt as though he was not alone, even when he wanted to lose himself in his addiction.

We talked for a long time about Jesus and His love and how He does not let go of us even when we let go of Him.

Before I went home, Ed did his fifth step. He also committed his life to Jesus Christ, something he had never done before although he had been raised in a church. When his wife, Chloe, saw the change in her husband's whole aspect a few days later, she asked to see me and ended up committing her life to the One who had so obviously restored her husband to humanity. When Ed was released, I baptized his wife and children, and they steadily moved deeper and deeper into the life of Christ over the years that I knew them. It was not easy. Their issues did not disappear when they received Jesus, but neither did He.

Ed and Chloe, who had lived together before marriage and refused to commit their lives to one another or to God after, had a lot of sin in their lives to repent of. They did not see this, and they did not repent prior to Jesus entering their lives. In their case, it was the very entry of Jesus into their lives and their acceptance of Him that paved the way for their lives to become repentant lives. Their marriage, the covenant containing their sexuality, was the first thing to be healed in them as a couple, but it would not be the last.

You are probably asking, "What does a story of the healing of an addict and his marriage have to do with reconciling the sexually broken, heterosexual or homosexual?" The quick answer is: everything! If we take a look at two chapters of the New Testament, Acts 15 and Luke 19, that quick answer will become crystalline in its clarity.

Acts 15 deals with the first general council of the Christian Church. The crisis that called this gathering into existence was about whether new Gentile believers could be held accountable for the whole of the Jewish Torah once they enter the Church. Jewish believers held Yeshua (Jesus) to be the fulfillment of the Law, and they believed it had become that much easier to observe the Law through faith in Him. But Jesus had said that He had sheep in other flocks and that He meant to bring them all together in one sheepfold (see John 10:16). When Gentiles from Syrian Antioch, who did not know the Law and the Prophets as the Jews knew them, began to come into the fold, an administrative problem erupted and the apostles sat down to pray and to deal with it. The result of their deliberations was the famous letter that prefaces their instruction with, "It seemed good to the Holy Spirit and to us…" (see Acts 15:23-29).

The letter goes on to declare that only the very foundational practices of covenant faith would be required of the Gentiles who gave their hearts to the Son. Those core concerns were that they should avoid idolatry, eating the meat of strangled animals, and sexual immorality.

The common thread in these prohibitions is the dishonoring of the very personality of those sinning and sinned against. In the Old Testament, idolatry was often spoken of as committing adultery, as dishonoring God, who had taken His people as His bride, and it frequently included that marital dishonor quite literally. Most pagan deities demanded sacred prostitution in the temples dedicated to them, and Jeremiah inveighed against the spiritual and literal adultery of Israel and Judah with the idols they served (see Jer. 3:3-6). But idolatry also defiles the spirit of the sinner who has turned his back on the source and spirit of life. The Bible clearly had no problem with slaughtering animals for food. But strangulation was a form of assassination as well as a particularly shameful death meted out to criminals and traitors; to kill an animal in this fashion was not simply to take its life but to dishonor the life that God had given to it and to dishonor the soul of the perpetrator who tramples as he kills. And sexual immorality, whether heterosexual or homosexual, was a clear defiance and dishonoring of the One who decreed that a man and his wife shall become one covenant flesh (see Gen. 2:24). But that too was more damaging to life even as it was less than authenticating of life.

Sexual immorality, understood as any sexual activity outside of the covenant of monogamous union between a man and a woman, is more than a dishonoring of God who established the nature and parameters of human personality. Paul calls it a crime against our own bodies, inasmuch as it is committed inside of our own bodies (see 1 Cor. 6:12-20). Whatever we may think about that, sexual relations, with their seemingly infinite potential to present one with bliss or consign one to misery, is one of the three core issues on which the apostles felt compelled to write. And the sound and fury that are generated in contemporary circles whenever the subject is raised is more than ample confirmation that it really is crucial for us to get it right, if such can be achieved.

Luke 19 details the story of Jesus and the tax collector. Zacchaeus, like Ed, was not repentant of the many sins he had committed as he collaborated with the hated Romans and preyed upon his own people in order to make the money he believed he needed to survive in an unjust world. He was, like

Ed, desperate enough, when he heard that Jesus was in the neighborhood, to risk radical rejection in order to see Him. When Jesus stopped and invited Himself to lunch at the sinner's home, Zacchaeus was so moved that he returned half of his wealth to the poor and returned what he had stolen fourfold. The unrepentant sinner became a repentant and authentic human being in response to the love of God, just as Ed finally dealt with the disaster his own life had become when he was reminded of the Jesus who had saved his life years earlier and was still hanging around waiting for a response.

Like the prodigal son in Luke 15, Zacchaeus had committed at least one of the big three prohibited acts. He had made idols of money and collaboration with the Romans. Jesus treated Zacchaeus just like the father treated the prodigal son in Luke 15. The father did not enable the sin. There was no provision of extra money to continue his debauchery. But when he saw the son coming home, when he spotted the teachable and redeemable moment coming down the road, he declared that nothing mattered except that the boy wanted to come home. His love overwhelmed and overtook any thoughts of retribution for the dishonoring that he had previously received. Jesus embodied this spirit when he invited himself to Zacchaeus' home for lunch. If we only saw fit to treat each other that way when we are sexually broken, what face might we present to the world as the Body of Christ in place of the one we all too often present.

Make no mistake—repentance has to come. In order to enter fully into the life of Christ, the only authentic life there is, we have to begin a process of letting go all of the counterfeits that pass for our own life. But Jesus could not care less which comes first, the chicken or the egg.

ENGAGING HOMOSEXUAL PEOPLE

One of the hottest topics in the national news during the summer of 2003 was the action of the Episcopal Church to approve an openly homosexual man for a top leadership post in the denomination. The General Convention of that body approved the blessing of same-sex unions at that same meeting and has reaped a worldwide whirlwind since that time since national member bodies of the Anglican Communion have broken communion with her and many of her own congregations have ended their affiliation with the parent organism. I am, and remain, an Anglican priest in good standing. I am grieved and ashamed of what my church has done in this action, but I am both proud of and energized by what I see God doing in its wake. He who says that He can raise the dead is doing just that.

On the Sunday following our General Convention, the Los Angeles Times (not known for its sympathy to God or to the values He holds dear), sent reporters and photographers to a well-known liberal bastion and to an equally recognizable orthodox congregation in Los Angeles. They expected invective against the unrighteous in the latter, and a plea for tolerance and compassion in the former. They got a big surprise, at least at St. James in Newport Beach.

The pastor entered the pulpit and began to speak of his enduring love for his Episcopal Church despite her embrace of apostasy. He spoke of the need to continue in love and forgiveness even as he asserted the necessity of resisting the action of the convention with the forthright good news of the whole gospel of Jesus Christ. He spoke of the calamity as a wake-up call to go forth and stand fast at the same time, to rediscover identity in the Great Commission and the Great Commandment. He called on the people in his care to name sin as the death rattle that it is while actively remembering that every one of us is saved by grace alone and is absolutely obligated to love one another into the Kingdom. When he finished speaking, a man rose in the congregation to say that he wished to introduce his wife and children to the rest of the assembly. He said that he had attended the church more than a decade earlier as an active homosexual man who had since been healed and made as happy as he was whole. And he wished to thank the congregation—he called them the reason he was still alive—for both loving and confronting him during that time when his life was a seemingly inescapable living hell.

The people from the LA Times found a reality 180 degrees from the bigotry they had expected to find in a conservative church. They were, however, honest enough (and conscientious enough) to recognize the real story and place it on the front page of their edition covering the fracture of the Episcopal Church. The story they reported was of a man deeply grateful to people who engaged him with the love of a Lord who died for him while confronting that which was disintegrating him. They saw, whether they could put it into words or not, the abundant life that is only released in the Body of Christ when we take our identity from the Great Commission and exercise the Great Commandment wherever we then find ourselves.

The Great Commission of Matthew 28:16-20 is presented in three distinct parts. The first part depicts the disciples coming to the mountain on which they had first recognized Jesus in His divinity and worshipping Him, even though and despite the fact that some doubted (see Matt. 28:16-17). The first call on our lives is to worship our God as He presents Himself, bringing our doubts along with us as an offering and as a cry for healing. If we wait until we are pure in heart and mind before we present ourselves to Him, we will wait a long time, likely forever. But if we come as we are, He will speak to us as He spoke to Peter in Luke 5:1-11 and John 21:1-19. He will say that we should come with Him as we are, that the process of our coming to perfection will be completed as we catch and feed His people in His name. In Matthew 11:2-6, Jesus depicted the Kingdom as populated not by those who are already perfect in their comprehension of Him, but by those who are faithful in taking no offense at Him.

The second part of the Great Commission is, of course, the command to go into all of the world and baptize those we find in the name of our Triune God (see Matt. 28:18-19). This is not a command to bring into the Kingdom those we deem worthy. We are called to baptize all as they are willing. "You catch them, and I will clean them," seems to be the way He puts it. Although it is a given of the gospel that each of us must choose Jesus to be our personal Christ, we should understand that He will not be satisfied while even one of us refuses His offer of abundant and eternal life (see 1 Tim. 2:3-5). As people made in His image we should be as unsatisfied with a partial harvest as He is.

The corollary to the command to baptize is to teach one another to observe all that he teaches (see Matt. 28:20), including His instructions for the enjoyment of our sexuality. I think one of the saddest episodes in Scripture is the one in Luke 18:9-14. The Bible tells us that the Pharisee "was praying to himself" as he thanked God that he was not like others, especially the sin-filled tax collector standing next to him and crying out to God for forgiveness and relief from the life of shadow in which he lived (see Luke 18:11 NASB). When Jesus commended the latter and dismissed the former, it was not because he saw the penitent one as somehow less sinful, and it certainly was not because he was merely expressing the humanity he had been given in his sins. It was simply as the Scripture says—the one prayed to himself and to the idol he had made of his own understanding of a selective obedience. And the other prayed to God, begging to be released from addiction to his brand of idolatry. The best way to seek that perfection to which we are called is to cling to nothing in ourselves and to seek Him by embracing the gospel along with those we think of as being in even worse shape than we are. As we feed His sheep, we become His lambs, or so He says.

The third part of the Commission is the awesome promise He makes to be with us always, even to the end of the age (see Matt. 28:20). That promise is not conditioned by our behavior. It is His response to our hunger and thirst for the fullness of His righteousness. But we become capable of recognizing His presence in our midst to the degree that we let ourselves be as compassionate as the Samaritan who cared for the victim of the robbers (see Luke 10:25-37).

The most poignant scene that I recall in *The Passion of the Christ* is the one concerning the woman taken in adultery. There is no dialogue in the scene as Mel Gibson brings it to the screen. There is only the woman, the crowd of angry self-righteous ones, and Jesus drawing His line in the sand.[1] But when I witnessed this scene, it was as though I clearly heard Jesus speak from the screen. He said to the crowd, "This woman is a sinner, and you have caught her in the act. You have three alternatives. You can judge her according to the law; the penalty is stoning. You can throw down your stones, as you recognize that not one of you is worthy of casting the first one. Or you can acknowledge that each of you needs me as much as she does, and you can join me with the woman on this side of the line that I have drawn." Let's remember that the Scripture records Jesus' words to the woman, "Go now and leave your life of sin" (John 8:11), even as He stood with her. Let's also remember that the crowd threw the stones to the ground and dispersed, but not one of them crossed the line to stand with Jesus among the sinners. How can we appropriate His promise to be with us always if we will not stand where He stands?

As a young man, I dealt with the grief and horror of one of my best friends announcing that he was gay. To add gasoline to the fire, he also announced that he was in love with me and that he expected me to become his lover. The tension eventually resulted in a fistfight between us and the end of a friendship that was part of the warp and woof of who I was. Some months later, after he had moved to another city, I became convicted that I had to find him and talk with him. I went to his city and tracked him down, declaring that I had come to find him and that I meant to spend the night in his home. He asked if I was now ready to become his lover and I said, "No way. But I am your friend, and I am going to stay with you (on my terms, and not on yours), but I am going to stay with you." When we arrived at his apartment, he showed me a gun and threatened to shoot me if I did not either leave or jump into bed with him. I slept on the sofa that night, and I left the next morning. Some weeks later, I heard through the grapevine that he had renounced homosexuality and today he is happily married and the father of grown sons.

Blessing the Broken

Is it really so simple? Of course not. When God moves as miraculously as He did in the face of my friend, He compresses His intervention to a size small enough for us to see its shape and dynamic. Homosexuality is as difficult to heal as any other addiction, and it usually takes a long time and a deep infusion of the grace of God. But who will deliver that grace but one who loves the sinner as much as he hates the sin? Who will minister to the leper but one who knows how deeply he also needs God's cleansing? Taking our identity from the Great Commission helps us to avoid the sin of the Pharisee in Luke 18 just as it inoculates us against the sin of the Sadducees in Matthew 22:23-33, in which they mock marriage in order to indulge their own rebellion against the Word of God.

I have taught Christians for over two decades to oppose the gay agenda at every turn, not because homosexuality is a worse sin than those that I and my friends commit, but because it is sin, and therefore a dealer of death to those caught in its grip. Members of the gay community have a life expectancy of between half and two thirds that of the straight community because of the much higher incidence of suicide, substance addiction, sexually transmitted diseases (AIDS is but one of these), and domestic violence. I have always said to my people that if they cannot speak against this scourge from the standpoint of a heart broken for people suffering on account of their own behavior, they would do better not to speak at all.

The sin of social and sexual conservatives is that they all too often condemn the sin while hypocritically claiming to love the sinner. But it does not come across as love until and unless they engage with that same sinner in the humility and commitment demonstrated by the congregation of St. James who walked with the gay man when he was trapped in a lifestyle he never chose and from which he seemed unable to escape. They engaged him where he was but with integrity for where God had told them to stand. The sin of the liberals is that they claim a *laissez faire* attitude toward the sexually broken, especially those of the homosexual variety, which is actually an even more radical form of disengagement. It is as though they are saying, "We can't help you and so we leave you to your own devices." Yet God calls on us to engage with one another and even to bear one another's burdens.

My own Episcopal Church has shot itself in the head with its defiance of the Word of God. But that defiance is rooted in a deeper rejection of the Great Commission, our identity and marching orders, which dates back many decades. Many Christians of many denominations are content to parse and memorize Scripture without ever acting on its imperatives for mission, and they too face disaster in their denominations if they fail to repent. Those Episcopalians who constitute the core of a faithful remnant have chosen to view themselves as a faithful vanguard of the resurrection promised by our Lord and our Christ. They embrace the gay and the straight, not in terms of whom these people believe themselves to be but in terms of who God calls all of us to be. Revival and transformation are the only possible destinations of such a course.

But is homosexual activity the only sexual expression singled out for condemnation in the Word of God? Frankly, the issue is not, and has never been, the actions that are condemned; rather it is the actions that are commended and why.

A record of the Word of God that includes the Song of Solomon cannot possibly be opposed to sex for the pure joy of it. When Sarah, Abraham's wife, was told that she would bear a child in her old age, her question was, "Will I now have this pleasure?" And although she refers to the pleasure of having a child, she was also well aware that it would be preceded by the pleasure of sexual union with her husband (see

Gen. 18:12). When we read that God spoke of Israel as His bride (see Hos. 2:19-20), that He commended human faithfulness in marriage as a state of bliss akin to that of the Kingdom of Heaven, which He did through the mouth of Paul (see Eph. 5:32...), and that Jesus performed His first miracle at a wedding feast (see John 2:1-11), we must conclude that God invented sex for the joy it would give and for no other purpose. (There are other ways to procreate, as nature demonstrates.) Yet His Word cautions, continually, that the joy is compromised and even destroyed when sexuality is expressed outside of the ultimately intimate relationship for which it is intended. And, just to be sure we know that we are all sailing in the same precariously leaky boat, Jesus pointed out that if we even lust after one other than our spouse in our hearts we are as guilty of going out of the bounds as if we had taken a lover into our bed (see Matt. 5:28). The good news is that alongside the revelation that all have sinned and fallen short of the glory of God is the companion revelation that all are redeemed in the blood of the Christ. It is the perfect context for reconciliation.

Reality is that heterosexual sin is just as serious a matter in the Kingdom as homosexual sin. (The difference is that, for heterosexual people, repentance can lead to complete healing, while in homosexual people, a re-orientation must precede full healing.) Just as important is the statement Paul made in Romans 6:16-18,

Don't you know that when you offer yourselves to someone to obey him as slaves, you are slaves to the one you

obey—whether you are slaves to sin, which leads to death, or to obedience, which leads to righteousness? But thanks be to God that, though you used to be slaves to sin, you wholeheartedly obeyed the form of teaching to which you were entrusted. You have been set free from sin and have become slaves to righteousness.

The point is that we are incomplete in ourselves; that is why sexuality as the means of joining ultimately with another is so crucial to our being. Because we are incomplete, and therefore inadequate, in ourselves, we cannot choose to recreate ourselves in whatever form we think will work best at the moment. We must choose between one form of servitude and another. God maintains that the one kind leads us into freedom and that every alternative to it leads us only from servitude into bondage. But the very fact of our inadequacy opens the door to that bondage if we strain and strive against it.

If My People...

Second Chronicles 7:14 is one of the best known verses of the Bible, and it is the inspiration for this book and the one that will follow it. "If my people, who are called by My name, will humble themselves and pray and seek My face and turn from their wicked ways, then I will hear from Heaven and will forgive their sin and will heal their land." The Hebrew that we translate into English as "wicked ways" is actually more akin to inadequacy than to moral wickedness. The fact is, there is nothing morally reprehensible about our being inadequate. That is just the way we were created; it was God's plan to create beings designed for community with Himself and with each other. But when we are wounded at an early age, as most if not all of us are, we become less capable of achieving our destiny in fellowship. If I am betrayed by someone I trust, I become less willing to trust in the future; if I am ridiculed by one to whom I have made myself vulnerable, I learn to protect myself in the future. But God presents Himself as the healer of all of our wounds and the sole source of our developing adequacy. What if I seek a shortcut to healing, perhaps learning to cope with and minimize the pain of my wounding because I have decided that this is the best I will ever be able to do? What if I, when challenged to seek a fuller healing in Christ, declare that my inadequate method of self-care is the best for which I can hope and that I will consider no other; this is the hand I have been dealt and that is all there is to that?

At that point, I have chosen my own inadequacy as the ultimate reality of my life, and thus, I have made an idol. For whatever is ultimate in my life is what I worship, and if I am not worshipping God, I am worshipping an idol. In fact, any idol (whether it's a golden calf smelted because Moses was gone on the mountain too long, a Sunday morning golf game chosen because I find the sermons boring and I seek God in the great outdoors, or a favorite pornographic alternative to treating my wife like a person) is simply a shortcut to the abundant life promised in Christ and His way. But it never turns out to be a shortcut to anything but bondage and death.

If, for example, I had a father who was either unavailable or abusive, the chances are fairly good that I am still seeking appropriate male love as an adult. But having never seen it before, I don't know what it looks like. I find myself attracted to men who look like they might be able to supply what I lack, although they never do, and I drift from one gay affair to another. This is not at all farfetched since most researchers believe that most homosexuality is triggered by a dysfunctional relationship with the parent of the same gender or by a childhood sexual trauma. (Exceptions would be those researchers who are convinced there is a gene for homosexuality, although there has never been a shred of credible scientific evidence to support that view.) I can either cry out to God for relief and genuine healing until it comes, believing Jesus' promise in the Great Commission that He will never leave me alone, or I can do the best I can with what I have to work with. Reality is that promiscuity, to a massive degree, is the rule rather than the exception in the gay community because the lifestyle simply does not deliver on its promises. Reality is that there are many thousands of healed homosexuals out there proclaiming that genuine help and health are available to the broken. I know a number of these healed and sexually resurrected ones personally while others, such as Joe Dallas, Sy Rogers, and John and Anne Paulk, maintain a high public visibility and profile.

Suppose I had a mother who was mentally ill, addicted to drugs, and abusive to me throughout my childhood. (I am not being hypothetical here; my mother was all of those things.) Suppose further that I have an ache in my heart that reminds me that women cannot be trusted and that I should get some of my own back by using them as objects for my gratification since I was not gratified as a child. I am then a prime candidate for heterosexual promiscuity, and I may not even understand why I seem to be incapable of the kind of fidelity that is lauded in the Word of my God. But, if I choose to do the best I can with what I have to work with, the truth is that my real god is the limitation of my program of self-care. Yet the choice is mine, not of what compulsions I may experience, but of whether to worship my inadequacy or to assault the gates of Heaven (and of my brother and sister Christians) until I receive the fullness of healing. Reality is that my wife deserves the latter, God certainly deserves the latter, and I too deserve the latter.

I have chosen the path of healing, and Diana and I have recently celebrated thirty-two years of a happy and faithful union. I have, of course, greatly oversimplified the scenarios I described above. And they do not even begin to cover all of the varieties of sexual brokenness or their causation. But I think the picture is clear enough. Healing, for all of us, is a lifelong process. But the alternative is one addiction or another based on our (dysfunctional) predilections. And what looks at first to be harmless can be the most seductive of all. More than four hundred studies, for example, show the addictive and escalating quality of pornography and how it tends to desensitize the user to all human relationships. There is a correlation between porn use and domestic violence as well as other types of abuse, and there are many millions, including millions of Christians, who are hooked on the seemingly secret temptations of the internet. But only the spider thrives on darkness.

So what about the perfect context for reconciliation?

AUTHENTIC, HUMBLE, AND REAL

John Stott once opened a sermon with, "Authentic humility is a realistic appreciation of who we are in relation to God and one another."[2] I have never heard it put better. This kind of humility is a great place to start with sexual brokenness, ours or theirs, or any other kind of brokenness.

Some years ago, I was asked a question in an adult confirmation class that found its way into my sermon for the following Sunday. A woman in the class asked if it was true that homosexuality is an abomination according to the Bible. I answered that it was, but no more so than heterosexual immorality or the decision to play golf rather than going to worship on Sunday morning. "Sin," I said, "is sin. There are no gradations from a biblical standpoint." After having preached that same point the next Sunday, I was amazed at some of the comments I received after church. One woman asked me if anyone from our congregation was likely to make Heaven. Another congratulated me on telling the congregation that homosexuality was not a sin. Still another said that, since her husband was on the golf course at that moment, he was going to be pretty steamed to hear that I thought he must be gay!

Sexuality is so close to the bone for all of us that we tend to hear what we want or need to hear to justify ourselves in the way we have chosen. But God did not create us for bondage of any kind. He says in Galatians 5:1, "For freedom Christ has set us free. Stand firm, then, and do not let yourselves be burdened again by a yoke of slavery." But He adds a note about the route to our freedom in the next chapter when He says, "Brothers, if someone is caught in a sin, you who are spiritual should restore him gently. But watch yourself, or you also may be tempted. Carry each others' burdens, and in this way you will fulfill the law of Christ" (Gal. 6:1-2). The word is much more blunt in First Corinthians, where He says, "Do you not know that the wicked will not inherit the Kingdom of God? Do not be deceived: Neither the sexually immoral, nor idolators, nor male prostitutes, nor homosexual offenders, nor thieves, nor the greedy, nor drunkards, nor slanderers, nor swindlers will inherit the Kingdom of God. And that is what some of you were..." (1 Cor. 6:9-11).

No one is saying that people caught up in sexual sin are not redeemable in the blood of Christ; but we are told that sexual sin is an impediment to authentic life and should be treated as such. Likewise, we are cautioned against judging one another because there is nothing in the above list that we have not partaken of to a greater or lesser degree. So how can we be reconciled with brothers we look down upon because their sexual brokenness is other than our own?

For openers we can lighten up on one another. The gay community members and those who believe they are being supportive by endorsing the lifestyle can drop the smug questions such as, "Have you ever met a gay person or actually talked to one? Perhaps if you got to know us, you wouldn't be so quick to demonize us." Truth is that every reparative therapy ministry is staffed by people with many years of experience caring for the sexually broken, usually both heterosexual and homosexual, and most of these ministries are staffed by sexually broken people who have experienced deep healing in the love of Christ and properly applied therapeutic methods. People such as Drs. Joe Dallas, Joseph Nicolosi, and Jeffrey Satinover have impeccable credentials. Ministries such as *Exodus, Imago Dei*, and *Focus on the Family* have excellent track records. And they only seek to treat people who desire change. I am personally acquainted with many who have received healing in this most sensitive of areas.

The gay community can also drop the completely bogus position that the serious health consequences of their way of life, the higher incidence of depression, suicide, disease, and so forth, are the result of straight society's rejection. There has never been a time in our land or in the world when homosexuality boasted greater social acceptance, and the statistics are unchanged. It is a life that deals nothing but death to those who live in it and are trapped by it.

For those of us who walk in heterosexually broken temptations to sin, we can swear off of making comparisons between ourselves and those we think are "really messed up." Multiple studies have shown that people live longer and happier lives when they are in faithful and committed marriages. Children of those covenant relationships are more likely to be able to enjoy the same types of blessings. Likewise, hundreds of studies have shown that living together out of wedlock, and being sexually involved outside of wedlock, makes stable commitments more difficult and less likely. Adultery and abusive sexual practices hurt all concerned, consenting or not. Pornography of all kinds destabilizes and dehumanizes all concerned and poisons relationships, even when one party knows nothing of the porn use. There is no such thing as a private act with consequences for only one person. But there is healing for all of these things, and the dynamic element is the love of God applied through human hands and heavenly insight. The only contribution required of us is that we abandon the shortcut to God that we have chosen; it is always a counterfeit.

As I told the confirmation class, "Sin is sin. There are no gradations." The reason we need a book on reconciliation is because we all echo Adam when he excuses his sin by telling God, "The woman you put here with me—she gave me some fruit from the tree, and I ate it" (Gen. 3:12). It is our disengagement from God and from one another that leads us into unhumanity, in a profound sense, and only our reengagement, through the process of reconciliation with God and man, can lead us back. So long as we look at ourselves in the mirror and find our brother less beautiful than we are, we remain in the trap described in James 1:23-25, we do not long remember even what we look like. But if we keep our attention on God and on doing what He calls out of us, bearing one another's burdens in the process, we will know what God looks like and we will know just how beautiful we have become in His eyes.

Paul described a path to healing the state of sin, from which Christ rescues every one of us, in Colossians 3. The arrangement of material was no accident. First he called on all Christians to put aside the areas of their lives in which self is central. Every listing of sins and virtues in the Bible has this in common: all of the sinful acts are self-centered and all of the virtuous behaviors are others-centered, whether we compare lust to faithfulness or cursing to blessing. Then he spent a few verses teaching on how to reengage by exhibiting compassion, forgiveness, and love. Finally, he described a covenant relationship between husband and wife for which they are now prepared, having walked the path of healing activities.

And for those of us who have removed enough of the planks in our own eyes that we are ready to begin surgery on the specks that plague our brothers (see Matt. 7:3-5), we are given the wonderful formula for reconciliation found in Matthew 18:15-20. But we need to be clear that this is a formula for reconciliation, not for expulsion from fellowship. We should go to the brother who is sinning, presupposing that he is a brother, and we share our concern with him. If that is ineffective, we should return with two or three witnesses. If we still come up dry, we should bring the matter before the church. And only if there is danger of infecting the body, should we treat the brother as though he were a tax gatherer. Such a process is always risky, because it calls for real vulnerability and engagement on our part, but it works so well that we can undertake the process even if the planks are not all out of our own eyes. This is because the process itself requires that we walk by faith and not by sight.

Is it all so simple? No—there are many years of struggle ahead for some of us; and we who are smug on either side of the sexuality debate might be shocked to find out who has the greatest number of struggling years ahead. But Paul also spoke of what is at stake in the third chapter of Philippians. He said, "But whatever was to my profit I now consider loss for the sake of Christ. What is more, I consider everything a loss compared to the surpassing greatness of knowing Christ Jesus my Lord, for whose sake I have lost all things. I consider them rubbish, that I may gain Christ" (Phil. 3:7-8).

FOR FREEDOM SET FREE

When I met Jesus Christ, I was 22 years of age. I had almost no experience in the church and was led into one of the more traditional denominations. And the congregation I attended still practiced what is called auricular confession of sin. That meant I was invited to go into a little box that was very dark and quiet and confess to the priest everything I had ever done or failed to do that might stand between me and God. This was the Episcopalian equivalent of saying the sinners' prayer.

The priest told me to prepare for my confession by sitting down with paper and pen and asking God to show me my sins. He told me that whatever was revealed to me in prayer I should confess, even if it seemed trivial to me. He also told me that if I remembered something really gross after having completed my confession, I should ignore it; if

God had wanted me to deal with it, He would have reminded me before I was finished, and I should attribute any afterthoughts to the devil's effort to trip me up.

What the priest did not know, and I was not thinking about, was that two years earlier I had helped two friends of mine obtain an abortion. They had come to me for help because they knew I valued friendship more than anything else. In my own mind, that was the only issue—two friends in trouble. I believed that what grew in their bellies was flesh, but not human life. I borrowed enough money and found a doctor willing to do the procedure (this was before Roe vs. Wade), and my friends had their abortions. I had not the slightest guilt over what I had facilitated, and nothing changed on that score when I received Jesus as my Lord and Savior.

When I entered that confessional booth, I had quite a laundry list of sins for someone who did not even understand the concept of sin. I knelt and said, "Bless me, Father, for I have sinned, and especially since my last confession which was...never, I have..." and I began to go down my list. About halfway through the list, I heard a little voice whisper in my ear, "Don't forget the abortions."

That was all I heard; there were no recriminations and no excuses offered for ignorance. I confessed the abortions as sin, and when I left that little booth, I knew two things. I knew that I had just been acquitted of two murders for which I was indeed guilty, and I knew that I would never dare to judge someone who had done what I had done. I know today that if I can be forgiven for what I did, the taking of innocent human life because my friends' panic was more important to me, then there is no sexual sin that cannot be forgiven and no sexual bondage that cannot be broken by the blood of Jesus Christ. We have only to ask.

I know also the truth of the parable of the two sons who are commanded by their father to go into the field to work. One said that he would go, but he did not. The other said that he would not go, but he went (see Matt. 21:28-32). I know that we need to take all kinds of sexual sin and bondage as seriously as the Lord takes them, and I know that we need to do this because we love one another as He first loved us (not because we hate or would ignore one another). We need to be serious about engaging one another and lightening up on one another when we do come together. Finally, we need to remember that Jesus Christ takes sin, all kinds, far more seriously than we do. He takes anything that separates Him from His people so seriously that He is in nowhere near the hurry we are to cut people off, whether we stand for or against the Biblical witness about human sexuality.

A number of years ago, He gave me a vision of what it was like to witness the story of Zacchaeus and the triumphal entry into Jerusalem that immediately followed it (see Luke 19). In the vision, I too had heard that Jesus was passing through Jericho. I knew that He would be stopping under the tree in which Zacchaeus was hidden, and I thought that if I ran through the back alleys between me and the tree, I would be able to beat the crowds there and get a really good up-close look at Jesus. As it happened, I had outsmarted myself with too elaborate a plan, and each time I was within range, I saw that I had just missed Him since my shortcuts kept becoming longer cuts.

Knowing He would be entering Jerusalem, I ran all the way to the Temple mount and arrived, breathless, in the court in which Jesus was already teaching the people. I did see Him clearing the Temple of the money changers, from a distance, but I had to content myself with a seat in the back of the crowd. And then it happened. I could look over Jesus' head from my distant vantage point, and I could see that the money changers He had just cleared from the holy precincts were sneaking back in. They were approaching Him from the rear, and they were armed. They meant to kill Him right then and there!

I began pushing my way through the crowd, trying to get His attention so that I might warn Him of the dirty trick these dirty sinners were about to pull. I pushed and darted and shoved until I found myself standing a few feet away from Him. He stopped what He was saying and looked right at me. He spoke in a voice both kind and firm, "Do you really think I don't know who is approaching me from behind? It was never my intention to expel them permanently; I just had to clear a place for myself so that I could teach. They have as much right, and as much need, as you do for my presence and my voice. And I don't need you to protect me."

We really do need to be very serious about engaging one another in the name and in the Spirit of the Lord Jesus Christ who hates sin and loves sinners. And we really do need to be both broken and light of heart when we do come together in the presence of Him who says, "Who will step across the line that I have drawn? Don't worry about who you see standing with me."

ENDNOTES

1. *The Passion of the Christ,* DVD, directed by Mel Gibson (Beverly Hills, CA: Twentieth Century Fox, 2004).

2. John R.W. Stott, sermon preached at First Presbyterian Church, Evanston, IL, Fall 1982, title unknown.

Chapter 9

AGAPE LOVE BETWEEN THE GENDERS

D IANA and I are no more perfect in our marriage than is anyone else this side of Heaven. But we have been happily married for more than 30 years and we are more in love every day—except when one or the other of us is considering murder. The rest of the time, we just enjoy being together, even as we struggle to resolve a breach between the genders that has its roots all the way back in the garden at the beginning of the world. In 1992, God gave me grace for a significant step in that direction.

We had just begun a new ministry in the town of Gilroy, California, the garlic capitol of the world. Alongside getting to know the people of a new congregation and establishing a new home, we had also to deal with the deaths of Diana's aunt and my mother within 30 hours of each other. We were 700 miles from everything and everyone that we knew, and I decided that I had to attend a workshop being offered by Fuller Seminary back in Southern California.

I can not imagine a more supportive bride than my own. She has always been there for me in whatever I wanted or needed to do professionally. She not only kept the house and hearth going while I was in seminary, and later in graduate school, but she was also the breadwinner during the seminary years to boot. All of that was on top of dealing with health issues of her own and the loss of a number of our children to miscarriage and one to stillbirth. She is also the most creative artist and craftsperson I have ever known, and she is a tower of faith and spiritual giftedness. Yet in the face of the move and death in the family, coming on the heels of several difficult years personally and professionally for both of us, it seemed to me that there was a distance between us. (Naturally, I assumed this was in no way my fault.) We were not fighting or ignoring one another; it just seemed to me that we were going through some motions without the fire that we both wanted and expected in our marriage. And then I got into the car one day to drive to Pasadena with her full blessing and support.

God did an amazing thing when I was on the road that day. Over every mile that I drove, I could hear God singing a love song to Diana. He was singing to her, but He let me hear His voice. The tune was from that old and wonderful praise song, "You Are My Hiding Place," but the words He kept crooning to my wife were, "You are my special one; you always fill my heart with joy indescribable, whenever I think of you, I am overcome." As He sang, I could see Diana through His eyes and she was (oh, she was) indescribably beautiful. I made up my mind that, the moment I returned home, I would tell her how much I too loved her and that I would find a way to carve out some special time for us to be together. But He kept singing the same refrain and showing me the same vision. It took several hours of praying and thinking about her before it finally dawned on me what God wanted me to do. And how dull of heart I must have been not to have figured it out a long time before that. But when I did realize what God was trying to say to me, I turned the car around and headed for home as fast as I could without bringing the entire highway patrol down on my head.

God was not merely showing me how He saw Diana. He was asking me why I did not instinctively and from my heart see her in the same way—all of the time. I know, and everyone should know, that when God asks a question He is not seeking information. I also know that I would not trade anything for the joy I saw in her and on her when I walked into our home. I don't recall whether or not this was the first time I had literally dropped everything, including what I thought of as weighty professional requirements, just to be with her. I do know that there have been far too few such moments even since that time. Why is it that we so seldom look at the wife (or husband) that the Lord has given to us exactly the way He always looks at them? Whatever the answer, it is the reason that reconciliation between the genders is needed.

I know that I have not the slightest memory of what the conference was about that I missed; yet I will never forget how much it meant to both of us when I walked through the door that evening. I also know this: I did not come home that day because I am really such a nice guy underneath it all. I came home because I listened to God, for once. But then, that really is all that is ever required of us.

Diana has always been several steps ahead of me in this process. Four years before we met in 1972, the Lord spoke to her about the husband He had chosen for her. She had always believed that she did not need to go out of her way to meet me. In her opinion, the Lord would honor our choices in deciding to have or have not a relationship, but He would make it impossible to avoid the opportunity. In the meantime, she felt no need to go to singles' bars with her sorority sisters or to do any of the other things that are designed to put young women in the way of eligible bachelors. She simply went about her life of school and work and social events that interested her and expected that I would turn up when the time was ripe, whoever I was. And then God spoke to her.

He said that He wanted her to begin daily prayer for the man He had chosen as her life mate. She answered, "But I don't know who he is." And God replied, "But I do." From that day on, Diana prayed every day for a man whose name she did not know. She asked the Lord to give me a good day, to be a very present help in time of trouble, to draw me close to Him, especially if I did not already know Him, and to give me joy as well as protection. It would be another two years before I even met the Lord my God; two more years would pass after that before Diana and I would meet and fall in love. I know in my heart and in my bones that the prayers she prayed during that time in which she did not know my name, but God did, prepared me to be with her and to be with Him. Diana is a faithful and dependable person, but she will be the first to say that she is not *that* faithful and dependable. She is a lover, but no one is that loving all of the time. Like me, she listened to the voice of God, who requires nothing more than that of us.

COMPLETED ONLY IN ONE ANOTHER

God made men and women for each other, one for each. I do not mean by that to imply that there can only be one man for each woman and vice versa. The Word of God does not support that notion and the story of Ruth and Boaz is just one case that defies it. But Jesus did say in Mark 10 that the union of one man and one woman, becoming one flesh in their union, is of the very warp and woof of the Creation itself (see Mark 10:6-9). It is clear that God made each of us incomplete in ourselves and that the coming together of a man and woman in the relationship of covenant marriage completes the humanity, and the image of God, in both of them. God is so explicit about this that He described the creation of the first man and woman thus, "So God created man in His own image, in the image of God He created him; male and female He created them," (Genesis 1:27). When He described the special act that brought forth the woman from the side of the man, God said that He decided to give the man what we translate into English as a helpmate (see Gen. 2:20-22). But the original Hebrew word ezer described Eve as "one who can look him in the face." We could not ask for a more clear statement of the equality of the sexes—or of their need for one another to be completed in their mutual being.

At the same time, the so-called war between the sexes also goes all the way back to shortly after the Creation, in the garden and the events described in Genesis 3. Eve was in the garden one day, accompanied by her husband, Adam, when the serpent offered her the chance to die from the inside out. Of course, it was not presented that way, but the offer was to live independently of the source of her life. The image that comes to my mind is of a deep sea diver who is seemingly self-sufficient inside his diving suit but whose need for life is supplied through the air hose and lifeline that attaches him to the boat above. If the air hose is detached from the suit, he will be cut off from the source of his life, although he will not know it for a brief period of time because of the small supply of air that is already inside his helmet. But he is dead where he stands unless he quickly reconnects or reengages with the source of his life. Of course, the serpent said nothing of the kind. He just invited her to experience the joys of untethered living—and she bit.

After she bit, she untethered herself from the man as well. It is always this way. When we disengage from the relationships into which we are called, there is no place to stop. And Eve, who knew very well (and said that she knew) that she and Adam had been commanded to leave that particular fruit alone, gave some to her husband. She believed, because she had rationalized her disobedience, that she was giving her husband a gift. The truth is that she was betraying him as she stepped out of relationship with God, which made authentic relationship with anyone whom God had made impossible. She was behaving no differently than the alcoholic who gives a drink to another alcoholic because he does not want to drink alone.

It does not matter one little bit, by the way, who committed the first betrayal in this economy of the Fall. Adam blew off his chance to care for and redeem his wife when he obeyed her in defiance of the Lord and accepted the fruit. Her eyes were not opened to the realities of good and evil, and her own nakedness, until the transaction was completed in the sin of Adam. The destruction of relationship was not consummated until both had eaten, for the text says, "Then the eyes of both of them were opened and they realized they were naked…" (Gen. 3:7). It would have been the same if Adam had eaten first; they were not whole without each other. Now their wholeness had been savaged in their lust to live free of that pesky air and life line. But Adam carried the betrayal even further in the next few verses.

When God came to walk with the couple in the garden, He found that the intimacy they had enjoyed was already gone. In this passage, "in the cool of the evening" is the way we translate the Hebrew, but the word is *ruach*, which is the word for the Holy Spirit. God had to call out to locate Adam instead of simply finding Himself intrinsically and spiritually together with them, as they had been before. And when God sought an explanation for this dislocation, Adam compounded the betrayal and death of relationship when he said, "The woman you put here with me—she gave me some of the fruit of the tree, and I ate it" (Gen. 3:12).

None of this was Adam's fault in his mind. God set him up by giving him this woman, and the woman led him into sin with the fruit, he said. In fact, God had given them everything and they (the two of them) had thrown it away, and then they competed with each other to blame the other. From that point on, they go their own way, still with each other because they can't seem to function apart, yet grimly determined to remake the other into a mirror-image instead of respecting the other as a person with his or her own integrity whose differentness completes what is missing in self.

I oversimplify to make a point. But let's face it—men and women are different from each other, and we all think that the way we are is the way any decent and intelligent person ought to be. There are gradations of what I will call the "guy" traits and there are likewise gradations in what I will label the "girl" traits, which is why God does not mass-produce husbands and wives but makes us one for another. But guys, after their masculinity, are problem-solvers, while girls, after their femininity, are relationship-builders. Guys are speakers and girls are listeners. Guys are initiators and girls are responders. Guys build walled compounds; girls make the compound livable by being there and arranging things inside. Guys need to take risks; girls need to protect their children by holding them close. Guys pioneer; girls settle and consolidate. The more a man is the way that I described, the more difficult it is for him to fathom, and respect and cherish, one who is the way that I described a woman. The converse is just as true. Relating to the other gender would be a challenge, before God knits us together, even if we had not begun our life together with a series of mutual betrayals. As it is, without redemption and resurrection of the possibilities of relationship, it is impossible. Given our differences, it is not remarkable that so many marriages endure in misery or end in divorce; the miracle is that so many are happy and provide places of nurture for children and joy for one another.

Men and women are different from each other. We are so utterly different that there is no natural way (in ourselves) for us to be compatible with each other if we think of ourselves as complete and okay within ourselves. Only when we commit to sacrificing our differences, which does not mean eliminating them, but rather placing them at the disposal of the other in the name of Christ Jesus, does our very incompatibility become the vehicle of our union as the one flesh God created us to be. That is why a Bible passage like Ephesians 5:21-31 is so perplexing and so liberating at the same time.

> *Submit to one another out of reverence for Christ. Wives, submit to your husbands as to the Lord. For the husband is the head of the wife as Christ is the head of the Church, His Body, of which He is the Savior. Now as the Church submits to Christ, so also wives should submit to their husbands in everything. Husbands, love your wives, just as Christ loved the Church and gave Himself up for her to make her holy, cleansing her by the washing with water through the Word, and to present her to Himself as a radiant Church, without stain or wrinkle or any other blemish, but Holy and blameless. In this same way, husbands ought to love their wives as their own bodies. He who loves his wife loves himself. After all, no one ever*

hated his own body, but he feeds and cares for it, just as Christ does the Church – for we are members of His Body. For this reason a man will leave his father and mother and be united to his wife, and the two will become one flesh.

The operant statement in the passage is the first one that we read. "Submit to one another out of reverence for Christ." It is not about hierarchy in relationships between the genders; it is about differentiation of function to enrich both parties. But God has laid down the method of mutual submission as the vehicle for realizing these riches. The rest of the passage gives detailed instructions for just how this mutual submission is to occur, after our kind. The woman is to treat her husband as though he were Christ Himself (and all of us are expected to receive Christ), which is a very feminine way of relating, but then the Church is the Bride of Christ. And the man is expected to sacrifice himself for his wife, which is a very manly thing to do if we recall that Christ is the manliest man who ever lived and that He sacrificed Himself for His Church and Bride.

It should be mentioned here that a covenant is always a reciprocal relationship. Both parties need to abide by the terms and conditions or there is no relationship and no commitment binding on either party. There has been much abuse in the Church because of men who come running to the pastor or the church council complaining, "My wife will not submit to me," when, in fact, no one ever said she should submit to bullying or a self-centered and authoritarian leadership of the family. The wife is called to submit to the godly leadership of her husband, and the husband is called to sacrifice himself for the godly submissiveness of his wife. If either is out of the will of God, the law of love would indeed call on the other to take initiative in winning the errant one back with the tenderness of real and sacrificial love, the kind Paul describes in First Corinthians 13. But no one commands obedience in the marriage; it must be freely earned and freely given.

There has been just as much abuse in the Church from women running to the pastor, or more often simply seething in passive aggressive silence, they believe their husbands are not sacrificing to bring them everything that they could possibly want. It is about mutual submission. It is about what we can give, not what we can get. Yet when a man is self-sacrificing for his wife, it is astounding how much pleasure she finds by giving herself to him. And when a man knows that the woman God gave to him is eager to give herself to him, it is amazing how much he will give to maintain that joyful status quo.

GOD'S WAY OR THE HIGHWAY

For those of us in a relationship which seems to have lost the loving feelings, the first thing to recall is that love is not a feeling followed by action. Love is a series of actions that, as they become habit-forming, will be followed by feelings that are appropriate to them. There are, of course, unions that are so disintegrated by addiction, abuse, or adultery that there is no going back. God makes allowances for such disasters to be redeemed through dissolution (see Matt. 19:9), but those cases are the exception, and our culture is all too ready to say, at the first sign of offense, "I'm out of here unless you want to straighten up and be what I want you to be!"

I have no formula and no procedure for reconciling the genders. Neither does God. He has only an economy of relationship that brings peace and joy when we choose to adopt the attitude of heart and the behavior that shapes that attitude toward one another. That attitude, and that behavior, is called sacrifice. Sacrifice is not just appropriate as a way of making peace between men and women. When we become people of sacrifice, we reengage the economy of the universe. Sacrifice is literally what makes the world go round. It is the thing that was lost to our kind when Adam decided to take care of himself at Eve's expense and when Eve decided to look out for herself at Adam's expense.

We are taught in school that only the strong survive in nature. We are, if we are educated in a Christian setting, taught that the Kingdom of Heaven poses an alternative way of being that is grounded in the sacrifice of the Christ for the people He was sent to save and heal. But we accept the status quo of a nature read in tooth and claw as normative, and then we wonder why so many of us scoff at the teachings of the Church and maintain, "That's all well and good for protected people, but I have to live in the real world." Reality is that we have not lived in the real world since the episode of expulsion from the garden. When Jesus mounted the Cross, emerged from the tomb, and sent the Holy Spirit to birth and nurture the Church, He launched a process of redemption that is progressively restoring the real world. But He did not come to create a world that never before existed. He came to redeem and fulfill what His Father had intended and initiated from the beginning. If His way is the way of sacrifice, then it is, and always was, the authentic way of the world.

Look at how nature perpetuates itself. Every species of animal, from spiders to salmon to she-bears, sacrifices itself so that the young can be born and survive. The white blood cells that rush to defend our bodily systems any time a hostile microbe gets under our skin have independent existence of their own. Yet they throw themselves on the intruders in a kamikaze style attack and obliterate themselves in their zeal to absorb and destroy the invader. Anyone studying astrophysics (especially the writings of Dr. Hugh Ross of the Reasons to Believe Institute) will soon discover that any number of stars were obliterated near the beginning of time in order to free up and relocate the right concentration of heavy and light elements that make up this rocky planet. When Jesus used the image of a kernel of wheat falling to the ground in death so that a mighty stalk might grow in its place, He used only images so familiar and normative to His hearers that they could not fail to get the point (see John 12:24).

Diana's prayer for me on a daily basis was a small sacrifice that she regularly gave because she was obedient, and afterward saw that it was good. It had an impact on my life that I cannot calculate even more than thirty years into our life together. Her decision was after her kind, but submitted to God. My return to her on that day in 1992 was a small sacrifice that I gave because I was obedient, and afterward I saw that it was good even though I had gone on the trip with her whole-hearted blessing. It had a permanent impact on our marriage as we began to seek new opportunities to reciprocate and expand the reach of it. My decision was of my kind, but submitted to God. What if we spent more than a token amount of time (all of the time) choosing to rejoice at the larger scope a woman's commitment to reciprocity and responsiveness brings to a man's capacity for visioning and adventuring? What if we made a serious commitment to focus all of that masculine capacity on the needs of the woman and the children that she gives to us? The marriage service in my church's prayer book says that the purposes of marriage are their mutual joy, the help and comfort given to one another in adversity, and (when it is God's will) the procreation of children, in that order. What if we actually took that seriously?

Scripture is laced with stories of how we stick to our guns—I will be a guy after my own image come hell or high water. And the women are no slouches at doing it their way in the serene confidence that they are only doing what they must. Take, for example, the visit Abraham made to Abimelech as it is recounted in Genesis 20.

Abraham moved into the Negev region, a territory ruled by Abimelech, the king of Gerar. Abraham decided that Sarah was so beautiful that it was possible that the king would kill him so that he could take her for his own wife. He rationalized the situation into, "I've got to do what I've got to do in order to keep both of us alive until I can move on," and he told the king that she was his sister (a statement that was technically correct, since they shared the same paternal bloodline, but which was clearly intended to deceive his host). Since Abimelech was attracted to Sarah, he sent for her and took her for his wife. Before he had a chance to consummate the marriage, God spoke to him in a dream and told him that he was messing with another man's wife and thereby risking his own life at God's hands. In other words, God has a much higher regard for Sarah than did her own husband. Abimelech returned Sarah to Abraham and, instead of killing him, gave rich gifts to both of them and gave them the run of his territory. One can reason here that, if Abimelech was the kind of man who treated Abraham the way he did when he caught him in deception, how much more honorable might he have been when he discovered honest dealing in his guests?

The problem here is that Abraham did exactly what so many of the sexually broken do, as I described them in the last chapter. He refused to place his trust in the Lord and did what he thought was the best he could do in a difficult situation. He worshipped his own inadequacy instead of the Lord His God who had never let him down. He made an idol of his own poor resources and dishonored his wife in the bargain. It was small wonder, by the way, that Sarah did not think herself worthy of the pleasure of childbirth when her husband treated her in this way (and it is hardly likely that this was the first time it had happened in their life together).

Even worse, when Isaac was born he learned the ways of this form of idolatry from his father, and he treated Rebekah the same way when he visited a Philistine king also named

Abimelech (see Gen. 26). The pattern of abuse was perpetuated instead of dealt with. Abraham was, of course, merely
seeking a shortcut to the solution of his problem (we men
are, after all, problem solvers) instead of taking it to the Lord
for what would have been a far less messy and complex resolution. The bad news is that every time we take a shortcut to
the fruit of relationship with God, instead of working with
God, we end up with an idol of one kind or another. This is
true whether we are smelting a golden calf in the desert,
stealing a blessing from Esau, or dishonoring a wife by refusing to acknowledge her as a wife. The fruit is never good.

Jezebel is the most maligned woman in the Bible—and
with good reason. She was a woman who truly did love her
husband, King Ahab, but she too sought a shortcut to the
solution of her problems. As a woman she was culturally, and
perhaps naturally, prevented from taking the kind of direct,
executive action that a warrior would go for. But when confronted by a problem such as the refusal of Naboth to give up
his vineyard (after the king has already offered to buy it at a
kingly price), she did what women do at their worst. She
sought a relational solution, but a perverted relational solution. She arranged for Naboth to be falsely accused of blasphemy so that, after he had been stoned to death, the king
would get his vineyard (see 1 Kings 21). In the short run, her
shortcut worked just fine. But in the end, it was her blood that
was licked by dogs after she had been pitched from a window
by Ahab's successor (see 2 Kings 9:30-37).

She did what she did out of love for her husband. But
divorced from the love and the ways of God, her love could

only be perverted. It brought a legacy of bloodlust into the government of Israel that lasted for centuries. It also made her name a household symbol for all that is wicked, treacherous, and partaking of witchcraft (which is nothing more or less than a human effort to manipulate God).

The story of Amnon and the rape of his sister, Tamar, is covered in an earlier chapter, along with the rebellion the incident inspired in Absalom because King David refused to be a proper parent. Amnon also rationalized, or should I say absolutized, his need borne of lust into a good thing in his own eyes. He got what he wanted from Tamar by way of sexual gratification and then decided he did not want her at all when she asked him to do the honorable thing (see 2 Sam. 13:1-22). He had made an idol of his feelings, and when they were gratified they changed so that his desire to be left alone was the idol. He paid for his abuse with his life, and the kingdom was splintered because of him. It is so very easy to say, "Amnon—what a jerk!" But how easily do we as men decide that what we want and need is the best for all because it is a shortcut to our happiness—and how often does the thing, when we get it, turn out to be an idol that can neither speak nor hear?

And what of Bathsheba, the widow of Uriah the Hittite? The Bible tells the story of David's sin, that when he spotted her bathing he became consumed with lust for her. He became so obsessed with what he wanted that he actually had her husband murdered in order to keep quiet what he has done—impregnate her. But the Bible says that both of them were punished through the death of the child Bathsheba carried (see 2 Sam. 11-12).

At first glance, Bathsheba appeared to be swept along by events. How could she refuse the king, and what was she to do when she found out she was with child by him? Reality is that David was guilty of all of the charges Nathan the prophet leveled against him, including murder. But reality is also that David was no Amnon; he did not rape Bathsheba. And the kings of Israel did not possess absolute power over the lives of their subjects. (If they did, Naboth would not have dared to refuse Ahab.) Bathsheba chose to bathe on her roof, where David, looking down from an upper window, could not fail to see her. She would most certainly have been in his confidence about how to deal with the pregnancy when Uriah could not be mistaken for the father. Her passivity was nothing but passive aggression as she did (or failed to do) what needed to be done to assure her ascension to the position of queen of Israel. She chose a relational shortcut because she was a woman acting at her worst, and the consequence was not only the death of her first child but also the eventual death of Israel. She was the mother of Solomon, the builder of the first temple in Jerusalem, but also the king who made idolatry popular and acceptable and set the stage for the revolt of Jeroboam and the eventual destruction of the two kingdoms (Israel and Judah) that were established in the place of God's intention for a united people of God.

The disengagement of the genders has major league consequences beyond whatever misery individual men and women inflict upon one another. Each time we take a shortcut to what we believe is the fruit we are entitled to, we set up an idol, and the fruit is never good. Yet each time we make the sacrifices for one another that God is always calling us to, the fruit is good—indeed, it is very good.

AN ECONOMY OF SACRIFICE AND HONOR

Diana prayed sacrificially for me before we met because the Lord prompted her. The story of Steve and Susan Nichols is shared in Qaumaniq and Suuqinna's book, *Warfare By Honor.*[1] In this story, God spoke to the couple about their sons' wives early on. They made it a family custom to have the boys pray for their future spouse each night as part of their bedtime prayers. They bought a charm to give to the woman who would marry each of them once each year, and they wrote a letter telling her of how they had spent the year. They were, of course, much too young to appreciate the significance of what they were doing when they began doing it. That is the whole point—they learned of the importance of honoring the bride by honoring her before they even knew her. It was implanted in them from the beginning that they were preparing for a lifetime spent with and for someone else. On the wedding day, the charms and letters would be presented to the bride as a wedding gift and as a welcome into the new family. Qaumaniq and Suuqinna wrote, "They will have taught each son to pray for his wife, to save himself for her, and to give himself to her, the totality of himself, including his history. What a welcome! What an act of protocol!"[2]

What a way to train and raise up ambassadors of reconciliation between the genders. How much reconciliation will still be needed for young men and young women who have been raised in this way? How much will such members of the Body be serving as icons of relationship in the eyes of our God and of His people? One can only say Amen to that.

God takes the reconciliation of the genders so seriously that He made it a repeated metaphor for His reconciliation with His people Israel. In the third chapter of Jeremiah, for example, He accused both Israel and Judah of repeated acts of adultery with foreign gods. Yet He also promised that the merest gesture of repentance would fully restore the marriage covenant between them. "...Return, faithless Israel...I will frown on you no longer...Only acknowledge your guilt....Return, faithless people...for I am your husband. I will choose you..." (Jer. 3:12-14). The whole prophetic book of Hosea is an essay on the marriage covenant entered into by the prophet with the prostitute, Gomer, as a microcosmic expression of the covenant between Jacob and Yahweh and the Lord's pleading with His wild bride to come and remain at home with the One who will not live without her.

In Ephesians 5:32, God said, by the mouth of his servant Paul in the exhortation to husbands and wives, "This is a profound mystery—but I am talking about Christ and the church." The same type of material, linking marriage to the covenant with Yahweh, is found in the letters to the churches at Rome and Colossae, and it is difficult to count all of the references to the wedding banquet that Jesus made in the Gospels when He referred to His final coming and reign. God was not spiritualizing marriage in this way; He was simply and profoundly calling for it to be on earth as it is in Heaven.

In Colossians, Paul went so far as to implicitly link the conduct of a marriage (from both sides of the gender line) to the process of sanctification in each person (see Col. 3). He first outlined the rejection of sin in terms of every self-centered pursuit. He then described the embrace of the Christian life in terms of a process of other-centered behavior. At last, he described, as though we are now ready for the ultimate consummation of our humanity, what we must do and become in our marriages and in the raising of our children. His instructions, of course, are a restatement of the call to mutual submission and sacrifice found in the letter to the Ephesian church (see Eph. 5:22-33).

Is it really that simple? Is the reconciliation of the genders in terms of the marriage covenant really the path to the consummation of our common and complex humanity? Is it really all about recognition and acceptance (dynamic acceptance) of the fact that when we take care of our own survival we end up dead and that when we focus on the life of another we end up receiving abundant life? The prescription sounds suspiciously like, "Seek first His kingdom and His righteousness, and all these things will be given to you as well" (Matt. 6:33).

Scripture is filled to bursting with examples of men and women being ambassadors to one another (which is what we are called to be to the world). In each case, they were walking out the unique blessings God has assigned to men as men and to women as women, nothing more. But they were sacrificing these traits for the benefit of others instead of marshalling their puny resources in a vain effort to win survival for themselves as the people they cannot quite become in isolation.

The prostitute in Luke 7:36-50 washed the feet of Jesus with her tears and dried them with her hair before breaking open the jar of spices to slather her Lord with the special ministries of the burial office while He was still present to enjoy the honor done Him. The profession of prostitution is nothing but a perversion of the call to servant ministry, the call to the office of the pastor. In caring for Jesus, who had forgiven her sins, she was recovering the vocation she had thrown away. It was the same as the way that my city surrounded the red light district for many decades with ministries of service and honor so as to heal the entire downtown section of the city.

When Joseph vowed to care for Mary, even though he knew she carried the child of another, even carrying her to his birth city to claim her and enroll her as his family in the census demanded by Rome, he was simply stepping beyond the pioneering spirit of adventure and exploration that we rightly attribute to men (see Matt. 1:18-25). He had become the shepherd of the flock he was leading into new places of pasture and fresh water, that all may live and prosper. He was exploring the greatest adventure that ever was, but without leaving behind those whom God had entrusted to his care. He was following in the footsteps of Abraham, Moses, and King David at their best. And he was lining himself up to receive a love for the ages.

Mary and Martha of Bethany may be the most famous sisters of all time. Both served God the Son in different ways that were equally appropriate to their gender personality. Mary sat at the feet of Jesus and hung on His every word— not because He was a famous man but because she recognized the voice of God in what He had to say. Martha served to make the household comfortable as she brought and took away the various dishes and accouterments of a Jewish social occasion. She lapsed briefly into a dysfunctional aspect when she complained that Mary was not helping her enough (see Luke 10:40), but she was at her best when her very feminine assertiveness drives her to call the Lord to the side of her dead brother, Lazarus. "Lord...if you had been here my brother would not have died. But I know that even now God will give you whatever you ask" (John 11:21-22).

Her dependency on Jesus, as an active and dynamic quality rather than a passive quality, was exactly what moved Him to raise Lazarus from the dead. The very same dynamic was at work in John 2:1-11 when, after Jesus had first refused to turn the water into wine, his mother told the servants to just do whatever He told them to do. From the Old Testament to the New, God was forever telling His people that He could resist their manipulations forever but that He has no defense against their humble dependency.

And let us remember that even when Martha served at the house in Bethany, she was doing something quite outside of ordinarily accepted gender roles, as was Mary, during a gathering of men in Jewish culture. It was not the cultural roles that were decisive but the fact that the women were functioning as Kingdom women, in a truly womanish way.

Solomon was functioning as a man in the best sense when he wrote the Song of Solomon. Here was the wisest man in the history of Israel who poured his wisdom into two primary books—the Proverbs about holy living and the Song about holy loving. To the extent he fills this erotic classic with agape love, Solomon functions in the same way as did Jesus and John when the Lord instructed his youngest disciple to care for Mary, His mother, after His death. John took that charge as the most important of his apostolate.

We live in a time of acute confusion about how men and women are supposed to relate to one another. On one level, this has not been news since the expulsion from the garden and the events that led up to it. But as first women and then men have become dissatisfied with the gender status quo over the past half century, a guilty truce between the two that has led much abuse and subjugation for women and plenty of debasement for men (from King Ahab to Ted Bundy), has withered and died. The opportunity today is for resurrection of the economy of mutual sacrifice and submission, after our respective kinds, that God clearly intended from the beginning.

This means the restoration of men to a Godly leadership in family, church, and society and the restoration of women as the essential and equal partners in the shaping of that endeavor. It does not call for a self-conscious and self-righteous wrestling match over whether women can lead. There are plenty of wonderful women leading ministries, congregations, and even the United States state department. And they are usually the exception rather than the rule, just as Paul greeted and honored the women leading some of his own churches in his letters, knowing and accepting all the while that most of them were led by men. Restoration does call for a self-aware acceptance of the nature of godly leadership and a stepping up to the plate for those men who have preferred to order women around from the comfort of their loungers while watching the football game or to win the bread at a distance both spiritual and physical. It is about making things on earth as they are in Heaven. God's promise is that inasmuch as men and women choose first the path of sacrifice for one another, they will quickly discover exactly what it means to be one another, and one flesh in one another.

I can never forget the famous O. Henry story called *The Gift of the Magi*. In it, the woman sells her beautiful hair in order to raise the funds to buy a silver chain for her husband's watch that he prizes—but not as much as he prizes her. He sells the watch in order to buy a set of tortoise shell combs for his wife's hair that she so values and cares for—but not as much as she cares for him. When they see the incarnated love that is between them, they collapse into each others' arms, amazed not at the seeming futility of their mutual sacrifice but at the wonder of it all.[3] When we make a habit of behaving this way toward each other in the name of the Lord, so that He even informs and orchestrates our sacrifices, the gates of hell shall not prevail against us.

Yeah, it really does sound like, "Seek first his kingdom and his righteousness, and all these things will be given to you as well" (Matt. 6:33).

ENDNOTES

1. Qaumaniq and Suuqinna, *Warfare by Honor: The Restoration of Honor: A Protocol Handbook* (Nashville: Healing the Land Publishing, 2005), 170-171.

2. *Ibid.*, 171.

3. O. Henry, *The Gift of the Magi* (New York City, Publisher unknown, 1906).

Chapter 10

GRAFTING JEWS AND GENTILES

A story is told of a time that tensions reached such a climax in the city of Rome that the pope decided to expel every one of the Jews from the city. When the chief rabbi heard of the planned expulsion, he went to see his rival in order to plead for a change of heart. The pope admitted that his mind was not open to change, so the rabbi made him a proposition. "I challenge you to a debate. The rules are these: You may use any visual aids that you desire, but the debate must be conducted in silence. Whoever wins the debate gets to determine the fate of the Jewish people of Rome." The pope was so intrigued by the concept of a silent debate that he agreed to the terms. The men came together in his office the following day at noon.

Since the rabbi was the challenger, it was the pope's privilege to go first. He held up three fingers. The rabbi's reply was to hold up his index finger only. The pope then swept both hands out and away from his body, as though he were indicating some sort of panoramic view. The rabbi replied by jabbing the index finger of his right hand into the palm of his left. The pope indicated the bread and wine on the small table beside him, which was spread out on the ceremonial cloths of communion. The rabbi took a ripe red apple from his pocket, bit into it, and displayed it for the pope to see. At that, the pope threw up his hands and exclaimed, "You have won the debate, sir. You and your people are welcome to stay in Rome for as long as you like. I know when I have been completely outclassed. May God bless you and your people always."

After the chief rabbi was gone, members of the pope's staff entered the office. Breathless with anticipation, they demanded to know who had said what and who had won the debate. "This chief rabbi is a master debater. I was outclassed from the get-go," said the pope. When his staff members demanded again to know what was said and how it all went down, he replied, "First, I held up three fingers to symbolize that God is one in three, Father, Son, and Holy Spirit. His reply was to hold up one finger, reminding me that God is one, a belief we share. Then, I swept my hands apart to indicate that God is everywhere. But he simply jabbed his finger into his hand to show that God is right here before us. Finally, I pointed to the elements of the Holy Communion, which everyone knows have been entrusted to us in the Church. But he took an apple from his pocket, the symbol of the sin which unites us even when love does not, for we all share in its harvest. At that point, I knew I had lost the debate; I told him that he could stay."

In the meantime, the chief rabbi had returned to his office. All of his staff members were frantic to know how the debate had gone, who had said what to whom, and especially if the Jews would be permitted to remain in Rome. "This pope is really a good man," said the rabbi. "You just have to take the time to get to know him and he is really quite reasonable. You just have to talk to him; talking always makes things better." But they demanded all the more to know what was said and what was the outcome of the silent debate. "Well," said the rabbi, "first he held up three fingers to let me know we had three days to get out of town. I held up one finger to let him know our determination that not one of us was leaving. When he saw that, he swept his hands apart to tell me that they were planning to scatter us to the four winds. I jabbed my finger into my hand to tell him that not one of us was leaving. When he saw that we meant business, he settled down and took out his lunch. I took out my lunch too, and we became friends. I am looking forward to getting to know him much better over the years."

If this story teaches us anything it is that God can bring about His purposes in the midst of our confusion and misunderstanding, if we will humble ourselves and be faithful to the covenants we make, regardless of the degree to which we see clearly and understand all that is before us. The context of relationship between Jew and Gentile is no exception. Although there is confusion on both sides about who the other may be in Christ, there can be no doubt of God's intention to gather all of His family under one roof and within the folds of His one great love. Just as certain is the determination of our sovereign Lord to do this gathering in the midst of our confusion and misunderstanding. His plan has been visible for quite some time.

When I was privileged to speak at the Jewish synagogue in 1999, I did not ask them to become other than the people God had created them to be. I simply gave thanks for what we shared of God and expressed my hope that one day we would share a good deal more. I was quite clear on what I thought that "more" would be in Yeshua Hamashiya (Jesus the Messiah). But I was equally clear about leaving the sorting of the wheat and the tares in our respective spiritual communities to the Lord. I was able to be so clear on that because I was willing to live in the tension of knowing God's heart without necessarily knowing His mind. The situation had not changed much when I attended some meetings in Redmond, Oregon, in the Spring of 2004 where the avowed agenda was to prepare the way for reconciliation of Messianic Jews with Gentile Christians first, and later of Expectant Jews with Gentile Christians, within the Body of Christ. At those meetings, I was moved to prophesy to the gathered Christians.

"Your fathers longed to see what you see, and they did not. The prophets longed to see what you see, and they did not. The patriarchs longed to see what you see, and they did not. To you have been given the keys to the Kingdom of Heaven. These are not spiritual keys but keys of flesh. The keys are the people who are called by my name. See to it that you take good care of my keys. For a bent key will not open any lock, but a straight key will enter in and will open the doors wide."

God does nothing without telling His servants the prophets what is on His heart (see Amos 3:7). This prophecy does not call the Jews out as though they were the whole people of God. Jesus said that He had other flocks to tend and gather (see John 10:16). But it clearly marks the Jews as the core and heart of this people for whom the Jewish Jesus gave His life, to whom He first returned, and to whom He promised, by the Spirit, that He would again return (see Acts 1:7-11). They are described in the prophecy as the incarnate keys to the Kingdom of Heaven while at the same time depicted as being in the hands and care of the Gentile Church. We are instructed to care for them and to guard their structural integrity. In other words, we must maintain the straightness of the keys or they will be of no use. How does Scripture speak to these issues?

Genesis 12:3 reads like this: "I will bless those who bless you, and whoever curses you I will curse; and all peoples on earth will be blessed through you." The Hebrew word *arar* is translated as "curse" but it has more to do with the effects of cursing than with the act of cursing. It is as though God was saying that if we permit the Jews to be cursed, then we ourselves will be permitted to be cursed, that God will withdraw His protection from those who fail to protect the Jews. Conversely, God clearly promised Abram that all peoples of the earth will participate in the blessings bestowed on the Jews, and He reiterated this promise in Zechariah 8:20-23 when He declared for the returning Jewish exiles a harvest so abundant that it would impact the whole world.

If the Babylonian Exile, occasioned by centuries of Jewish sin, could not negate the covenant of God, can anything cancel it? In Isaiah 61, after He declared the captives set free in Israel, God promised to "make righteousness and praise spring up before all nations" (Isa. 61:11). In the next chapter, He swore that, once the savior had come to Jerusalem, "Never again will I give your grain as food for your enemies and never again will foreigners drink the new wine for which you have toiled" (Isa. 62:8). In Isaiah 56:7, He called His house a house of prayer for all nations. The next verse reads, "The Sovereign Lord declares—he who gathers the exiles of Israel: 'I will gather still others to them besides those already gathered'" (Isa. 56:8). All nations are indeed called, but all are called to Jerusalem, the capitol of the Jews, because the firstborn of Yahweh (the Jews) remain the core of the family of God. When the new covenant was prophesied in Isaiah, Jeremiah, and Ezekiel it has always been understood by Christians as encompassing the Gentile world in Christ. But we dare not forget that the covenant was made with the Jewish people, while we Gentiles were only grafted in, to use Paul's term (see Rom. 11:11-24). Likewise, when Joel prophesied the general outpouring of the Spirit of almighty God on all people (see Joel 2:28), that outpouring followed the prophesied repentance, cleansing, and healing of the land of Israel.

If no Old Testament idolatry can negate the promises of God to the descendants of Abraham, which were fulfilled in the coming of Messiah Yeshua, can the rejection of the Son negate those promises? Paul wrote in Romans 9 that he would give up his own salvation in order to see the salvation of the brothers of his own tribe. "Theirs is the adoption as sons;

theirs the divine glory, the covenants, the receiving of the law, the temple worship and the promises. Theirs are the patriarchs, and from them is traced the human ancestry of Christ, who is God over all, forever praised" (Rom. 9:4-5). Not that Paul considered there to be anything automatic about the salvation of the Jews through their ancestry—he told the Church plainly that this must come by faith and through the confession of Jesus as the Messiah. But Paul must have known that the same God who spoke through the mouth of the prophet Malachi to decry the incidence of divorce and infidelity in Israel toward the wives of their youth would hardly harden His heart toward His own covenant people. Indeed, Paul wrote to the Gentiles, "If...you, though a wild olive shoot, have been grafted in among the others and now share in the nourishing sap from the olive root, do not boast over [this]...You do not support the root, but the root supports you" (Rom. 11:17-18). God assured the Jews that when they believed, they would be grafted in again, and Paul stated in Romans 11:29, "For God's gifts and His call are irrevocable."

Jesus said that not one jot or tittle of the Law and the Prophets would be abrogated until all was fulfilled (see Matt. 5:18). And if all was fulfilled in His first coming, then why must He return and why must He return to Jerusalem? All is indeed fulfilled—the full debt for sin is paid and the foundation laid for eternal life in the death and resurrection of Jesus who is called Christ. But with God, the reality is proleptic— the promise and the fulfillment are one as the acorn and the oak tree are one. The abundant life that we are promised in Christ is here, and we are living it today. Yet the people of God have not yet grown up into the fullness of the stature of

Christ; the world has not been swept clean of sin and suffering; the children have not been gathered to the bosom of the Father. Seen from this perspective, even the resurrection and ascension must be viewed as a deposit on the promise of the Kingdom. But the end of the beginning will be when Jesus returns to claim His throne. The gifts and call of God irrevocably await acceptance from those He has sworn to bless, from all of the nations, beginning with Israel.

RECONCILIATION TRUMPS REPLACEMENT

There is simply no Biblical justification for the idea that God is finished with the Jews or that He has replaced them with the Gentile Church. Likewise, if there is no replacement for the Jews, then there is no reason to suppose that when they receive their Messiah they must leave behind their Jewishness. Paul is explicit in Romans 10:9-11 that only the confession of Jesus and the belief in His name are necessary for salvation. Trust in Christ alone brings life. Yet many in the Body teach that the Jews have forfeited all claims to the love of Yahweh, and many more believe that when a Jew meets Jesus, he must abandon the faith of his fathers—something that Jesus never did.

In Acts 15, the Jerusalem Council deliberated over how to deal with the new Gentile Christians. There had never before been Christians who were not also Jewish. Did they need to observe the whole of the Law or could they be grafted in on the basis of their profession of faith in Christ alone?

The Council wisely decided, in the power of the Holy Spirit, that the profession was sufficient, although the new converts were exhorted to avoid immorality and idolatry as affronts to the Holy Spirit dwelling within them. In this way, the Gentile Church was guided into being by the Jewish Church. Can the Gentile Church justify any other approach (after two millennia of hostility and mutual resentment) when God is calling once again to His firstborn and they are beginning to answer and come into the sheepfold? Is it not now time to say to the Jewish Church, "Worship and adore your Messiah as you choose. We will ask nothing more of you than that you avoid idolatry and immorality, as you once asked those things of us. You need not become Episcopalian or Methodist or Assemblies of God to take your place alongside us in the olive tree. What you are doing in receiving Jesus is finding the ultimate fulfillment of your Jewish faith, and we simply praise God for you."

PrayNorthstate launched a prayer project on Yom Kippur 2004. We sensed a calling from the Lord to be in daily prayer over the last one hundred days of the year, and that meant our project had to begin on Yom Kippur and end on the first day of the new year, the traditional feast of the naming of the Christ child. Our project was modeled after another and very successful project undertaken in nearby Nevada County in which three teams of intercessors were formed from representatives of many congregations and denominational backgrounds, each praying for specific issues of community-wide scope and, therefore, of Kingdom significance. We gathered approximately 130 volunteers from a cross-section of the Body of Christ. We asked one team to pray for peace in the county, while another prayed for an economy of prosperity, and the third prayed for public health. We planned to measure God's response in terms of easily documented reductions in the rates of the eight most prominently-tracked crimes against persons and property, the rate of unemployment, and the numbers of traffic fatalities and cancer admissions to local hospital. We also asked all team members to pray for protection of the county's young people against sudden and violent death (we were averaging about two each month when we began to pray). And God insisted by revelation that we call the project *Paah-ho-ammi*.

The name of the earlier project was simply Arrowhead because the prayers were specifically and consistently targeted on issues of public importance and visibility across the spectrum of Nevada County. The name, like the project, was simplicity itself and presented no difficulties in understanding its import to any of the perspectives embodied in the congregations of the county. It immediately drew broad support from churches across the spectrum of that county's Body. When I went before the Lord to ask His blessing for undertaking a similar project in Shasta County, He waited for a seeming eternity before giving it. Then He said, as clearly as you are reading these words, "Call it *Paah-ho-ammi*." He did not tell me what it meant or even in what language it might be found. He simply told me to call it *Paah-ho-ammi*.

Weeks went by in which I met with many pastors and community leaders to enlist support for this project. The name, in its very mystery, became a turn-on for some and a stumbling block for others. The Lord finally led me to look in the very incomplete Hebrew dictionary located in the back of my Bible concordance. I discovered the word is a perfectly good, and biblical, Hebrew compound meaning, "Cry alas, my people." Why had the Lord insisted that a cross-section of the Gentile Church of Shasta County pray for His intervention in the language of His first-born?

The results of the prayers were spectacular. Traffic fatalities were reduced by about 20 percent, as were cancer admissions and crime in those areas patrolled by the sheriff's department, when compared to the same time period of the previous year. There were no traffic fatalities at all on the most traveled holiday weekends of the year (Thanksgiving, Christmas, and New Year), all of which occurred during the time of prayer. Unemployment went down slightly, even while it was spiking across the nation. But this has proved to be the gift that keeps on giving since building has begun to boom and tourism has broken its own records in terms of hotel room sales. The greater Redding area is now a national leader in housing starts and investment housing. Prophetic statements, released in 2001 and 2004 respectively, to the effect that Redding would be renamed Abundant Springs and that economic renaissance would find its epicenter in the heart of the hotel and motel district are coming true.

Perhaps the most dramatic fruit of the project was that only one death impacted the generation of our children during the time. To see God move from permitting two deaths per month of His young ones to only one in three months is worthy of much prayer and more praise and a whole lot of testimony.

This is a testimonial, not to the power of prayer, but to the power of a God who cannot resist it when His people humble themselves and pray and seek His face. But why did He insist that prayers be framed in the language and during the holy days of the Jews?

The only disappointment in this project was that we were unable to enlist the churches to participate as bodies. There were no Sunday bulletin announcements, no breaking into regularly scheduled Sunday routines to call entire congregations to prayer, and only a scattering of local pastors committed to pray each day. As I write this chapter, we are in the midst of a second wave of *Paah-ho-ammi*, and we have the corporate participation of twelve churches in our county, including some of the powerhouses of the evangelical and charismatic streams. I expect the results of this wave to be even more spectacular with this even more broadly-based participation of the Body of Christ. And I can only answer my own question with two statements from the New Testament.

Paul showed us in Romans 11 that while the Jewish Jesus was both a cornerstone and a stumbling block to the Jews, so also the Jews are both a cornerstone and a stumbling block to the Gentiles. "If some of the branches have been broken off, and you, though a wild olive shoot, have been grafted in among the others and now share in the nourishing sap from the olive root, do not boast over those branches. If you do, consider this: You do not support the root, but the root supports you" (Rom. 11:17-18). And Jesus Himself said, while speaking in the Nazareth synagogue, "The Spirit of the Lord is upon me, because He has anointed me to preach good news to the poor. He has sent me to proclaim freedom for the prisoners and recovery of sight for the blind, to release the oppressed, to proclaim the year of the Lord's favor" (Luke 4:18-19). He went on to say, after He closed the scroll He read from, "Today this scripture is fulfilled in your hearing" (Luke 4:12).

More than two years have passed since we prayed the first phase of *Paah-ho-ammi*, launched and landed on two traditional Jewish holy days and couched in a Jewish name. The second edition was couched between two traditional Christian holy days, the day on which baby Jesus was presented in the Temple at Jerusalem and the National Day of Prayer in the United States, and the results were even more dramatic. Today the testimony of how God responded to the petitions of a small band of intercessors, in a county of nearly two hundred thousand, has overcome the discomfort with the mysterious name of the project. But the name of the project is still *Paah-ho-ammi*—"Cry alas, my people", and the name of the Savior is still Yeshua Hamashiya—the Hebrew equivalent of "Joshua the Messiah" or "Yahweh's salvation the Anointed One."

BLESSING THOSE WHO BLESS THE FIRSTBORN

If we believe that Jesus has set us free and has given us the recovery of sight, then we had better look hard at the reality that He always presented Himself as coming first to give those gifts to the Jewish people. If we believe that God speaks to His people today, as He did in the day when His Son walked our world, then we had better believe that His insistence on a Hebraic framework for prayer telegraphs His insistence that today is the day when He says to all of us, and especially to the firstborn, "Today this scripture is fulfilled in your hearing." He means to make us one Body in Christ now, and He means to do it without permitting any of us to lord it over the others. But He also means to give the firstborn the place at the table that has always been prepared for them.

The history of hostility and bloodshed between Jews and Gentile Christians is long and shameful. No so-called Christian nation can claim clean hands. Edward I of England, the infamous king in the story of *Braveheart*, treated the Jews with far greater brutality than he reserved for the Scots, and he eventually expelled them outright from his kingdom. Spain and Portugal established the Inquisition primarily to force Jews to become Christians and to root out any whose conversion may not have been wholehearted enough to suit the torturers. The history of pogroms in France, Germany, Poland, and Russia would require more space than this chapter can support. And our own nation and Canada refused refuge to those Jews who escaped the Nazi holocaust on ships like the St. Louis. We refused to block UN Security Council resolutions that labeled Israel and Zionism the sole aggressor in the many wars that are really episodes in one great war aimed at exterminating them from the Middle East. Even today, our government pressures Israel to abandon territories it has taken in response to aggression and which it holds for the sake of its own safety, territories that were given to Israel by God within the bounds of the recorded history of the Bible. And each time we side with the enemies of Israel and persuade the Israelis to make territorial concessions, the violence in the Middle East only escalates. This has been the case following their recent withdrawal from Gaza.

At the same time, God's promise to Jews and Gentiles in Genesis 12:3 has proven reliable and demonstrable time after time. The United States, led by President Lyndon Johnson, supported Israel with the materials they needed to wage war and with the political muscle of our nation in the United Nations in 1967, and we saw unprecedented economic prosperity and moral growth (in terms of great leaps forward in the Civil Rights Movement and the enfranchisement of millions of citizens who had been denied the vote and access to our prosperity for centuries), and we are stronger for it. Two of the most far-reaching revivals in our history were launched during that decade—the Jesus People movement and the Charismatic Renewal, which sprung from the unlikely foundation of the liturgical churches. Mission ministries like Youth With A Mission and culturally cleansing streams like Focus on the Family bubbled from that spring and have shared the light of abundant life in Christ with millions at home and abroad. When God says that He will bless those who bless Israel, He is not speaking philosophical concepts; He is making the most pragmatic of commitments!

President Ronald Reagan was one of the best friends Israel has had. The economic recovery that framed his presidency in the eighties eclipsed even that of the sixties and corresponded with a rise in American prestige around the world that had dipped since the tragic events of the Vietnam War.

The leadership triplex of Reagan, Margaret Thatcher, and Pope John Paul II brought down the Soviet Empire and defanged world communism as a threat to international freedom. One of the principal character traits the three leaders shared was their outspoken love for Eretz Israel.

The economic good times, with a two-year wrinkle of recession during the first Bush administration (which was one of the mildest recessions ever recorded and was far less devastating than the one that swept an increasingly anti-semitic Europe and Asia), continued and expanded during the two terms of President Bill Clinton. Clinton attempted to establish his legacy as a peacemaker by demanding concessions from Israel during the second half of his presidency, and the fruit was a deep recession, inherited by his successor in office, the younger George Bush, and the frequent terrorist attacks on Americans and American installations with seeming impunity for the terrorists. This legacy reached a ghastly conclusion on September 11, 2001 and came to a dramatic halt during the last four years of an administration that, for the most part, is strong in its support for Israel and her right to life, liberty, and the pursuit of happiness.

It would be ridiculously over simplified to imagine that all of our fortunes are nothing more than a reflection of our national attitude toward Israel, but the relationship cannot be denied. It played out just as surely in the recovery from post-war recession that plagued the late forties, a recession that broke following President Harry Truman's recognition of Israel (we were the first great power to do so), which then erupted in the prosperity revolution of the fifties when

Dwight Eisenhower, also a friend of Israel, led the land and people of America. And it played out just as surely in the high inflation and cultural disarray during the years Richard Nixon and Jimmy Carter occupied the White House, years in which abortion on demand, divorced and broken families, addiction to drugs, and defilement by pornography became the epidemics with which we still contend.

GOD'S LONGING TO GATHER

It would be just as oversimplified to paint the Jewish people as the helpless and wholly innocent victims of all that has happened to them. Jesus Himself said to His people,

O Jerusalem, Jerusalem, you who kill the prophets and stone those sent to you, how often have I longed to gather you as a hen gathers her chicks under her wings, but you were not willing. Look, your house is left to you desolate. For I tell you, you will not see me again until you say, "Blessed is he who comes in the Name of the Lord" (Matt. 23:37-39).

The Jews were chosen out of all of the peoples of the world to enjoy a unique revelation and relationship with the King of the universe, the Creator of all that is, and the great lover of all that He has created. Their history in their own sacred books is one of repeated rejection and betrayal of the One who brought them out of Egypt and who continued to lavish His love on them. The cavalcade of martyrs found in Hebrews 11 is primarily composed of Jews who were sawn in half and worse for the crime of calling their people back from the abyss of idolatry. They were sent into brutal exile, to Assyria and later Babylon (both of which were located within the present-day borders of Iraq), because they would not soften their stiff necks toward their Father in Heaven. They lost even the restored Eretz Israel because they were so divided among themselves that they asked a Roman general to sort out their politics, and he obliged by bringing his army and setting the stage for Herod the Great and the desperate times into which the Messiah strode. They rejected their Savior, and then they provoked the Romans to destroy their temple and their city in A.D. 70. And they were so embittered against the newly-named Christians that they expelled us from their synagogues when we thought of ourselves as nothing more than a fulfilled sect within Judaism, long before Christians ever thought of excluding Jews from the life of worship we are called to share.

I know personally people of Ukrainian descent who tell of how the Jews slaughtered their relatives. The headlines of the world press tell how the Israeli government, in its understandable quest to protect the people from the scourge of fanatical suicide bombers, chooses to build fences across land shared with Palestinians who are then cut off from both work and water. By depending on their own engineering and military skills instead of on the One who built Israel over the largest fresh water aquifer in the world, they take a far deadlier risk than that offered by the bombers. There is a reason behind God's prophetic word, "Out of Egypt I called my son"

(Hosea 11:1), that reaches beyond the mere circumstances of Joseph seeking refuge for his family and even beyond the fact of the pre-Mosaic exile. Perhaps the Jews need us Gentiles for the wholeness of their faith just as much as we need them.

I have personally witnessed people of German descent, in settings of corporate reconciliation where other tribes were representationally coming together after centuries of enmity and genocidal hatred, repenting and begging with tears for forgiveness from representatives of both Israel and the Messianic Jewish community for the Holocaust. And I have seen them refused. The Jews are indeed a stiff-necked and rebellious people who need to receive their Messiah, and one wonders what to do with them.

God has an answer, of course. Love them. If we are family with God, then we are surely family with the Jews. Family loves and receives family and lets family be who they are. Family has your back, not because they think you deserve it, but because you are family. And, at least for Messianic Jews, that sword cuts both ways.

I carry the blood of Abraham and Isaac and Jacob in my veins. I was raised in no faith at all and in a totally Gentile culture. I met Jesus in 1970, at the age of twenty-two, and I entered the ordained ministry of the Gentile Body of Christ fifteen years later. I was shocked and devastated to learn of my Jewish roots on my mother's side in my mid thirties (I would have been proud to know who I really was all of my life) because my mother had kept the information back due to her own shame over the Holocaust. Today I rejoice with my Gentile relatives in the faith of Christ once crucified because we have the grafted branches and leaves of the tree of life, and we are both called and empowered to share with the whole world. And I rejoice with my Jewish relatives in the faith of the One long promised who would lead all people, even those of the other flocks He mentions in John 10, beside green pastures and still living waters that become a mighty river of life issuing from Messiah's throne in the Jerusalem of the Jews. The Gentile Church is the community that has spread all over the world, but the Jews have always been and will always be the keepers of the flame. And we will not see Heaven in all of its fullness without one another.

One of the proudest and happiest moments of my life came about when I stood on the banks of the Sacramento River with a group of Gentile and Jewish Christians and worshipped the Lord our God one night in 2002. Arni and Yonit Klein are Messianic Jewish leaders of American birth and Jewish lineage who at that time led a 24/7 worship ministry in Tel Aviv. They travel the world seeking to foster reconciliation between Jews and Gentiles and they were guests in our home for this purpose. We had gathered at the river so that we might pour a bottle of water from the Jordan River into our own Sacramento River and celebrate the Supper of the Lord together. We had just shared the news with each other that northern California is the roof over the second largest aquifer in the world as well as the home to the first Jewish community on the west coast. After pouring the Jordan River water, we presented the Kleins with a bottle of Sacramento River water we had taken from the headwaters that morning—they would pour it into the Jordan when they returned home.

During the course of several days of visiting and meeting with many leaders in our home while we hosted the Kleins, they told of a remarkable thing that had just happened in Israel. Forty Messianic rabbis had covenanted to place a full page ad in an Israeli newspaper that enjoyed national circulation. The ad would simply express the patriotism of the Messianic community and their commitment to bless the nation with every prayer and every breath. What was truly mind blowing about the story was that these Jewish rabbis, world-renowned for millennia over their inability to agree on anything, had come together on the wording of the ad in about 30 minutes.

Looking over the group on the river bank on that last evening of their visit, I reflected on the worship and prophetic declarations of the joining of our two communities in ushering in the Kingdom of God, the one in which all of the blind and deaf are restored and all of the dead are raised and all of the poor are blessed with the good news of abundant life in Christ Jesus because no one is taking offense at Him or His (see Matt. 11:2-6). I thought of the miracle of agreement that had been given to the rabbis in Israel that day, and of the miracle of God's own presence among us in the Supper that bears His name. And I could not resist the pastor's urge to count the house that seems to come over us at every worship service. There were 40.

It is time, today, for the Body of Christ to become the Body of Yeshua and vice versa. If the Body is to be One, then all of the branches and certainly the root need to be brought in. All have a piece of the revelation of God to share at the table. God said, in Isaiah 56:7, "...Their burnt offerings and sacrifices will be accepted on my altar; for my house will be called a house of prayer for all nations." Surely the Jews, just as they are, while clinging to the hem of the garment of Yeshua Hamashiya, are included in that calling. I speak principally to the Gentile community, for I have more of the blood of the Celt and the Viking and German in me than of the older (in Him) kind. But the truth is that He is waiting for both communities to approach each other with the words of Isaiah, when he said, "I am a man of unclean lips, and I live among a people of unclean lips, and I my eyes have seen the King, the Lord Almighty" (Isa. 6:5). To an approach like that, the Lord can only interject His words, "...I have come that they may have life, and have it to the full" (John 10:10).

Chapter 11

FIVE-FOLD LEADERS WORKING TOGETHER

IN the spring of 1997, a group of about a dozen pastors gathered in an upper room of the gym of the Sacred Heart Catholic Church in the little town of Anderson, California. We were a rag tag cross section of the Body of Christ that included charismatics, evangelicals, and liturgical types (both Catholic and Protestant) all praying together. We were seeking God's face in the Scriptures and asking Him for a vision of how the Church might respond to the coming federal welfare reform law in our community, which boasted one of the highest unemployment rates in the state. We spent most of the day together, and by the end of it, we were convinced that God meant for the Church to lead in this move of His to resurrect the nation, beginning with our county. One very dynamic dimension of the vision He had given to us was to be an agency of the Church; we would call it Faithworks Coalition.

This coalition would be a collection of volunteers and paid staff from many churches in Shasta County; it would cooperate with government agencies without being subservient to them; and it would operate on the principal that giving a man a fish was good but teaching a man to fish was much better. Implicit and explicit to the vision was that we would not limit our activities to helping people leave the welfare roles. God impressed on our hearts that economic self-sufficiency was only the tip of the iceberg of the grace He meant to pour out. We would, while cooperating with secular servants, offer life as eternal as it was abundant to those who asked our help. We spoke this vision with the authority of the Lord who gave it to us; we prophesied it.

Within eighteen months, Faithworks Coalition, working with County Social Services, had cut the welfare rolls of the county in half. Approximately 70 churches in the county had signed on as partners in the ministry. Every client had been offered, without having anything forced down their throats, a shot at eternal life and the fellowship of a local church that seemed compatible with that client's needs and background, regardless of denomination. Restoration Enterprises had been birthed along the same lines in order to minister to people recently released from prison and to keep them from going back. The Good News Rescue Mission had received a gift of 700 acres of agricultural land in the east county, the direct application of one of the features of the vision we had seen in the gym that day, and people were coming from all over the state to see the wildly successful faith-based recovery ministries that Shasta County boasted. Faithworks Coalition became one of the nationally recognized points of light, and sister ministries of the same name were being established in other states as well as in other California localities.

Today, Faithworks of Shasta County is operating twelve grant-funded apartments for transitional housing for the people that God is moving into independence from government handouts and into a more total dependence on Him. The complex is called Francis Court, after the saint who said to preach the gospel by every available means, using even words if necessary. It grows from the vision of one man, the current executive director, who does not think of himself as being the least bit prophetic. Robert Scott is a retired Air Force fighter pilot who met the Lord in a near fatal plane crash. He wants to do what Jesus does, and he believes that he and the Lord are on the same page in that desire.

The premise on which all of this is based is as simple as Proverbs 29:18. "Where there is no revelation, the people cast off restraint...." When we gathered in that upper room, we had covenanted with one another to use the brains God gave us, but only after receiving the vision He had promised to those who seek His face. He said it literally in Jeremiah 29:11-13,

> *"For I know the plans I have for you," declares the Lord, "plans to prosper you and not to harm you, plans to give you hope and a future. Then you will call upon Me and come and pray to Me, and I will listen to you. You will seek Me and find Me when you seek me with all of your heart."*

The most literal translation of Proverbs 29:18 is something like, "If you would live, you must look God in the face." When we gathered in that gymnasium, we decided that we would use our brains to think and plan and act upon, not what our brains could produce, but only on the vision that only God could produce. What He showed us was far too grandiose for us to handle; but it was just the right size for what He had in mind, and it is still unfolding today.

This is not the only prophetic manifestation in the region. In the Spring of 2001, the ministry of PrayNorthstate, which Diana and I lead, was just launching. While on my way to a pastors' prayer meeting in the county north of Shasta, I was praying as I drove, and the Lord released another dimension of the vision He had set free in 1997. He simply spoke out that He was renaming the City of Redding "Abundant Springs."

I knew that the first name given to the region now called Redding, California was Poverty Flats. The appellation was birthed in the derision of the gold miners who found no gold inside the limits of the city. The current name is actually a misspelling of the name of the pioneer landowner, of European stock, in these parts, one Pearson B. Reading. A moment's thought can make it seem as though everything about Redding is the fruit of accident or disappointment. But there are no accidents and even fewer disappointments in the Kingdom of Heaven. And God had just spoken clearly that He knew this place as the City of Abundant Springs. My options were to either sit on the knowledge He had imparted or to speak the prophetic word, however foolish and unsupported it may seem to be. I chose to speak the word and to speak it repeatedly.

The past three years have seen some remarkable changes in Redding and the surrounding area. Many people have taken to calling, and praying for, Redding as Abundant Springs. The Sacramento River has been spanned by what we call the Sundial Bridge, a landmark that has been featured in national magazines. The city has broken its own records for hotel room sales the past two year, and this too was prophesied. New commercial zones are being developed, and housing is booming so much that Redding was declared the top market in the nation for investment housing in 2005. The locally owned utility is selling power to other cities and even other states. Big League Dreams is a family sports park that is now operational. The downtown is beginning to bloom as a cultural center anchored by a fully renovated theatre called the Cascade on one end and a block under development for Christ-honoring businesses on the other. Light manufacturing is returning for the first time since the timber industry downsized in the early nineties, and orders for timber are again healthy and nearing their pre-1993 levels.

Redding is now home to an international school of supernatural ministry with campuses in six locations and an institute of Kingdom Business that teaches business people to seek their vision from the Lord before they make a move. Public schools, which once seemed to be black holes for academic failure, are becoming magnet schools; several have even been named California Distinguished Schools in the past year. It even turns out that, – unbeknown to a newcomer to the area like myself, Redding and its environs are literally placed over abundant springs of water. The springs are so abundant that, in earlier times, the biggest construction challenge in Redding was keeping the artesian water from coming up through the floor boards.

Early in 2004, a prophetic word was released over Redding's downtown mall. The mall has long been a political football as politicians and commercial leaders jockeyed for position and method to revive the commercial vitality that has transferred from the mall to another part of town. The prophecy said that the mall was intended by the Lord to be a center for service and ministry. In the intervening months, the long-awaited removal of the mall's roof has begun, and this will eventually permit traffic in the downtown to assume a more normal pattern. Shasta College has plans underway to become the mall's anchor tenant. And it turns out that most of the existing concerns in the mall are either ministry or service, while commercial spaces remain largely vacant. At the same time, a prophetic word was released over a business concern on Redding's hotel row that this company would become the heart of a business revival in that strip. But first the management would become believers, either by transfer or conversion. At last report, the first part of the prophecy is being rapidly fulfilled. The fun part is watching the rest of the revelation unfold, in the mall and on that strip.

Prophecy, of the biblical kind, is alive and well in northern California and in the rest of the modern world. But the challenge for ambassadors of reconciliation is to avoid making an idol of the gift (on the one hand) or shunning the gift (on the other) in the name of honoring the source of all gifts.

HIS SPIRIT POURED OUT

Joel 2:28-29 is one of the most well-known pieces in the Bible. "And afterward I will pour out my spirit on all people. Your sons and daughters will prophesy, your old men will dream dreams, your young men will see visions. Even on My servants, both men and women, I will pour out My spirit in those days." But is every spirit that is poured out the Holy Spirit? Is there a way that anyone of devotion to God can tell His voice?

I had the privilege of meeting Dr. Jack Hayford in the summer of 1995. I was attending a Congress on the Holy Spirit in Orlando, Florida, and Hayford was one of many speakers at that event. I had admired him as one of the finest teachers and prophetic voices of the twentieth century, and I made a point of attending the workshop for which he was scheduled. I have long since forgotten the topic on which he was speaking that day, but I will never forget the shock of hearing him give a ringing endorsement for something that I was pretty well convinced was of the devil.

At that time, the so-called Toronto Blessing was the hottest topic of conversation in the charismatic and Pentecostal wing of the Church, not to mention on the covers of *Newsweek* and any number of other national magazines.

The phenomenon had broken out in a little congregation of the Vineyard Fellowship in Toronto, Canada, right next to the international airport. It was characterized, or so the secular media presented it, by groups of Christians erupting in prolonged laughter. The laughter was sometimes replaced by weeping and, sometimes, by animal noises such as the barking of dogs. People were flocking to the Toronto Airport Vineyard Church by tens of thousands and the church itself had grown from a membership of a couple of hundred people to more than four thousand. At least that many attended their nightly revival services, and the pastor, a man named John Arnott, had no explanation for it except that the Holy Spirit had shown up one day and taken up residence.

I was not raised in a church of any kind; when I became a Christian, I had no tradition and no churchy baggage to shed. I met the Lord Jesus in a public high school classroom while I was proctoring a test for a class of business students. I was promptly led into a liturgical church, and I cut my teeth on the rituals and sacramental practices of that branch of the Body. Most of my friends were evangelicals, and I was soon steeped in their way of doing and understanding theology and the Scriptures. In 1987, two years after my own ordination into the professional ministry, I received the baptism in the Holy Spirit and, by the time I was attending this congress and listening to one of my heroes speak, I was both familiar and comfortable with the gifts of the Spirit and the mind-set that all things that make a difference are indeed a gift (a charism) from the Lord of life. Tongues, healing, words of knowledge, and prophecy were special to me but neither unusual nor threatening. But I believed in testing the various manifestations of the gifts against the witness of the Bible as thoroughly as I believed in the gifts themselves.

And then Jack Hayford said that the Toronto Blessing was a gift of the Holy Spirit to bring revival to a hungry world, and I could find no reference to holy laughter in my Bible. And he admitted that he hadn't even been to Toronto to see it for himself, but he still he blessed it! I decided at that moment that I had to talk with him personally and ask him what he believed about Toronto and why he believed it. At the same time, it was obvious that each of the thousand or so people crowding his workshop would love to have the same privilege. I was in the back of a cavernous room; clearly, if I was to have my private conference with this man, it would have to be ordained and orchestrated by God. I spread my hands right there and said, "Lord, if You want me to talk to him, if this is as important to You as it seems to be to me, well, it is all in Your hands, and if not, that's okay with me. Your will be done."

As he concluded his talk, I began to move forward. As I had imagined, there was a solid mass of humanity between me and the speaker. He was talking with those who had managed to press in close, but as I watched, the crowd seemed literally to part in front of me, and I found myself walking up the aisle that had opened. I was the last to reach him before he moved on to his own next engagement; he asked me to walk with him as we talked. I recounted my own recollection of what he had said about Toronto, and he confirmed that I had heard rightly. I said that I knew of no biblical referent and I added that I was troubled by his serene acceptance of something he had never seen up close and personal. He stopped and turned to me, eyes kind but with an edge in his voice. "Tell me," he asked, "do you see the hand of the Lord in this?"

I thought back over everything I had heard about this movement, how the church had exploded with new people who had never before heard the gospel, how the joy they received was moving out from Toronto, how even the secular media was talking about Jesus in magazine cover stories and nightly news broadcasts, how tired church leaders were returning from Toronto on fire and on mission again. I said, "Yes, but..." and he never let me finish. "No buts," he said, "Do you see the hand of the Lord in this?" I said that, yes, I did see His hand. He gave me that trademark Hayford smile and said, "Then lighten up." No stranger to prophecy, I had just been initiated into the latter day prophetic movement.

Nine months later, in the spring of 1996, Diana and our children and I went to Toronto to see for ourselves. We found little to remind us of our previous charismatic experience, not to mention our evangelical and liturgical background. We also saw little of what the national magazines seemed to be so energized about. What we did see was a multitude of people from many denominations and traditions within the Body of Christ united by their common hunger for a fresh breath of the Spirit of the living God. We saw people worshipping with abandon, shamelessly, and we saw many experience a deep healing and cleansing of heart and mind while seemingly in a deep trance or, in some cases, while convulsively jerking on the floor but obviously free of pain or discomfort. We saw some of the famous laughter, although we encountered no barking or other potentially obnoxious noisemaking.

The principal complaint about Toronto, and the outbreaks in Pensacola, Kansas City, and even my home city of Redding, California, has always been that it is not properly pastored. What critics mean is that the outbreak is not managed or structured, as though one could manage the Holy Spirit! But what I witnessed in Toronto was the most accountable outbreak of the Spirit that I could imagine. People who believed they had a prophetic word had first to submit it to a team set apart for evaluating such words. People desiring to pray for others in the services were asked to refrain from that unless they were part of another team trained and set apart for that purpose. Every effort was made to release the Spirit of God and quench any other spirits that might have found their way inside.

I left Toronto fully prepared in my heart for the ministry I would begin in the greater Redding area in a scant three months. The words of Jack Hayford rang in my head as my family and I packed and placed our home for sale and prayed that God would have His way with us in a freshness that we had not previously known. Everybody thinks that the way they met the Holy Spirit is the only way it can be done. But the Lord is forever saying, "Behold, I am doing a new thing. I come to tell you about it."

So, why are so many people afraid of the prophetic?

STRAW IN THE MANGER

For one thing, as someone once said, there is a lot of straw in that manger along with the baby. Prophecy is nothing but a euphemistic anchor term for every word that God has spoken, is speaking, and will speak. Every word of Scripture, for example, is a prophetic word because it is a word that God spoke. One of the words that God spoke, in Amos 3:7, is that He never does anything without first revealing it to His servants, the prophets. Another is the word in Joel 2:28 that says that in the latter days He will pour out His Spirit on all mankind and all men and women will have the privilege of prophecy. If this is true, and it is, then God must be continuing His prophetic activity with the prophetic partnership of human beings right now and today. But there is straw in that manger; there are words released as though they came from God but about which God knows absolutely nothing. It was the same in Jeremiah's day.

The Old Testament is full of stories of men who claimed to speak for Yahweh and did not, but Jeremiah devoted more than two whole chapters to this material. He predicted in Chapter 27 that many false prophets would promise a quick end to the Babylonian exile, and then he opened Chapter 28 with the story of Hananiah, who made a big splash with his claim that God would remove the Babylonian yoke from the necks of the people of God in two years. Jeremiah did not openly challenge Hananiah, but he simply remarked that he hoped the false prophet was right and noted that the prophecy should soon come true if it was the truth. What actually happened, of course, was that Hananiah died within a few months.

In Chapter 29, Jeremiah wrote to the exiles, unmasking the false prophets Ahab (not *that* Ahab), Zedekiah, and Shemaiah, all of whom had been complaining that Jeremiah was such a downer of a prophet! Jeremiah prophesied that the exile would last for seventy years, and history would show that he was absolutely right. But that chapter also contained some of the most encouraging words in the Bible: "'For I know the plans I have for you,' declares the Lord, 'plans to prosper you and not to harm you, plans to give you hope and a future. Then you will call upon Me and come and pray to Me and I will listen to you. You will seek Me and find Me when you seek Me with all your heart" (Jer. 29:11-13). The Lord was actually promising that when we seek Him we cannot fail to find Him, and He has a much better track record for keeping His word than we do.

Yet, if we believe Jeremiah, then most of the prophets were false. (He indicated a multitude of them in Jeremiah 29.) How can we tell them apart? The Biblical witness is consistent, from Deuteronomy to Jeremiah to the Lord Jesus, that a prophet can be believed when his words come true. It sounds simple enough, but some prophetic utterances call for action before it will be possible to verify them through performance. That calls for some risk-taking.

Chuck Pierce is a contemporary prophet with an excellent track record. It has already been told in an earlier chapter how he predicted the wildfires that devastated southern California in 2003 and the way in which God would make

weather miracles to bless the Herculean efforts of firefighters. In the same prophetic statement, Chuck also predicted
the torrential rains that fell all over the state in December
2003 and for the first two months of 2004. People of prayer,
armed with the prophetic warning and knowing how much a
good snowpack was needed, prayed that rains would turn to
snow, even in the cities. When the downpour began in
Redding, three and a quarter inches fell in a little more than
24 hours. Most of it fell as snow, and we praised the Lord for
His goodness in our land. Once again, the Lord spoken true
while expecting His servants to partner with Him.

Wendel McGowan is a pastor and friend of mine from
Redding. He is a well-known prophetic figure locally, and he's
gaining acclaim more and more beyond our local region.
Some eight years ago, he spoke a prophetic word over me to
the effect that I would become an apostle to my own denomination, the Episcopal Church, and would have a part in leading my own people back to our roots in the Great
Commission. Prior to that time, I had done some extra-
parochial preaching and teaching within my denomination,
and I had held several localized leadership posts, but nothing
of the grandiosity of what my friend predicted was even
remotely on the horizon. When Diana and I founded
PrayNorthstate in 2001, no one could have been less interested in our interdenominational ministry and vision than my
own denomination. My friend just kept faithfully speaking the
word God had given him for me.

Then came the General Convention of 2003 and the beginning of the end of the American Episcopal Church as I have

known it. A big part of my function in PrayNorthstate is to come alongside leaders in all denominations and settings, both sacred and secular, and serve as God gives me opportunity and insight. Many orthodox Episcopalian congregations were in deep despair at the apostasy of the national authorities and many of the bishops. I found myself with numerous opportunities to bring interdenominational teams that I have trained and to bless the ministries of these churches, some of whom were already under fire for their stand for the Word of God and His command to make disciples. Each of these churches has experienced a jumpstart of Holy Spirit empowered authority for ministry in their communities and a strong impulse to push out into their communities in partnership with the rest of the Body. In many cases, the pressure on them from denominational headquarters has been eliminated or reduced as God has come in answer to our prayers. And I am finding that my conference schedule for this spring alone is more than a quarter filled with Episcopal churches hungry for transformation. Wendel's prophecy is beginning to come true, and all that is required of me is that I do the ministry to which I am called and include Episcopalians in it wherever possible.

On the other hand, there have been multitudes of false prophecies in the current prophetic revival, just as there were in Jeremiah's time. There have also been misguided and ham-handed efforts to shoehorn people into compliance with prophecies that have not yet manifested at ground level and may never do so. When the jury is clearly out, our place is to wait on the Lord, in all of the tension that may generate, until the jury is in.

Prior to the opening of the Iraq war, there were numerous prophecies about American prospects in the coming conflict. One very prominent national figure called for a million people to pray each day and asserted that, if that happened, Sadaam Hussein would step down from office and war would be averted. Some two million people registered at the man's website and presumably prayed each day, and the prophecy was just dead wrong. Another prominent prophetic figure assured his disciples that the war would be over in two weeks, and still another said God had told him that American armor would be trapped, ambushed, and destroyed in the Iraqi desert. Yet another claimed that God had told him that Americans would face high casualty rates in this war (it has actually claimed fewer lives than any comparable conflict in modern times). None of these men recanted or apologized for misleading many people.

Back at home, where the stakes were not life and death in Iraq, a prophecy was delivered several years ago to the effect that California would be divided into eight regional spokes for purposes of concentrating prayer for transformation of the state. A ministry fellowship called Pray California grew out of the response to this word, and an effort was made to identify leaders and representatives from each region for purposes of worshipping and ministering together whenever that might be feasible. The rub was that only seven regions had actually identified themselves when Pray California was formed, and some of those did not have an identifiable leadership, at least one which was known to the leaders of the fellowship. Most of the leaders were content to let things plunk down and manifest themselves over time (the prophecy had been uttered, after all, by a very reliable person), but some insisted that eight regions had to be identified at once, along with their leaders, because the prophecy had said it would be so. The counsel of Gamaliel in Acts 5 is that, if the word is from God, it cannot be stopped, and if it is not from God, it will collapse under its own weight. Those who thought they were defending prophecy could have saved themselves a lot of stress by consulting Scripture.

But how do we tell them apart if we cannot easily wait them out for fulfillment? The Spirit of God in First Thessalonians 5:19-21 calls on all men and women to test the spirits without quenching the Spirit. It is not that difficult to do.

Testing the Spirits

If we return to Jeremiah and the false prophets, we see right away that Jeremiah's word was consistent with the Bible as his contemporaries would have known it. Moses called on the children of Israel to choose life in obedience to the commandments of God or death in defiance of them. The judges of Israel, and such recognized prophets as Samuel and Elijah, offered the same message. In Jeremiah 28, the prophet spoke in concert with the recognized words of God, while the false prophet, Hananiah, offered Jacob an essentially free pass. Biblical consistency is the first test of authentic prophecy, whether the speaker is a Chuck Pierce or a Joe Doaks.

Jeremiah also and always called Israel back to her original vision and identity that she had straight from Yahweh. His book is laced with Yahweh's pleadings to return to Him and to the worship that He had commanded. The false prophets had no sense of history; the dreams they attributed to the prompting of God were complete in themselves and offered nothing but immediate gratification to those who hungered for it. I do not mean to say that every word of prophecy must contain chapter-and-verse references to the genesis events of its subject and audience. But there must be at least an implied consistency because the Lord has always presented Himself as a God of history who reveals Himself in history. Whether or not the prophetic word maintains continuity with the original vision for the people is a second test for its authenticity.

Jeremiah also looked ahead to the future destiny of the people because God looks to the fulfillment of His purpose in calling and creating them. He related to them the hard truths of reaping what they have sown, but he was also well aware of the fact that God never changes His plans or His promises. Jeremiah does not stubbornly repeat the promise of God to make all nations blessed because of Abraham's faithfulness, but he was on the lookout for a renewal and freshening of that vision. When God began to speak to him of a new covenant to be written on the hearts of every Jew, he recognized the voice of God in the contents of the message, something the false prophets would have likely blown off because of the very grandiosity of such a message in the face of the national debacle. The third test of prophetic authenticity is that the message calls out or renews the prophetic destiny of those to whom it is addressed.

When a prophetic word meets all three stands of the test, although it cannot be finally confirmed until it comes to pass, it has demonstrated that it is worth risking for. It has placed itself in a new wineskin, and that skin can now be stretched as the revelation ferments and bubbles to full potency. The hearers become like the man with the five talents (see Matt. 25:14-30), and the only question is whether we will invest in the Kingdom now that we have our marching orders. The investment is the same one for which Isaiah called some 600 years before Christ. Put watchmen on the walls; give yourselves no rest, and give Yahweh no rest until He comes and establishes Jerusalem (see Isa.62:6-7).

But some leaders in the Church fear those very watchmen, and some of the watchmen resent the gatekeepers we call the leadership of the Church. Since both receive their calling from the Lord Himself, reconciliation leading to a renewal of covenantal unity is imperative. The potency of the five-fold ministry (as depicted in Ephesians 4:11-16) is at stake. And neither camp is without sin.

Bob Jones is another prophet with national and international credentials. He came out of the Kansas City movement that grew around the ministry of Mike Bickle and the International Houses of Prayer. He has served in a durable ministry for some two decades. I was privileged to hear Bob speak in Redding a couple of years back, and the thing I remember most was his exhortation to think of the five-fold ministry as though it were the crew divisions for the Starship Enterprise. He had a place on the starship for everyone—apostles, prophets, evangelists, pastors, and teachers. He was quite clear that the prophets belonged in the engine room, right alongside Scotty.

Mr. Scott may not seem very prophetic to many of us, but he was indeed the vision-caster for the ship. He knew more of the structure, the potentialities, and the limitations of the ship than did even her captain. He was the one who guarded and exhorted and continually returned attention to the mission and vision of her five-year voyage. His zeal, his creativity, and his perseverance were both contained and released in his duty post. It is a fitting, and prophetic, tribute to James Doohan, the actor who played Scotty for three decades of Star Trek, that he would be the first of the principal personalities associated with that movie and TV series to have his ashes shot into space (although he was not the first of that elite group to pass away). His remains go where no man has gone before, like many other prophets.

But Bob Jones was equally clear that the prophets should not be permitted to occupy other spaces in the ship, especially the bridge. The very zeal that makes them such effective and relentless stewards of the ship's power plant will likely inhibit their ability to see the big picture, the stuff that lies between the prophetic vision and its realization at ground level. Prophets tend to be poor leaders of men because their eyes are not on the men themselves but rather on the goal beyond the immediate relationship. They too often lack the qualities of mercy and flexibility, and sometimes see these qualities in others as a lack of commitment. Apostles and pastors belong on the bridge, although Bob Jones placed the latter in the medical department, under the watchful and compassionate eye of Dr. McCoy. To paraphrase Bob's comments on the prophets: Put them in the engine room, and your ship will never break down or falter. Put them on the bridge, and the ship may blow itself up.

Yet many prophets, because they see the destination so clearly and tend to think in black-and-white terms, demand to serve on the bridge. No prophet in the Old Testament was ever called to be king, although some of the kings did prophesy. (The office is not the same as the gift.) They were never called to military leadership (Samuel and Moses were primarily judges in Israel.) and they never had charge of the treasury or the temple. The prophets exhorted and encouraged the king; they clarified his situation and rallied the people. They were the stewards of the vision that was and is Israel. But they observed proper protocol when addressing the king; even Elijah spoke to Ahab only when permission was granted. And when the word had been duly delivered, the prophet went away; having done his duty, he let it go and left it between the ruler and the One who reigns. If there is to be reconciliation between prophets and apostles, and I sweep the pastors under the apostolic mantle here for the sake of the conversation, the prophets will have to recognize and embrace their place in the engine room.

PROPHETIC PROTOCOL

I always teach the folks who minister as intercessors for PrayNorthstate that if they have a word from the Lord, or think they have a word from the Lord, for the pastor, school principal, or business owner that we came to bless, they should give the word, however outlandish it may sound even to them, and then let it go.

In the Body of Christ, it is the apostles who have the command or leadership function. Yet Captain Kirk would have shot himself in the head with a photon torpedo launcher before he would have attempted to micro-manage every department. He was the first to acknowledge that he did not know the power compartments as well as did his chief engineer. The final decision was his to make. But as a good leader, he made it only after carefully hearing, considering, and usually deferring as much as possible to the input of those that he trusted enough to make department heads. If there is to be reconciliation between prophets and apostles, there will have to be, if not a sharing of power, a profound sharing of honor and respect, flowing from the apostles to the prophets.

I always defer to the apostolic leadership of the pastor, school principal, or business or government leader to whom we are ministering in PrayNorthstate, and so I expect that as we honor that person he or she will become willing to be influenced by the prophetic material that we may bring into the relationship. This deference is without reference to what I think they understand about apostolic leadership.

We also need to spend some time on the connection between prophets and intercessors; it is an intimate one. Prophets mediate between God and people; there is no presupposition that mediation is necessary and certainly no necessary sense of an adversarial relationship. It is simply a mediating office. Intercessors are people who stand between adversaries; the adversaries may be God and people, or they may be two or more people at odds with one another. My favorite illustration of the work of the intercessor concerns my son, Chris, when he was about two years old. Chris was a very active boy and his energy, curiosity, and creativity got him into trouble more than once. One day, he had done some harm to a little girl named Shannon who was visiting. Chris was sent to time-out in his room, and Shannon, without waiting for or expecting an apology, planted herself in front of the closed door to his room and began chanting (parental consumption) "Chrissofer out! Chrissofer out!" With his victim leading the charge for his early release, we could not resist for long. Neither can God.

There is no office of the intercessor in the Bible. It does not appear in any of the lists of spiritual gifts. On the contrary, all Christians were exhorted to pray without ceasing in First Thessalonians 5:17, and Jesus described His Father's house as a house of prayer for all nations (see Mark 11:17), quoting from Isaiah 56:7. Isaiah also gave the word of the Lord that all of Israel should give themselves and the Lord no rest from their intercession until He came to establish Jerusalem (see Isa. 62:6-7). Yahweh told Solomon directly that if the people called by His name, the whole people, would humble themselves and pray and seek His face, that He would hear from Heaven and come and heal them (see 1 Kings 8:22-61). Jesus held up the widow who pestered the unjust judge in Luke 18:1-8 as the model for all prayer warriors. And if the widow is called to this calling, then who is not called to it?

On the other hand, there is and should be great honor for those who answer the call to intercede. If anyone who prays for others and seeks the reconciliation of adversaries is an intercessor, then it is just as true that all too few answer this call. Even fewer are faithful to it over the long haul. There can be no more thankless calling, and no more honorable one, than that of the intercessor. These are the people who pray in the paving of the straight highway in the desert for God. They bring about the atmospheric change that makes communities where sin has abounded into hospitable places for the Spirit of the living God, who is then free to come by invitation and transform these communities into provinces of the Kingdom. These are the ones who activate, with their prayers, the prophetic visions cast over a city.

I love to tell the story of acclaimed prophetess Cindy Jacobs when she was preaching in the Hemet, California, church of Pastor Bob Beckett, shortly after that city had entered into the process of transformation in a visible way. Cindy interrupted her sermon three times to fix the pastor with her gaze and declare, "You were not God's first choice to lead this movement in your city!" On the third time she added, "But when you said yes to God, you became His first choice." The same reasoning applies to intercessors wherever they may be. And God loves His intercessors with unlimited passion for the simple reason that they have said yes to Him.

To be sure, there are various levels of gifting and experience in intercession. My wife, Diana, thinks nothing of spending hours on her face before God whenever He calls her into intense travail, and she has spent as much as eight hours in prayer for a woman with a bad back and a badly wounded heart. I am attention deficit disordered, and I think nothing of spending seconds, sometimes minutes, in undistracted prayer. Both of us are prophetic, although we are not prophets; but our visions and prophetic words come in very different forms and on very diverse topics. We are two different members of the same Body, energized by the same Holy Spirit. What we have in common is our willingness to spend a little more than we have whenever God calls for us to steward an initiative of His, and we always find that the next time He calls we have more to spend. There are various levels of gifting and experience, but there are no levels of calling or ranking in the Kingdom. It is a Kingdom of beggars who have the keys to the vault in their possession by right of inheritance.

How can we account for the gaps in giftings? The answer is simple enough when we remember that the Holy Spirit outpouring promised in Joel 2:28 did indeed fall on that first Pentecost Sunday (see Acts 2), but not in all fullness. We received what I like to call a sacramental outburst of God's grace and glory.

SACRAMENTAL OUTBURSTS

A sacrament is a foretaste, a deposit on God's promise for the Kingdom. Baptism is a washing for citizenship in the Kingdom, but neither God nor anyone else expects that we will never wash again after baptism. On the contrary, the bathing we take in the River Jordan is meant to whet our appetites for an eternal swim in the river that extends from the throne of the King in the City of Zion. Likewise, Holy Communion is presented as a foretaste of the Heavenly Banquet; no one expects us to be satisfied, but rather to become all the more ravenous for the eternal feast of which the communion bread and wine are but a crumb and a sip. In the same way, the outpouring of the Holy Spirit on Pentecost Sunday on 3000 people was but a foretaste of the outpouring on all flesh that is in process since that time. It is not yet complete, even today, when it has spread to more than two billion people, which is a bit less than a third of the population of our planet. Like all sacramental outbursts, it is "already but not yet."

Wine is used as a metaphor or symbol for the blood of God, in which the Spirit resides, on a number of occasions in the Bible, from Melchizedek's presentation of bread and wine when Abraham visited him after a military victory (see Gen. 14:18-20) to Jesus' transformation of water into wine at the wedding in Cana (see John 2:1-11). (In Cana the miracle symbolized the transformation of our cleansing with water into our bathing in the Holy Spirit after the Ascension.) The language of "this is my blood poured out for you" in the Communion event is the latest and greatest of these expressions (see Luke 22:20). But what modern Christians forget, or perhaps never knew, is that wine was not considered to be at full potency when it was placed in the wineskins of the first century. It was wine alright; but the process of fermentation was not yet complete, so the coming to potency was a process. That is why Jesus maintained that the wineskin must be new and stretchable; when wine ferments it also expands. The wine too is part of a sacramental outburst.

The point is that for as long as we live in the time between the initial sacramental outburst and the coming in all of its fullness of the Kingdom of God, there will be gaps in the evident giftings for God's people, whether apostles or prophets or intercessors who flow between the various offices of the five-fold ministry of the Body of Christ. There are no levels of ranking or calling for intercessors, they frequently flow in the prophetic gifts although they are not necessarily prophets, and so there is nothing about which to become puffed up. But there is the immense privilege, for those of God's people who respond to this shofar sounding from Zion, of actually reminding God of the promises He has made as we stand in the gap between the children and the Abba. There is the incredible opportunity to engage in strategic or prophetic intercession, to the extent of our gifting, in such a way that we focus on those topics of intercession that actually impact our communities in Kingdom terms. This is the meaning of strategic or prophetic intercession, and it is of more value than my words can describe.

It requires that the intercessors, especially the more prophetic ones, remember at all times that it is their task and their privilege to stand between adversaries, not to become adversaries themselves. This is true even when the Lord God is one of the adversaries; it is for this purpose that God has raised up the intercessors. They must cry out as Abraham did on behalf of Sodom and Gomorrah, "Will not the Judge of all the earth do right?" (see Gen. 18:25), and as Moses did on behalf of the idolaters in the desert, "But now please forgive their sin—but if not, then blot me out of the book you have written" (see Exod. 32:32). They, and the prophets under whom they serve, are required to bless and curse not.

It requires that the Body, and the apostles and pastors who lead its members, receive the ministry of the prophets and intercessors. They are not required to act on every prophetic word that they hear; theirs is the leadership function. But they are required to recognize and embrace that God is speaking to His people today, perhaps more than ever, and that after having tested the words they receive, they are to act on the authentic ones. And they are rightfully expected at all times to rejoice and praise the Lord for the special care He has taken at this time in history to include His people in the partnership of His mighty works on the land and in our lives.

I began this chapter with several stories of prophetic acts and utterances that had made a profound and pragmatic impact on the communities in which they were extended. These are indeed instances of prophetic or strategic intercession bringing prophecy to pass; they are a great gift to the Church and to the communities in which the Church serves Christ and the world He has won on the cross. Yet much of the Church today is skeptical or even downright hostile toward any suggestion that prophecy has continued beyond the pages of the Bible. This is wrongheaded at best and downright apostate at worst!

In First Corinthians 4:20 we read, "The Kingdom of God is not a matter of talk but of power." This is neither the first nor the last time this statement is made in the New Testament. Nowhere do we find the slightest textual indication that the power was only available during the first century. In First Corinthians 13, we are told that prophecy will pass away, but there is no indication of when that might be, prior to the return of the King. In any case, when I consider the thousands of healings and other miracles that occur on a regular basis in my city alone, I am pretty well convinced that the power has not yet gone out of the world. To the contrary, God is clearly stepping things up, and He is doing it more and more in the denominational settings in which He is not expected.

Gerry Sprunger is a pastor and friend of mine from Siskiyou County, a man who has given faithful service to Christ Jesus for more than half a century. When Gerry was diagnosed with cancer that was as terminal as it was systemic, his family gathered for a farewell dinner. They sang and praised God for his life and ministry, and they made no plans to assault the gates of hell on his behalf because they belonged to a denomination that understands (doctrinally) that the gifts have ceased. When a prophetic word was released at the dinner to the effect that they ought to "cancel the cancer" in prayer, they obeyed the exhortation, not from belief but because they loved their father and were willing to trust God to show them new ways if He were so inclined. Nothing discernible happened while they prayed.

Some weeks later, another prophetic word was released to the effect that "when word of Gerry's healing gets out, revival will break out in Siskiyou County." When this word was received, there was still no indication that Gerry had been healed. Today, however, he is alive, well, and cancer free. His county is on the brink of major league revival, and thousands of people are hearing his story about how God intends His power for today just as much as He meant it when He unleashed the gospel of power and not of mere words to the original apostles.

What has this to do with reconciling the apostles and the prophets, not to mention the rest of the five-fold leadership that we are promised in Ephesians? I mentioned earlier that it is imperative for reconciliation that the prophets become assertive enough to offer their words in the face of skepticism and the seeming strangeness of the words and that they become humble enough to then relinquish their words into the hands of the apostles or pastors to whom they have given them. It is at least as important for the apostles and pastors to recognize that these servant hearts are performing a most necessary service and that community transformation does not come along without reference to their ministry. Leave them in the engine room and not on the bridge? Yes, but recognize, embrace, and honor their work in that engine room.

Micah 6:8 is a verse that everyone in the Body should tattoo on their foreheads and brand onto their hearts. It says, "He has showed you, O man, what is good. And what does the Lord require of you? To act justly and to love mercy and to walk humbly with your God." If the apostles and prophets dedicate themselves to treating one another in accordance with those words, reconciliation between them will no longer be an issue. On the contrary, the prophetic wing of the Body will recognize that it needs the more conservative wings to evaluate prophecy on the basis of scriptural consistency and the other tests, while the conservatives will embrace the fact that the prophets are bringing the fresh revelation without which the Body becomes a collection of dry bones.

I will never forget Jack Hayford's words to me in the face of my consternation about Toronto more than decade ago. I knew he was speaking prophetically to me, even though I had no context for the origin and destiny criteria by which I now test every word of the prophets that crosses my path. I did not know what Hayford knew, that there are ample precedents in both the Bible and in American history for the very kinds of manifestations (and their far more important fruit) that were common to such moves of God as the Toronto Blessing. But I did know instinctively that he spoke God's truth when he said to me, "Lighten up."

Chapter 12

ON EARTH AS IT IS IN HEAVEN

A country cleric ran out of gasoline while driving along a back road to visit a member of his congregation. He spotted a farmhouse off the road and went up to the door, looking for some help in his emergency. And the farmer was only too happy to help. He had a tank in his yard, but the only thing he could use for a can to hold the gas was an old chamber pot from a bygone era. He filled the pot with fuel and sent the pastor back to his car. As the pastor was pouring the fuel from the chamber pot into his gas tank, another man drove past and mistook the contents for something the pastor had emptied from his own bladder. He was heard to shout as he drove past, "Oh, if only I had faith like that!"

Of course, the punch line hinges on the passing driver imagining that the pastor had such faith that he could believe God would turn his own urine into gasoline when, in fact, the chamber pot held gasoline borrowed from the generosity of the farmer. But "faith like that" has only a little to do with an unshakable conviction that what we think is impossible can happen in the face of that conviction. And it has everything to do with a living and life-giving relationship with the One who can and does make everything happen that He declares necessary to the fulfillment of His plans for us. God is making miracles happen in our presence every day. They range from the spectacular healings of cancer and heart disease and the raisings from the dead (all of which I have personally witnessed in the communities in which I minister), to the multiplication of fish, oil, and other things, and the breaking of drought, the quenching of wild fires, and the sudden cooling of a heat prostrated day because His people asked (which I have also witnessed), to the little miracles that no one remarks upon because they are so commonplace, like the continued beating of billions of human hearts that we foolishly ascribe to some sort of involuntary muscular activity. The pastor in the story did possess uncommon faith; it was embodied in the faithful commitment he had made to depend on the Lord his God and to do whatever God commanded. He walked in the confidence that whatever He needed to accomplish that willed command would be provided and is already available to him—because he is on intimate terms with the Provider.

It is all about transformation, this process of repentance leading to reconciliation and beyond. The process of Holy Spirit transformation is now underway in some 500 communities and approximately 20 whole nations around the world. It is clearly and wonderfully described in the books and films of world-class leaders like George Otis Jr. and Alistair Petrie. It is there to be witnessed by anyone who will take the time and trouble to travel to one of the named spots or, much better, to pray and minister until it comes to home. Transformation is as far beyond mere revival in scope, just as the Pentecost event was beyond the sending of the twelve original apostles to the villages of the lost sheep of the house of Israel where Jesus had not yet gone. Communities in transformation are places in which business, government, education, and the churches work together in the common hunger they practice in seeking the face of God. Crime is uncommon in these communities. Miracles of healed bodies and old societal wounds are flowing unfettered. Land that was once unproductive and polluted becomes lush and burdened only with bumper crops, like the Guatemalan fields that produce carrots the size of baseball bats and the Fijian reefs that were ecologically dead but now teem with fish.

Jesus told the fishermen that He would make them fishers of men (see Matt. 4:19). In communities undergoing transformation, it is normal to find 90 to 95 percent of the people in a born-again relationship with Jesus Christ. The human trigger for all of this grace is a critical mass of people, sometimes as few as half a dozen to begin with, who, like the pastor with the chamber pot, have chosen to walk in intimacy with the Provider of all that they need. They have taken seriously God's invitation and command in Isaiah 62 to post themselves as watchmen on the walls and to give themselves and Him no rest until He comes to establish Jerusalem.

Reconciliation, the commitment to be an ambassador of reconciliation, is foundational to the paving of the highway in the desert that makes way for the Lord to bring His transforming Spirit to bear in our communities once and for all.

Transformation is an out-breaking miracle that cannot occur while the people of God are at war with one another. And for God, peace breaks out not in the absence of open conflict but in the presence of fellowship, new or renewed. Whether the estrangement is grounded in denomination or culture, whether it's gender-related or generational (or what have you) issues, the effect is to hinder the coming of God and to hinder it very effectively. On the other hand, God says that when even two or three of us agree on anything we ask of Him, He will do it for us (see Matt. 18:20). Is he serious?

UNLIKELY AMBASSADORS

My relationship with the transformation phenomenon went from longing to participation when Diana and I visited Hawaii in 1998 and encountered an Alaskan Inuit man named Suuqinna in the Honolulu International Airport. We were waiting for our transfer flight to Maui, and he was seeing some friends off. He has a couple of doctoral degrees, it turns out, but all we saw was a man dressed in jeans and a t-shirt; the regalia was topped off with a very ratty windbreaker that had the words "Warriors for Christ" inscribed on it. The Holy Spirit was so evidently all over him that he fairly dripped with the presence of God. I mentioned it to Diana, who had seen the Spirit too, and began to rise from my seat, intending only to shake his hand and wish him God's blessing. But the Lord stopped me in my tracks. "Sit down," He said. "You will meet this man, but it will be where I say and when I say."

My act of obedience was a small counterpoint to Diana's act when God had called her two years earlier to pray each day for the salvation of the whole of the people of Hawaii. Our trip to Maui was the gift of a friend who knew how badly we needed a rest. But our time there, besides being restful and exciting, was part of God's plan for us to become aware of the just-concluded Spiritual Warfare Project. The brainchild of Daniel Kikawa and Leon Siu, the project eventually involved ten thousand intercessors who prayed daily for the salvation of all Hawaiians. Kikawa and Siu had recruited most of them, but Diana was not the only one who came on board at the direct command of God without knowledge of the project in which she participated.

The project had climaxed eight weeks before our arrival, as I described in an earlier chapter, with multiple signs and wonders including the end of a two-year drought and the res-urrection of a once dead coral reef, which is now alive with marine life of all kinds, off of the big island of Hawaii. Thousands of people had accepted Jesus as their Lord in the wake of these events. God brought us into the company of two of the leaders from Maui (when we thought we were hunting for gifts for our children on the last day of our time there), and Jill and Tia Tahauri eventually filled us in on all of these events. From there, we soon became caught up in a worldwide movement to reconcile the peoples who have hated one another (both with and without a cause) and not just to witness many miracles but to actually live inside an out-breaking process of escalating miracle.

I did not actually meet Suuqinna for another two years, and it was at the airport in my own city of Redding. But the encounter with him at the airport in Honolulu began a chain of events that rocked my world. It set in motion a process that softened my heart that was hardened against native peoples. I had believed that the Indian wars in my own country, as brutal and merciless as they had been, were simply the result of a clash of cultures. (We had won; they had lost. Now everyone needed to get over it.) Meeting, loving, and being totally received by ethnic Hawaiians opened my eyes. I reread old accounts of how my people exterminated the buffalo in order to destroy the lifestyle of the Plains Indians just because they stood in the path of what my people called progress. God and my friends, who called me family, opened my ears to listen as California tribal people told me how their people had been slaughtered by the poisoned beef given them to celebrate a treaty that would never even be ratified in Congress much less acted upon. The process opened my heart to people like my friend, Lynda Prince, who was taken from her family as a small child, for her own ostensible good, and made to live in boarding school where she was beaten if she dared to speak her own language. I came to see that I had radically disengaged from people who were different from me and whom I did not know. When I engaged with them, just because the Lord said to do it, I wept at what my people had done. But I also came to love my own people and these others in ways I could not have previously imagine. The compassion of God is real and transferable. He asks only that we come to desire it more than anything else.

Obeying the Lord's word to wait on Him for a meeting with Suuqinna began opening a fresh perspective for me on how to protocol (honor and respect) others. The humbling of that encounter and the Lord's word about it opened fresh opportunities to learn from others (and other cultures) about how to treat the other as though he were better than I am, which is what the Lord commands of all of us (see Phil. 2:3). In this way we will enter into the greatness that is reserved for all of us. It opened the way for revelations and relationships all over the world and the opportunity to actually play a part in His process of transformation in my own city and region, and in the world. It included the Lord convicting my heart for a tough message that He called me (a middle-class white guy from California) to deliver to a world gathering of indigenous leaders in Sweden in the summer of 2005, even though I had no invitation to speak and no right to demand a hearing. Yet the Lord, in a virtual turnabout to the encounter with Suuqinna in 1998, spoke to one of the organizers of that event, telling her that a man from northern California was coming with a word they all needed to hear. I was the only man from northern California who registered for the conference. And Marie Enokssen had the courage and the vision to offer me a keynote spot on the speaker's schedule, even though she had never met or heard of me or Diana.

We both addressed the gathering on several occasions over ten days. We found that many messages delivered by others hit the same themes God had planted in us; God had paved the way for all of us. We had the privilege of reminding the gathering earlier that God always has our backs and that He expects us to imitate Him in this. When I spoke God's message of repentance leading to reconciliation, many hearts were broken for the Lord and for each other. God did this through an unlikely ambassador, and my heart tells me that we are still nearer the beginning than the end of the story. Everything changes when we do it His way, His when, and His what—and nothing will ever change until we let His "yes" be our "yes" and His "not yet" be our "not yet."

Jesus loves to utilize unlikely ambassadors. He loves to wait until we show up so that He can show off, and He chooses people who will have difficulty claiming the glory for themselves because it would just be too laughable. He does that in the story of the miraculous catch of fish in Luke 5:1-11. Some of those He would soon call as disciples (*talmudim*, as the Jews say it), had been out fishing all night and had caught nothing. These were professionals, good at their trade, as we see from the fact that they owned multiple boats and had hired a staff to work with them. But this night had been a total bust, and they were more than ready to hang it up as soon as the nets were washed and ready for the coming night. Jesus, who was standing nearby, turned to look at the tired and discouraged men. "Put out into deep water, and let down the nets for a catch" (Luke 5:4). Simon, who would be called Peter, and who did respect the teacher whether or not he understood Him, answered, "Master, we've worked hard all night and haven't caught anything. But because you say so, I will let down the nets" (Luke 5:5). We know the rest—how they brought in such a tremendous catch that they nearly capsized the boat. But we often forget how essential the obedient presence of the disciples was in enabling of the miracle to occur.

I don't mean that Jesus lacked the capacity to create or harvest the fish without Peter's assistance. But it is clear from the record that the primary purpose of everything God does is self-revelation. The disciples had to show up and participate so that Jesus could show off in accordance with the purpose of the Father.

Did Yahweh part the Red Sea and then permit the Israelites to find it that way? Or did He bring them to the shore with Pharaoh in hot pursuit and then unleash the wonder for all—including the Egyptians—to see? And He expected Moses to obediently lift his powerless, except for the Holy Spirit, arms to initiate the parting (see Exod. 14). Did He knock down the walls of Jericho in the night and let Joshua take the unprotected city the next day, or did He perform His signs before the eyes of both camps? And He expected the Israelites to blow those trumpets in worship and warfare as they were instructed (see Joshua 6). Jesus never did a miracle that nobody saw and, most of the time, He waited until a real crowd had gathered. God said more than 60 times through the mouth of the prophet Ezekiel alone, "I do this so that you will know that I am the Lord your God." It is true: When we show up, He shows off, and not before.

But there is a lot more to this story.

Living Inside a Miracle

When Simon Peter saw the glory of the Lord in the action He performed, he also saw something else, perhaps for the first time in his life. He saw the astronomical gap between who he was and who the Lord is; he saw the true meaning of sin. He realized that it has not so much to do with the bad things we have done and the good ones we have neglected as it has to do with the simple fact that we are not adequate to the requirements of our existence, that we never have been and never will be. We do bad things in a vain effort to compensate for our inadequacy (which is the meaning of the Hebrew we translate as "wicked") instead of turning ourselves over to the One *in whom* we are more than adequate and more than conquerors. But that day, Peter got it right; he fell to his knees and asked the Lord to leave him because he was a sinful man, not fit for His presence. The Scripture does not record this, but I am betting that Jesus laughed and said something like, "No argument there, Bro," before He said what is recorded. "Don't be afraid; from now on you will catch men" (Luke 5:10).

The passage is the perfect scriptural expression of what I have called sacramental outbursts and what I mean when I refer to transformation as an out-breaking miracle. The disciples witnessed and participated in a bona fide miracle in the great catch they receive in obedience to Jesus' instruction to let down the nets one more time. There is teaching inherent in the event itself. Jesus asked them to do something, which they knew to be both foolish and useless, simply because He had told them to do it. After Peter's declaration of inadequacy, Jesus upped the ante by stating that He knew about the inadequacy, that He was glad that Peter wanted to work on it, and that He had no intention of waiting until Peter was fully prepped before using him in a much larger project—the catching of men for the Kingdom of Heaven. In other words, Jesus wanted the disciples to escalate the level of their foolish obedience, and He would then take crude and uneducated fishermen (the *am'haaretz* or people of the land) and raise them to their highest and best use for the Kingdom as His chosen apostles.

What we will fail to notice, if we believe that repentance is a one-time prelude to conversion rather than a life-long process of abandoning self and incorporating the image and likeness of God (in whom we are created to live and move and have our being), is that Peter's act of repentance is essential to his participation in the escalation of the miracle in his calling to be a fisher of men. It is the difference between the nine lepers who were healed and kept walking and the one who came back to thank, and follow, Jesus (see Luke 17:11-19). Without the recognition of the gap that separated their being, Peter would have never noticed that the miracle had only just begun. He could have conceived with the mind that he already carried—by supernatural favor and blessing—a whole lot of fish, but he could not even imagine that the Lord of life would use him as an ambassador. His repentance, which meant to turn about and implied humility, made possible the new revelation and the escalating process.

Sacramental outbursts always begin with a miracle, in which the disciples are participant observers. They always contain teaching inherent in the event itself. And they always offer escalation of the process until the outlines of the miracle are no longer visible but the Lord and His foot and fingerprints remain visible for those who are willing to follow His lead into new and uncharted territory. Escalation comes about as the witnesses of these things, the participant observers, continue to sow the inherent teaching into larger and larger occasions and venues in which God introduces the same dynamic. As Peter continued to obey the Lord, based on Jesus' identity rather than Peter's understanding, he progressed from catching fish to catching people. The opportunity was not just to see or be part of a miracle but to live inside the processing miracles of the Kingdom.

Diana has suffered from poor health for most of her life. She has a history of life-threatening food allergies (six in all), along with fibromialgia and a curved spine. In the summer of 2004, she fell while doing some banking on a Saturday morning. She blacked out (the only time this has ever happened) and exhibited signs of heart attack, stroke, or both. While being tested for everything under the sun in the emergency room, she heard the Lord say clearly that He was fed-up with the attacks against her and that He would no longer tolerate them. He declared that she would begin to enjoy a robust health that she had never before known and that He was actually going to begin to age her backwards.

Now, two years later, her fibromialgia is history. Her spine is visibly straightening, and four of her six food allergies have vanished. Each of the allergy healings have taken place in very public settings. Typically, she is served something she knows she cannot eat and the Lord says, in so many words, "Go ahead, Honey, enjoy it." She eats with no ill effects and bears witness to the goodness of the Lord who addresses her as "Honey." In two of the cases, swiss cheese and lamb, she had to seek out the forbidden food after God said she could eat it because the restaurant had run out. We drove forty miles back into Glasgow, Scotland, so that we and our hosts could find a place selling lamb so that Diana would not miss out on the treat the Spirit had promised her and the Lord would not miss out on His glory. One day, she asked in prayer why the Lord did not just go ahead and heal everything He had promised in one lightning bolt of grace and be done with it. He answered with a question of His own. "Would you prefer to have a miracle, or to live inside one?" The answer was obvious.

THE PRIVILEGE OF REPENTANCE

Just as obvious, but often overlooked, is the reality that we don't have to chase after God; we only have to let Him catch us. Matthew 4:17 contains what is usually called Jesus' first public utterance. "Repent for the kingdom of Heaven is near." The translation utterly fails to gather the meaning of the Greek word *eggiken*, which means literally "is pursuing you." God the Son is saying, "Turn about, for the Kingdom of Heaven is chasing after you." When Peter, the leper, Diana, or anyone else turns to face the God they have recognized in the miracle (the God who is offering us utterly more than we can ask or imagine and who is astronomically beyond us and adamant that this distance will not be permitted to define our relationship), they are simply giving Him the opportunity to catch up with them and to carry them from there.

Repentance is the direct precursor to reconciliation with God. Reconciliation with each other (dedication to that project) is both caused by and effected by our reconciliation with God. We (all of us) have been running away for a long time. But it is not too long, as long as God is in the world.

There is another crucial dimension to repentance. In Matthew 9:17 Jesus said, "Neither do men pour new wine into old wineskins. If they do, the skins will burst, the wine will run out and the wineskins will be ruined. No, they pour new wine into new wineskins, and both are preserved." The Holy Spirit, Jesus' first and last gift to the Church (because the Spirit is all that the Church will ever need and because that same Spirit is the gift that keeps on giving), is much like the new wine that Jesus and every other New Testament believer would have been familiar with. It was not fully fermented when it went into the skin. It was bubbling and churning and coming to full potency. It had all of its fullness within it, but that fullness has not yet manifested. And we should know that when something ferments, its inevitable expansion is just part of the process. But if the Spirit is the new wine, then the Christian must be the wineskin. What will happen to us if we cannot stretch with the fermenting Holy Spirit within us? We will burst, just as Jesus said.

This is the reason Christians can say that we receive the Holy Spirit when we are baptized with water and that, sometimes, we are baptized later with the Holy Spirit. It is not that we receive a new baptism but that the one we have received is explosively manifested at a point in time. And any who believe that this Holy Spirit baptism is the last time God means to explosively birth Himself in us are either deluded or stagnant in the faith.

Our repentance (the lifelong process of our repentance), which is the ongoing will to turn as Peter turned so that Jesus can escalate the process and declare that He is not waiting until we are clean (although we do need to become clean), is most often manifested in the process of reconciliation. When we recognize that all have sinned and fallen short of the glory of God and that God won't hold that against us so long as we don't try to defend our position, we must acknowledge at once that we have sinned against most if not all of the people who have sinned against us. Reconciliation includes both repentance of our own sin and forgiveness of the sin of others.

I recall a woman I encountered at a healing seminar many years ago. She had arthritis in her hands so badly that her hands had curled into claws turned back on themselves. As I prepared to pray for her, I was prompted by the Spirit to ask her if there existed any unforgiveness in her life. She burst into tears and confessed that she had been angry with some members of her church for more than 20 years. In her inner agony, she cried out that she had forgiven them many times but that the old anger always came back, and she did not know what to do with it. I spoke to her in the voice of my office, saying, "By the authority committed to me as a priest of the living God, I release you from your unforgiveness." I then reached for her hands, to pray for them, but as we watched, her fingers uncurled and she was fully healed.

When I addressed the World Christian Gathering on Indigenous Peoples, I began with a confession of identification.

I confessed and asked forgiveness for the many sins of displacement, exploitation, and extermination against native peoples that my people (the Celts, the Norse, and the Germans) stand convicted of. But I also pointed out that my people originated in the Caucasus Mountains and that we were so obliterated by those who drove against us that there is no trace of us left in the land of our birth. The only connection is in the name we still carry—Caucasians. I added that there is not a tribe on earth that has not done what we have done.

This is not an excuse for the behavior of my people; there is no excuse. It is simply an admission of the reality that my apology is cleansing for me alone. If the representatives of other tribes and peoples would be cleansed, then they must offer their own repentance to the God who heals them and to the peoples who need to forgive them as well. My job, of course, as an ambassador of God's reconciliation, is to offer my own repentance before calling on others to repent, removing the log from my own eye before attempting delicate surgery on the speck in my brother's eye (see Matt. 7:3-5). That holds true, regardless of who you are..

Reality is that God will not settle for less than the fullness of His Kingdom, on earth as it is in Heaven. In that Kingdom, as it is described in Matthew 11:2-6, the dead are raised without exception. Lepers are cured—all of them. The blind and deaf have their sight and hearing restored to them across the board, and one hundred per cent of the poor (in spirit) have good news preached in their resurrected hearing. And the place is populated with those who do not take offense at Jesus as He actually is. Only then can He actually reign as Lord of all.

Are 90 to 95 percent of the people in the community in a born again relationship with the Christ? Is there little crime? Are there fewer sick people? Are the pornographers and the drug dealers out of business because no one is buying? This is only another sacramental outburst for Jesus because He will not be satisfied until all of the people are born again and marching under His banner (including the pornographers and drug dealers) and every feature of the Kingdom just described is in full bloom. Even the first Pentecost in Jerusalem was only such an outburst, if we can use *only* when describing such a miracle.

When the apostles gathered on the balcony and Peter addressed the crowd in what would become the first Christian sermon, he quoted from the prophet Joel (see Joel 2:28-29). He said that what was happening was fulfillment of the promise that in the latter days God would pour out His Spirit on all flesh and that all would have the privilege of speaking the words of God as they prophetically left the mouth of the Father (see Acts 2:16-18). This was the new covenant promised in so many prophetic utterances, and it was indeed for all mankind; all who called on the name of Jesus would be saved. Three thousand heard the news with gladness as they repented and accepted baptism (see Acts 2:41); yet this is hardly all mankind. It is, at best, a deposit on the promise for all mankind; it is a sacramental outburst or outpouring of God's grace. In our time, the number on whom God has poured out His Spirit has climbed dramatically. There are now more than two billion in the Kingdom, and that is only a bit less than a third of the world's population. The numbers are growing by thousands daily, especially in places where the people are routinely poor in spirit like poverty-overwhelmed Africa and politically-oppressed China. But we are still in the early stages of the process of escalation. God will not be satisfied until all mankind has been swept into the river that flows from His throne, as described in Ezekiel 47 and Revelation 22.

Everyone must choose God for himself or herself. There are no shortcuts and no proxies in the Kingdom of Heaven. But God will not be satisfied while even one person is on the outside looking in, and He calls upon His people to share that dissatisfaction for as long as He harbors it. And so He calls us to be His ambassadors of the reconciliation that He has established through the death and resurrection of His Son.

Reality is that God loves each and every one of us just the way we are. He loves us whether or not we love back, whether we think we are of the elite classes like the Pharisee in Luke 18 or we know ourselves to be at best a miserable tax collector. He loves us so much that He has no intention of leaving us in the condition in which He finds us. It is our very neediness (the inadequacy that we go to such great lengths to hide, which causes us to look down on those we consider even less adequate), that is irresistibly attractive to God. There is a most enigmatic verse that follows on the heels of the wonderful Kingdom description that Jesus gave when speaking to the disciples of John the Baptist. After they had gone, He told His own *talmudim* that the Kingdom is taken by force and violence; and that forceful men lay hold of it (see Matt. 11:12).

I have always thought it absurd that anyone would think they could arm wrestle God for possession of His Kingdom. Yet Jesus invited this very absurdity; He declared that this is how it is! Indeed, I thought it absurd until it dawned on me one day, by the prompting of the Holy Spirit, that when we display and submit our dependency to Him, He cannot help giving us everything. "My grace is sufficient for you," He said in Second Corinthians 12:9, "for my power is made perfect in weakness." He really does love us so much that He will not leave us in the condition in which He finds us.

It was inconceivable to me that I would meet that man from the Honolulu airport in some other part of the world at some other time of God's choosing or that I would deliver a keynote address at a worldwide gathering of people whose history would incline them to view me with suspicion (if not outright hostility) if I claimed the right to speak the words for Sweden that God had implanted in me. I could have forced the issue and spoken to Suuqinna at the airport, and I could have explained to the Lord that He really ought to find someone more qualified to bring His word to that gathering. But everything changes when we do what He says and we do it when, were, and in the way He says to do it. And until then, nothing will ever change. Because I obeyed in those two occasions, I am privileged to count Suuqinna as a lifelong friend and to be part of a worldwide move of God's transforming Holy Spirit. I don't even want to think of comparing the excitement of what God has given me to the boredom of what little I might have claimed for myself.

WEAPONS OF OUR WARFARE

Reality is also that none of us will attain our destiny through the rehearsal or recovery of our history, especially the grievances that dot our history. We will redeem our history by seeking and attaining our destiny through Him who created us and our destiny. We will attain our destiny through a process of personal and identificational repentance, a progressive turning of our lives over to Jesus, including our grievances. Most of our grievances have at least some basis in reality, and many are substantially or even wholly legitimate. But whether we are discussing Catholics and Protestants, immigrant and indigenous peoples, young and old, liberals and conservatives, there is a world of difference between recognizing our history as something to be dealt with and choosing to live in the place where we do deal with it.

The best way to deal with our history is to repent of our shame over having been wronged, as I had to do with Lucas the Hispanic boy, and to seek forgiveness of those we have wronged. In both cases, this is an act of both personal and identificational repentance. It becomes a renewal, a making new, of the wineskin that is me, and it invariably results in an upsurge of the Holy Spirit that is bubbling and sizzling and fermenting within me.

We may grasp the personal component of repentance quickly, whether or not we enjoy what we are grasping. But the identification thing, for many, is controversial, and for some, it presents an additional point of grievance. "Why," we demand to know, "must I apologize for what others who may identify with me have done, possibly centuries ago? Does not the Bible say that every man will die for his own sin?"

First, we might make a note of the fact that the Bible is about life and not death. The God of the Bible is God of the living and not of the dead. We may face death only for our own individual sins, but we can only face life in the intimacy of the community of the Body and the blood, a community in which we have no rights, only righteousness. Logically, we can also reflect that we have no problem with inheriting the benefits of our ancestry. If I have the hands and the instincts of a craftsman that I inherited from my father, I am both proud of and grateful for my heritage. But if I have also inherited his bad temper and periodically take that out on my wife and children, I do not want to acknowledge that, and I certainly do not want to repent of the sins of my ancestry in the quest to lead a healthy family of my own. If I live on land that my great grandfather wrestled from the great plains, I am proud to consider myself his heir and to celebrate my heritage whenever I ride in the pioneer days parade. But if my great grandfather wrestled that land from the American Indians, I don't want to discuss it (it was such a long time ago that no claim can be still valid). And if my family acquired a fortune through the contacts my ancestors made in various unwholesome and perhaps even shamanistic associations, I am happy to receive the money and even to vow to spend it in more wholesome pursuits, but I don't want to deal with the sources of the wealth in a way that God might prescribe to right the wrongs of the past. The bottom line here is that if we receive the good things of our inheritance, which we did not earn, we must also bear responsibility for the bad things in which we also played no direct role. As Mr. Spock would have said, "It is simple logic."

Most telling is the simple reality that identificational repentance is typical of how the heroes of the Bible came before the Lord. When Moses discovered the golden calf in Exodus 32, he said to the Lord, "But now, please forgive their sin—but if not, then blot me out of the book you have written" (Exod. 32:32). Daniel begged God to forgive him and the people for their many sins even though Daniel was a righteous man (see Dan. 9:4-19). Nehemiah begged the same forgiveness before he undertook the rebuilding of the Jerusalem wall (see Neh. 1:4-11). Isaiah referred to himself as a man of unclean lips who lived among a people of unclean lips (see Isa. 6:5). It is the same with Jeremiah, Ezekiel, and Hosea. Jesus' act of self-sacrifice on the cross, for our sin, was the ultimate act of identificational repentance recorded in the Bible. We are called only to imitate Him and these others whenever God gives us the opportunity by placing us in a position where we can seek reconciliation with an individual or group.

Reality is, finally, that the world is always asking us what we consider worth fighting for, but God is always asking us what we consider worth surrendering over. We are, as I described in a previous chapter, in the midst of the third world war and the final and ultimate conflict in history. The Lord has called us to battle and instructed us to use only the weapons He furnishes in Second Corinthians 10:3-5. Those weapons are not mentioned by name, and I called them weapons of faithfulness, witness, and relationship-building in that earlier chapter, for so they are. More specifically these weapons are blessing, forgiveness, and Holy Communion. They are the weapons not of aggression, but of surrender to the Lord our God.

Romans 12:14 calls upon us to bless and not curse. Jesus called us, in the Sermon on the Mount, to love our enemies and bless those who persecute us (see Matt. 5:44); He even said that He expects us to leave our gift at the altar and go seeking reconciliation with anyone who claims a grievance against us, however unjustified it may be (see Matt. 5:23-24). He exhorted us in Matthew 18:15-18 to make every effort to restore the fallen brother or sister and, in that context, told us that whatever we set free on earth would likewise be liberated in Heaven. No one is calling on the United States to disarm in these pages; indeed, the New Testament states clearly that national governments are instituted to wield the sword in a righteous cause, and the most militant military empire of all time (Imperial Rome) was held up as the example (see Rom. 13:1-7). But it is just as clear that military and political resources are intended to clear a level playing field for the real engagement, in which the love of God in Christ takes sole possession of the stage for the balance of the drama of history. When Jesus sent out the 72 into all of the towns and villages where He had not yet gone, He called on them first to bless whomever they encountered, without regard to what those folks deserved. He is like that, and He expects us to represent Him as He is, not as we are.

In John 20, Jesus was among the disciples on the evening of His resurrection. He breathed on them and called them to receive His Holy Spirit, just as the Hawaiians do when they say "Aloha" and punctuate the word with their own breath. He told them that He was sending them as He has been sent and that they were to represent Him by forgiving sins in His name. He said that those sins they forgave on earth would be forgiven also in Heaven but that those they retained (in context) would be retained to pollute the apostolic band itself (see John 20:21-23). He was putting feet to all of the parables in which the one who failed to forgive was the one condemned (rather than the one who was not forgiven). I have seen it happen more than once that when sin is forgiven, the enemy can find no foothold. And the Lord seems just as concerned now as He was two millennia ago (in His encounters with the street woman in Luke 7:36-50 and the tax collector in Luke 19:1-10) about whether forgiveness or repentance comes first. But He is quite clear that forgiveness is a most potent weapon in the warfare in which we are engaged.

The third weapon in our heavenly arsenal is the Supper of the Lord. When we think about this one, we need to reflect on the fact that the Lord our God is the foremost party animal in the universe. Jesus came not fasting but eating and drinking enough to be accused of both gluttony and drunkenness (see Matt. 11:19). The Kingdom of Heaven is forever depicted in terms of the heavenly banquet table (see Matt. 22:1-14), and the prodigal is ever welcomed home with a party and the killing of the fatted calf (see Luke 15:11-32). Even in the Old Testament discussions of the tithe, God demanded that Jacob bring all of his substance to a designated place and throw ten percent of it into the common pantry so that all could celebrate the goodness of the Lord (see Deut. 14:22-27). The New

Testament simply expands on that theme, parabolically, by including the sick and the poor in the feasting. We need to consider also that the accuser is the lord of lack; he is the one who whispers to us that there might not be enough, that we should neither look nor touch nor enjoy, that our salvation is in our laws and not in the life we are given in Christ.

In Psalm 23:5, we are told that God sets a table for us in the presence of our enemies. This is an act of war. In First Corinthians 11:26, Paul tells us that each time we celebrate the supper we declare the death of Jesus until He comes again, and we already know that we are called to overcome the world by the power of His blood and the strength of our testimony (see Rev. 12:11). These are combined in one event each time we celebrate the Supper. Jesus girded His people with Communion on the night before He died, the opening salvo in the greatest battle ever fought. It matters little to the Lord how we "do this in remembrance of me" (Luke 22:19), so long as it is an exercise in reverential fine dining rather than fast food consumption. But it matters greatly to Him that we do it in His name and that we do it frequently, especially when we face great challenges.

I have personally witnessed traffic accidents and satanic ritual activity disappear from a community following the strategic application of indiscriminate blessing, unmerited forgiveness, and the celebration of the Supper of the Lord. The world wants to know what we consider worthy of combat; the Lord wants to know what we consider worthy of surrender. Only when we answer the question can we engage "on earth as it is in Heaven."

SEEK YE FIRST

Diana and I have a custom that has always been special to us. Because she is very sensitive to direct sunlight, she cannot go ocean swimming in daylight without risking a severe burn in a very few minutes. In Hawaii, many of the beaches have shade trees close to the water. When we are in Hawaii, we will go to the beach and she will hunker down in a cluster of trees with a good book while I swim. I always bring my mask and fins with me so that I can be sure to find and bring to her a piece of coral from God's ocean floor as an offering for the woman I love. God had been gracious to let me find a piece on every trip we've made to a Hawaiian beach. It was so regular and so special that it became inconceivable that I would not have a piece of coral for my wife, until the time I forgot my mask in California. There went my ability to see under water, even in the clear waters of Maui. I trusted in the Lord that day as I went into the water. I knew that He was capable of leading me to the coral without my having to lead myself. I would walk by faith and not by sight, and all would be well. I remembered my mentor years before telling me not to put my faith in my ability to hear the voice of God but in His ability to speak. Wasn't this the same thing? And so I dove repeatedly to the bottom and felt in the sand for the gift I knew that God would give to Diana and me. But I found no coral.

It never occurred to me that I was being silly to place such value on God leading me to a piece of coral; this was part of our relationship, and I knew that it was as special to Him as it was to me. I was a bit disappointed when I began to tire and knew that I would have to head in to the beach. But I chose immediate reconciliation with God, and I laid on my back on the water for a moment of worshipping Him and letting Him know that I was willing to let this go. I began to swim in, and I let the pure sea water wash over my body. I gloried in the blue of the sky and the breeze that freshened my skin each time I stopped to look. And I gave God glory for it all. When I reached a place shallow enough to stand, I put my feet on the sandy bottom and there, between my toes, were not one, and not two, but three pieces of coral to take to my bride. As I walked up the beach toward her, clutching my prize, I reflected on the fact that once again I was privileged to participate in a sacramental outburst of His love. I realized that the more I sowed this particular teaching (that it was good to give Him glory for what He gave and for what He appeared to hold back for awhile), the more I would be privileged to live inside an escalating miracle of stretching wineskins and a fermenting Holy Spirit.

God really does love us, and He does not find any of the desires of our hearts to be trivial. He simply asks that we give them up to Him since He intends to transform us into seekers-first of His Kingdom so that all other things can be given to us as well (see Matt. 6:33). When we seek reconciliation before vindication, whatever the issue, we free Him to do the transformation of our hearts and minds and to bless us in the bargain.

God really does mean to redeem and resurrect our history through the attainment of our destiny. Our repentance, as a process of our life, makes possible the full potency of the

Holy Spirit in us as the stretching of a new wineskin enables the full fermentation of the new wine without damage to either. But before any of this can happen, God really requires that we answer the question He poses. It is not about what we are willing to fight for but about what we are willing to surrender. When we come to see our growth in Him as an outgrowth of our commitment to represent Him as ambassadors of His reconciliation, no matter what, we answer His question, and we answer it well.

So from now on we regard no one from a worldly point of view. Though we once regarded Christ in this way, we do so no longer. Therefore, if anyone is in Christ he is a new creation; the old has gone, the new has come! All this is from God, Who reconciled us to Himself through Christ, and gave us the ministry of reconciliation: that God was reconciling the world to Himself in Christ, not counting men's sins against them. And He has committed to us the message of reconciliation. We are therefore Christ's ambassadors, as though God were making His appeal through us. We implore you on Christ's behalf: Be reconciled to God (2 Corinthians 5:16-20).

The call comes straight from Heaven. Let it now be on earth as it is in Heaven.

ABOUT THE AUTHOR

J IM WILSON taught for over a decade in California public schools before being called into the ministry. He graduated from Seabury-Western Theological Seminary in 1985 and pastored congregations for 16 years. From that vantage point, he has seen and celebrated the work of God's Holy Spirit in charismatic, evangelical, and mainline bodies with equal awe and enthusiasm. He and his wife, Diana, launched PrayNorthState in February 2001, making it their full-time ministry in June of that year.

Jim teaches on personal evangelism, congregational development, leadership, spiritual gifts, and the simple majesty of God's creation. His focus has been community transformation and reconciliation since 1996. His ministry crosses denominational and cultural barriers as he shares the wonder of God's call to the Body of Christ to become a genuinely cooperative Body. He has authored more than three hundred articles in newspapers and periodicals. *Living as*

Ambassadors of Relationships is his first book. He hosts a popular weekly radio and television program, teaches from coast to coast, and ministers in multiple nations from Sweden to Scotland, including New Zealand, Fiji, and the Philippines.

Since 2001, Jim has offered a series of weekend training events designed to teach the principles of prayer evangelism, warfare by honor, and prophetic acts with impact as they provide opportunities to practice these principles. He and Diana have established Prayer Vanguard, prayer teams that prepare and pave the way for transformation, in nearly twenty northern California communities. Jim leads an interdenominational vanguard team of intercessors who come alongside communities, churches, and ministries seeking the Kingdom of God and His blessing anywhere in the state of California.

Jim and Diana share a passion to seed ten thousand intercessors across northern California who will pray for their neighbors, their communities, and God's Kingdom harvest. They believe that God is on the move in equal parts of prophetic and pragmatic events for community transformation. Their passion, and their ministry, is PrayNorthState.

The Rev. James and Diana Wilson
PO Box 493743
Redding, CA 96049-3743
E-mail: praynorthstate@charter.net
Website: www.praynorthstate.org

Additional copies of this book and other book titles from DESTINY IMAGE are available at your local bookstore.

Call toll-free: 1-800-722-6774.

Send a request for a catalog to:

Destiny Image® Publishers, Inc.
P.O. Box 310
Shippensburg, PA 17257-0310

"Speaking to the Purposes of God for This Generation and for the Generations to Come."

For a complete list of our titles, visit us at www.destinyimage.com